Children's Literature

Volume 22

Volume 22

Annual of
The Modern Language Association
Division on Children's Literature
and The Children's Literature
Association

Yale University Press

New Haven and London

1994

Children's Literature

Published with the assistance of the Frederick W. Hilles Publication Fund of Yale University.

Founder and Senior Editor: Francelia Butler
Editor-in-Chief: R. H. W. Dillard
Editor: Elizabeth Lennox Keyser
Book Review Editor: John Cech
Advisory Board: Jan Alberghene, Margaret Higonnet, U. C. Knoepflmacher, Alison Lurie, Mitzi Myers, Sarah Smedman (representing the ChLA), Albert J. Solnit, M.D.
Consultants for Volume 22: Gillian Adams, John Allen, Norma Bagnall, Phyllis Bixler, Kathleen Blake, Frieda Bostian, Ruth Bottigheimer, Stephen Canham, Beverly Lyon Clark, Richard Flynn, Richard Gillen, Peter Hollindale, Lois Kuznets, Anne Laidlaw, James Holt McGavran, Jr., Roderick McGillis, Leonard Marcus, Jean Marsden, Opal Moore, Perry Nodelman, Frank O'Brien, Klaus Phillips, Judith Plotz, Suzanne Rahn, Barbara Rosen, Mary Shaner, Daniel Shealy, Richard Sherry, Harriet Spiegel, J. D. Stahl, Jan Susina, Eric Tretheway, Ian Wojcik-Andrews

The editors gratefully acknowledge support from Hollins College.

Editorial correspondence should be addressed to The Editors, *Children's Literature,* Department of English, Hollins College, Roanoke, Virginia 24020.

Manuscripts submitted should conform to the style in this issue. An original on nonerasable bond with two copies, a self-addressed envelope, and return postage are requested. Yale University Press does not accept dot-matrix printouts, and it requires double-spacing throughout text and notes. Unjustified margins are preferred. Writers of accepted manuscripts should be prepared to submit final versions of their essays on computer disk in XyWrite, Nota Bene, or Word Perfect.

Volumes 1–7 of *Children's Literature* can be obtained directly from John C. Wandell, The Children's Literature Foundation, P.O. Box 370, Windham Center, Conn. 06280. Volumes 8–21 can be obtained from Yale University Press, P.O. Box 209040, New Haven, Conn. 06520-9040, or from Yale University Press, 23 Pond Street, Hampstead, London NW3 2PN, England.

Library of Congress catalog card number: 79-66588
ISBN: 0-300-05874-8 (cloth), 0-300-05875-6 (paper); ISSN: 0092-8208

A catalogue record for this book is available from the British Library.

Set in Baskerville type by Tseng Information Systems, Inc., Durham, N.C. Printed in the United States of America by Vail-Ballou Press, Binghamton, N.Y.

10   9   8   7   6   5   4   3   2   1

Contents

Reviews

From the Editor

Volume 22 marks the transition of the editorship of *Children's Literature* from the University of Connecticut, where it has been so ably edited for the past twenty-one years, to Hollins College, where we hope to continue the tradition of publishing the most original and provocative work in the field of children's literature. Hollins College, like everyone even remotely concerned with the past, present, and especially the future of children's literature—the writing, reading, studying, and teaching of it—owes an immense debt of gratitude to the founder of the journal, Francelia Butler. The story bears retelling. When, over twenty years ago, Francelia asked a male colleague why the field of children's literature was so often denigrated, he responded that a field must have a journal to be considered important. That was enough for Francelia. She promptly established one (which is not to imply that all Francelia, the fairy godmother of children's literature, had to do was wave her magic wand). Since then the annual, together with its complementary publication, the *Children's Literature Association Quarterly,* has been invaluable in promoting the scholarly—but accessible and unpedantic—examination of books and, increasingly, other media that children of various ages, periods, and cultures have enjoyed. I can attest from personal experience, as can the many contributors to and consultants on this volume, that *Children's Literature* has succeeded in luring specialists in other literatures to the field.

As most subscribers to *Children's Literature* know, the journal has been edited in recent years by Barbara Rosen with the assistance of colleagues and graduate students at the University of Connecticut, as well as by an occasional guest editor. I want to thank Barbara for generously sharing her editorial knowledge and wisdom. Innumerable consultants and contributors have referred to her uncanny ability to identify a manuscript's weaknesses and strengths and to nurture those strengths. Fortunately Barbara will continue to act as a consultant to the journal, as will other members of her staff at the University of Connecticut. Margaret Higonnet, who has coedited volumes of the journal with Barbara, will remain on the editorial board, and Jean Marsden, coeditor of a recent volume, has served as a consultant on this one. Anne Phillips, coeditor of volume 21, has contributed a book review to this volume, and I trust that she and those who worked with her will continue to contribute to the journal in various ways as they launch their academic careers. I would like to thank John Cech for staying on as book review editor, thus relieving me of that weighty responsibility, and Rachel Fordyce for continuing to contribute the valuable feature Dissertations of Note. I am also grateful to the consultants who have helped me with this volume, especially the dozen or so to whom I have turned repeatedly, and to the contributors for their good-natured responses to consultants' comments and for revising their essays against tight deadlines. Above all I am grateful for my collegial relationship with Cynthia Wells of Yale University Press. This volume, as these acknowledgments suggest, is very much a collaborative effort, one that builds on the past and will, I hope, lay a solid foundation for the future.

Perhaps fittingly, this volume, which marks the transfer of editorship and thus encourages reflection on the history of the journal, contains essays of retrospection and commemoration. Without conscious design on my part, the volume celebrates and critiques the Victorian past and even, as in the Bixler and Sircar essays, analyzes others' attempts to do so. Phyllis Bixler's essay on the recent Broadway musical version of Frances Hodgson Burnett's *Secret Garden* (the collaborative effort of a four-woman team) demonstrates the power of a children's classic to inspire fresh works of art, which in turn invest the original with new meaning. In the Varia section Sanjay Sircar's analysis of the Australian novelist Miles Franklin's account of a 1932 Lewis Carroll centenary celebration presents the darker side of canonization—cult status and commercialization. Both deal with what has become a pervasive theme of this volume: the relationship between adult readers and children's literature. In Bixler's interviews with the adapters of *The Secret Garden* the four women discuss their childhood reading—of Burnett and others— and their adult responses to Burnett, which led to their nonliteral and revisionary interpretation. Sircar shows how the organizers of the Carroll centenary, and Miles Franklin herself to a degree, appropriate Carroll, Alice, and the original Alice, Alice Liddell Hargreaves, in a virtual orgy of materialism and nostalgia.

Just as Bixler reads the adapters' reading of Burnett, and Sircar reads Franklin's reading of the Carroll centenary, so, too, do

Suzanne Rahn and Angela Estes, in other contributions to Varia, read Leonard Marcus's recent reading of the life and work of Margaret Wise Brown, an author more popular with children now than at the time of her death forty years ago. And just as Bixler praises the adapters for finding openness in Burnett's text, Estes praises Marcus for finding openness in Brown; and she and Rahn discover further openness for themselves. Anna Smol, in contrast, takes to task Victorian adapters of *Beowulf* for children. Their "misreading" of the original, unlike the musical version of *The Secret Garden*, constitutes a misrepresentation designed to inculcate turn-of-the-century boys with an unexamined pride in nation, race, and gender. Finally, Peter Hollindale's essay on the centenary of Lucy Boston (a figure who, he convincingly argues, links the present to the Victorian past) exemplifies the intelligent, informed tribute sadly lacking, according to Sircar, in the Carroll centenary.

Other articles in the volume deal with Christina Rossetti's little-known collection of poems *Sing-Song*, Louisa May Alcott's little-known story "Cupid and Chow-chow," Kenneth Grahame's classic *Wind in the Willows*, C. M. Barker's Flower Fairies, and the tales of Beatrix Potter. Sharon Smulders makes a strong case for the structural intricacy and semantic sophistication of Rossetti's deceptively simple poetry for children. She also sees in Rossetti's domestic imagery "acute insight into larger issues relating to the generational and sexual dynamics of the family." In *Sing-Song* these issues are subordinate to the larger themes of birth, maturation, aging, and death, but in Alcott's story, as Angela Estes and Kathleen Lant persuasively argue, the sexual dynamics of the family are everything. As though inspired by such poems of Rossetti's as "I Have a Little Husband," Alcott has her child protagonists enact the roles of husband and wife with devastating effect. Estes and Lant not only explore the Victorian past in their essay but revisit the journal's past, referring to their own prize-winning essay in *Children's Literature* on *Little Women* (volume 17) and to an earlier essay on "Cupid and Chow-chow" (volume 14). Bonnie Gaarden and Cynthia Marshall in their essays on *The Wind in the Willows* also engage in a dialogue, both with Lois Kuznets's feminist reading of the novel (volume 16) and with each other. Gaarden sees Grahame's nurturing male characters as constituting a more benign family than the families that Alcott or even Rossetti envisioned. Marshall sees Grahame in his washerwoman episode as qualifying the misogyny that has been attributed to him. To a remarkable degree, all of these essays, as well as Carole Scott's on Barker and Potter, deal with the physical, sensuous life of the child as depicted in children's literature, with the child's relationship to his or her body, with the way in which the body experiences pleasure and pain, and with its vulnerability and expressiveness, both naked and clothed. These essays, along with the Varia selections of Rahn and Estes, explore the child's relation with nature and the way animals (and in the case of Barker, plants) are used to represent the child or figures in the child's life.

Readers of this volume of *Children's Literature* will be able to make many more connections among the essays assembled here, in part because their subjects share a common cultural context (for example, Smulders, Scott, and Bixler all mention the Pre-Raphaelite influence on or associations of their subjects). But volume 22 is not devoted to a special topic, nor do we plan any such volumes for the immediate future. We will continue to publish the liveliest, most thought-provoking essays submitted but would especially encourage submissions on contemporary and international writers, as well as the classic writers in English. We hope, too, to include more dialogue among contributors and would welcome responses from readers. To borrow Perry Nodelman's words about literature as quoted by Phyllis Bixler, "What distinguishes the most important literary criticism is its ability to engender new interpretations." This engendering has been, and will continue to be, the mission of *Children's Literature*.

Elizabeth Lennox Keyser

Articles

Sound, Sense, and Structure in
Christina Rossetti's Sing-Song

Sharon Smulders

Christina Rossetti's collections of verse sequentially elaborate, according to Dolores Rosenblum, "a female aesthetic" of "poetic inexhaustibility" (134).[1] Examining Rossetti's arrangements of poetry over the course of her career, Rosenblum nevertheless fails to address the relation between sequence and meaning in *Sing-Song: A Nursery Rhyme Book* (1872).[2] The omission is startling for a number of reasons. Rossetti's juvenile poetic progress not only occupies the central position in her oeuvre but contains several of her "best songs" (*Family Letters* 94). Indeed, as William Rossetti observes, "the series includes various lyrics which, though not unadapted for children, are truly in a high strain of poetry, and perfectly suited for figuring among her verse for adults, and even for taking an honoured place as such" (C. Rossetti, *Poetical Works* 489–90).[3] Yet owing to its status as children's verse, *Sing-Song* has rarely received the critical attention that it deserves, especially as a unified poetic sequence.[4] Certainly, Rossetti's playful experiments in form and language allow readers to "experience *Sing-Song* . . . as a coherent text" (McGillis 221), but her sequential arrangement of lyrics informs this experience with meaning. Unfolding a narrative from cradle to grave, from winter to fall, from sunrise to sunset, *Sing-Song* invites readers to understand life as an ordered totality.

Sing-Song begins and ends with the sleeping child in bed. In the interval Rossetti guides the reader through three different, but simultaneous, temporal sequences. Taken together, these three synchronic movements divide into three successive phases, each slightly more comprehensive than the last. Grouping her 121 lyrics within roughly twelve decades, Rossetti uses clock and calendar to posit progress within circularity.[5] In the first three decades she treats preparations and beginnings: birth and babyhood, dawn and morning, winter and spring. In the next four decades she focuses on

Children's Literature 22, ed. Francelia Butler, R. H. W. Dillard, and Elizabeth Lennox Keyser (Yale University Press, © 1994 Hollins College).

growth: childhood, day, summer. In the final five decades she dramatizes a ripening into maturity: adulthood, dusk, autumn. In the last of these five decades she turns the sequence back to beginnings and thus underpins her asymmetrical arrangement with a symmetrical design. Doubling temporal on textual experience, these movements provide a syntax in which the poet grounds her exploration of the endless emotive and cognitive possibilities facilitated by rhyme and rhythm, repetition and apposition, sound and silence. For all the childish charm of single rhymes, *Sing-Song* makes rigorous demands on readers to create meaning from the formal, thematic, and structural constituents of the volume as a whole.

"By forming part of a sequence," says Christina Rossetti in *Time Flies: A Reading Diary,* a "single note" becomes one "element" within an "endless progression, of inexhaustible variety": "Change, succession, are of the essence of music" (29). As the title so engagingly suggests, *Sing-Song* aspires to the condition of music. Appropriately, the volume opens with a fugue containing poems about the newly born child and the newly born day. In the first two cradle songs a maternal speaker assures the baby of loving guardianship. Succeeding and varying this keynote, the next two poems replace the soothing presence of angels and mother with the dispossessing absence of parents and baby. The fifth lyric blithely announces several beginnings in the conflux of "morn," "born," and "springing":

> "Kookoorookoo! kookoorookoo!"
>   Crows the cock before the morn;
> "Kikirikee! kikirikee!"
>   Roses in the east are born.
>
> "Kookoorookoo! kookoorookoo!"
>   Early birds begin their singing;
> "Kikirikee! kikirikee!"
>   The day, the day, the day is springing.   [5][6]

"Born" describes the budding of flowers; "springing," the rising of the sun and the coming of dawn—that is, dayspring. But the position of the lyric within the sequence increases the field of semantic possibility. The prepositional phrases ("before the morn," "in the east") in the first stanza create a mood of anticipation at one equally with the seasonal and the diurnal moment. Because of the onomatopoeic repetitions, the feminine end-rhymes and the thrice-iterated "day," the momentum of the second stanza increases as Rossetti speeds toward the joyous climax of the poem.

The next several lyrics, which follow the child through early morning activities—taking medicine (6), receiving the eight o'clock mail (7), eating breakfast (8, 9)—modulate the established mood of expectancy. The emphasis in the breakfast lyrics on the coldness outdoors, for example, prepares for the sad "Dead in the Cold, a Song-Singing Thrush" (10), which initiates a second decade of lyrics. For the most part, these rhymes deal with unfulfilled hope and winter. But because "in music . . . one harmony paves the way to a diverse harmony" (C. Rossetti, *Time Flies* 29), this chilly series also incorporates the warmer notes of maternal reassurance found in "Your Brother Has a Falcon" (13) and of spring promise in "Hope Is Like a Harebell Trembling from Its Birth" (17). Although winter is treated as a period of possible miscarriage, its gestative dormancy eventually gives birth to the new season heralded in "Growing in the Vale" (20) and "A Linnet in a Gilded Cage" (21). In fact, the latter lyric not only suggests that "a linnet on a bough" is the "luckier bird" once "trees burst out in leaf" (21), but also recalls "the mournful linnets" (14) that lost their nest in the previous part of the sequence. Whereas the earlier poem describes a kind of abortive or false spring, the later one implies loss overcome. In successive lyrics, then, the poet comprehends and delivers the momentary tragedy.

Besides marshaling the order of lyrics in *Sing-Song,* the rhythmic progress of time constitutes a major thematic concern. Between "Minnie and Mattie and Fat Little May" (29–31) and "There Is but One May in the Year" (35), Rossetti brings the sequence closer to summer. Many lyrics in this part of the volume are meditations on the brevity of the season and the brevity of youth. Thus, in "Minnie and Mattie and Fat Little May" the youngest girl's name and the posies the girls carry—"Half of sweet violets,/Half of primroses" (30)—indicate late spring. Furthermore, this lyric adapts the carpe diem motif to the requisites of nursery rhyme. Instead of exhorting her readers to "Gather ye rose-buds while ye may," Rossetti says, "Don't wait for roses/Losing to-day" (31). She subverts, therefore, the impetus of the seventeenth-century lyric toward sexual initiation. Although "Minnie and Mattie and Fat Little May," the longest poem in *Sing-Song,* holds the moment for nine quatrains, time is inexorable. Indeed, from "The days are clear" (37) to "Brown and furry/Caterpillar in a hurry" (39), the poet dwells on the impossibility of arresting time; but in the caterpillar who may "Spin and die,/To live again a butterfly" (39), she intimates that transformation supersedes transience and that life embraces death.

Moving from spring to summer in "The Summer Nights Are Short" (36) and again from May to June in "The Days Are Clear," Rossetti also advances the course of the child's daily activities. Here, too, she proceeds from the babies of the beginning of the book to older children. With "A Toadstool Comes Up in a Night" (40), she begins a section on various lessons involving numbers, coins, and colors, as well as clock and calendar time. In these poems, moreover, the concept of verse time emerges clearly in Rossetti's manipulation of metrical measure and duration. The lesson on sewing in "A Pocket Handkerchief to Hem" (fig. 1) is exemplary for a steady rhythmic and verbal repetitiveness that imitates the even stitches required "Till stitch by stitch the hem is done" (41).

Writing of her Italian translations, Rossetti speaks of her efforts to marry the sound of her verse—assonance and consonance, rhyme and rhythm—to its meaning. She was justly proud of "Cavalli Marittimi," originally "The Horses of the Sea" (94), because " 'Rotolandosi spumando vanno' gave . . . something of the accumulative on-come of the waves, mounting on each other's backs" (*Family Letters* 77). Although she represented herself as a spontaneous poet who eschewed "skilled labour" (*Family Letters* 65), her comments on her translations provide a unique glimpse into her poetic practice.[7] Even in these most unpretentious and artless of lyrics, she worked scrupulously to achieve the necessary correspondence between form and content. Just as she strove for the sound of the surf in the open vowels of "Cavalli Marittimi," she captured the rhythm of the silent activity described in "A Pocket Handkerchief to Hem." Rossetti's mastery of phanopoeia, her description of action in sequences of sound and rhythm, transforms the tedious task of sewing into a delightful aesthetic experience. Verse time ameliorates and supersedes workaday time.

When "the hem is done," both the poem and the handkerchief come to conclusion: "And after work is play!" (41). This ending makes a fitting prelude to the nonsense complement to the rhyme, "If a Pig Wore a Wig" (42). But in the tailoress of the second stanza, "If a Pig Wore a Wig" playfully returns to the preceding sewing lesson and so denies that any activity is ever "done." Indeed, the accumulative on-come of separate lyrics militates against closure in

Fig. 1. "A Pocket Handkerchief to Hem": The apprentice needlewoman puts work before play. She also appears on the title page of *Sing-Song*, where she serves to remind juvenile readers to finish their chores before opening the book.

Sing-Song. As in "A Pocket Handkerchief to Hem," the other lessons in *Sing-Song* not only contribute collectively to Rossetti's design but also address individually the relation of parts to a whole. Although the poems can be defined as mnemonic aids, their distinction lies in the felicitous complementarity of sound and sense. The poem "1 and 1 Are 2," for instance, ends with the following couplet: "12 and 12 are 24/Pretty pictures, and no more" (44–45). Here Rossetti comments ironically on the vignettes offered in each of the preceding couplets. They have been no more than pretty pictures. While recalling the "couple more" that ends the second couplet, the "no more" of the last couplet establishes the finality of closure. Reiterating "no more" in the first couplet of the following poem, however, Rossetti elides these two distinct poems and shows that closure is a highly artificial construct and is by no means absolute: "How many seconds in a minute?/Sixty, and no more in it" (46). But even a minute is not conclusive; it is part of a larger continuum. Requiring a more sophisticated knowledge than in the poem about addition, this lyric moves from the smallest units of time to the largest: "How many ages in time?/No one knows the rhyme" (47). Ending the poem with a riddle unanswerable because of the empirical limits of human knowledge, Rossetti achieves closure through a rhyme that calls attention to the inability to complete endless time except through a poetic contrivance. In *Sing-Song* as a whole, rhyme also negotiates the chasm between finite and infinite time, between different conceptual orders. In other words, Rossetti seeks to comprehend eternity within the singsong rhythms and singsong rhymes of verse time.

In accordance with the idea that after work is play, the next series of lyrics, miscellaneous in theme, all offer a respite from work. But the woman poet's work is never done. Thus, once again recalling "A Pocket Handkerchief to Hem," a riddle at the center of the volume exploits mere sewing notions for its conceit.

> There is one that has a head without an eye,
>   And there's one that has an eye without a head:
> You may find the answer if you try;
>   And when all is said,
> Half the answer hangs upon a thread!   [71]

Half the answer is the needle held by the mother in Arthur Hughes's illustration (fig. 2). The other half hangs upon the reader's willingness to try to organize the component parts of the poem into an intelligible whole. Strategically placing the direct address to the reader at the heart of the lyric, Rossetti uses conditional phrasing to stress how meaning is contingent on audience engagement: "You *may* find the answer *if* you try." Truly, half the fun of the poem hangs upon Rossetti's wordplay, for the thread of meaning in this riddle—and in others like "A City Plum Is Not a Plum" (12), "A Pin Has a Head, but Has No Hair" (54–55), and "The Peacock Has a Score of Eyes, with Which He Cannot See" (65)—depends on making sense of apparent nonsense.

In spite of its riddling nature, "There Is One That Has a Head Without an Eye" yields to meaning "when all is said." The paired conundrums in the opening lines deploy a thread of associative logic, for pin is to needle as head is to eye. At the same time, the riddle frustrates associative thought, for a pin has no eye, the needle no head. Syntactic constructions implying negation—here "without" and elsewhere "no," "not," "never"—draw attention to the doubleness of language. Rossetti asks her audience to distinguish what is from what is not and uses puns to investigate the nature of single words with several denotative possibilities. For R. Loring Taylor, the concentration on verbal ambiguity reveals a basic "distrust of language" (xii): "The vision represented is thus, in its way, as absurd as that of Edward Lear or Lewis Carroll, although its center is moral rather than mathematical like Carroll's or verbal like Lear's" (xiii).

Fig. 2. "There Is One That Has a Head Without an Eye": Illustration and poem, like pin and needle, complement each other. Whereas Rossetti encourages readers to use their heads to discover an answer, Hughes challenges them to use their eyes.

In confusing the poet's moral vision with an "overt didactic intention" (xii), Taylor misses the point. Even though Rossetti draws her opportunities for wordplay from needlework, *Sing-Song* is far less overt in its didacticism than, for example, *Speaking Likenesses* (1874). And as this volume of prose tales reveals, the poet distrusts fantasy, not language.

Repulsed by *Speaking Likenesses,* John Ruskin asked in horror, "How could she or Arthur Hughes sink so low after their pretty nursery rhymes?" (37:155). Although she does not so much sink as change her stroke in this "Christmas trifle, would-be in the *Alice* style" (C. Rossetti, *Family Letters* 44), an answer lies in the medium chosen and the end proposed. Taking Carrollian fantasy to task, the Aunt who narrates these three stories keeps her would-be Alices busy with sewing, darning, and knitting. According to U. C. Knoepflmacher, Aunt is Alice's doubly punishing adult nemesis: she not only exacts work from her recalcitrant seamstresses but repays their industry with tales "which relentlessly discourage their potential indulgence in Alice-like fantasies" and which mock their childish incompetence ("Avenging Alice" 314). Additionally, as Rossetti explains in one of her devotional treatises, the labor that Aunt performs for "many poor friends" (*Speaking Likenesses* 50) and demands from her auditors possesses spiritual as well as social utility:

"Whoso clothes the poor, weaves for himself (still more obviously weaves for *herself*) a white garment" (*Face of the Deep* 138). Whereas Aunt, intolerant of displays of feminine infantilism, frustrates her listeners' desire for regressive fantasy, the poet is gentler in her persuasions.

Like Aunt, the lyricist of *Sing-Song* submits Victorian idealizations of childhood innocence to the probation of experienced womanhood, but she is concerned to give her would-be Alices practice in mastering the delights of wordplay rather than the duties of needlework. Nevertheless, because *Sing-Song* validates a comprehensible, albeit endlessly flexible and permutable, linguistic order, as well as a comprehensive temporal order, it is undeniably moral. Unlike the riddle about ravens and writing desks in *Alice's Adventures in Wonderland,* all the riddles in *Sing-Song* are ultimately capable of solution. "Puns and such like," Rossetti readily admits, "are a frivolous crew likely to misbehave unless kept within strict bounds" (*Time Flies* 26).[8] Although the puns in "There Is One That Has a Head Without an Eye" might cause a temporary confusion of meaning, the poet's grammatical constructions exclude one range of semantic potential even as it is elicited. The frivolity of Carroll's wordplay contributes to Alice's growing irritation with the world underground, but Rossetti's riddles operate within the strict bounds necessary to temper linguistic misbehavior. In this respect, *Sing-Song* provides a good-humored initiation into the rites of language.

Such lightsome lyrics as "There Is One That Has a Head Without an Eye," playful though they may be, put into relief the more perplexing questions that Rossetti poses in the course of *Sing-Song.* Indeed, her riddling allusions to the mysteries of life and death provoked one Victorian reviewer, Sidney Colvin, to marvel at the presence of both "a music suited to baby ears" and "a depth of pathos or suggestion far enough transcending baby apprehension." Because *Sing-Song* allows the "more complex self" to discover "the reward of its affliction of self-consciousness," it ranks among those children's books that are "more delightful still" for "the properly constituted grown-up reader" (23).[9] To prove the appeal of *Sing-Song* to little listeners, other contemporary readers co-opt the pre-literate child to the task of criticism. One notice ends by prefacing "If Hope Grew on a Bush" (68), a lyric of meditative pathos, with the following testament to the charm of the volume: "We know one who doesn't know her letters yet, and already knows half of it by heart" (review of *Sing-Song, Scribner's Monthly* 629). Still another, after abandoning the "limited little jury" consulted for opinions, decides the question of "whether or no Miss Rossetti would have done more for the children if she had done less for us" by simply being "very sincerely thankful to her for this as for her other poems" (review of *Sing-Song, Nation* 295).

By deliberately pitching her singsongs at two different audiences, Rossetti follows a precedent established in the title poem of *The Prince's Progress and Other Poems* (1866). To her brother Dante Gabriel, she confided that she had written "The Prince's Progress" to meet the "mean capacities" of a "general public" but had also included "refined clues" for a more select readership (W. Rossetti, *Rossetti Papers* 81). Directed to a general public composed of children, *Sing-Song* similarly contains refined clues for Colvin's properly constituted grown-up reader.

Although the two answers offered for each of the four questions in "What Are Heavy? Sea-Sand and Sorrow" (34) plainly accommodate two orders of readers, many of the amusettes in the central section of the volume refrain from the provision of obvious answers. Toward the end of the second movement of the sequence, "Sing Me a Song" (73) is perhaps the most interesting of these enigmas. Like the first line of "Dead in the Cold, a Song-Singing Thrush," its first line plays a variation on the titular singsong. Like "Minnie and Mattie and Fat Little May," it employs the three-sisters motif also found in such adult poems as "A Triad," "Maiden-Song" and "A Ring Posy." And like "There Is One That Has a Head Without an Eye," it tests the reader's capacity to link and synthesize sequences of words and phrases to make meaning when all is said. In fact, the relation between the first and second stanzas of "Sing Me a Song" typifies Rossetti's method of balancing complementary halves in *Sing-Song* as a whole (fig. 3).

In "Sing Me a Song," Rossetti constructs a single narrative from two seemingly discrete experiences—a song and a tale. The parallelism of the opening petition and question of each stanza establishes not only a symmetrical but a tacit causal connection between song and tale. The contrast between three sisters in the first stanza and two in the second provides an implicit rationale for the shift between mirth and mourning. In the ellipsis between the two stanzas, the circle of girls suffers a rupture. Interestingly, Hughes's illustration for "Sing Me a Song" occupies this interstitial silence,

Fig. 3. "Sing Me a Song": Hughes draws on Rossetti's symbolism to construct the missing narrative. Personified as an angel, death removes one of the dancing sisters from the circle of the living.

for it shows the third girl loosing her hold on a sister and tightly grasping an angel's hand: she is both part of the dancing ring and apart, separated from her sisters by the arc of an angel's wing. That the poet particularly admired this "charming design" of "the three dancing girls with the angel kissing one" (*Family Letters* 35) attests to Hughes's perfect understanding of the requirements of the text.[10] Describing the illustrations as "in the right spirit for such semi-childish semi-suggestive" lyrics (*Selected Letters* 278), William Rossetti astutely points to the interactive vitality of text and pictures in *Sing-Song*. The genius of Hughes's illustrations lies not only in their individual charm but also in the way they pick up on the refined clues in Rossetti's verse and contribute to the whole sense of *Sing-Song*. Although his depiction of the intercessory angel softens the experience of loss described in "Sing Me a Song," Hughes draws on the suggestive intersection of temporal and eternal realms in *Sing-Song* as a whole, making the illustrations into another level of the volume's meaningful dynamic.

Between "Sing Me a Song" and "Ding a Ding" (89), Rossetti advances into the third and final phase of *Sing-Song*. In the last five decades, she includes poems about autumn—or at least the end of summer—and homecomings. Many of the lyrics, like "Minnie Bakes Oaten Cakes" (82), concern adults rather than children. Although this poem marks a contrapuntal return to "Minnie and Mattie and Fat Little May," the later Minnie is a busy housewife. No longer part of a childish trio, she now anxiously watches "the church clock" as she awaits "her Johnny's coming/Home from sea" (82). This adult consciousness of time also informs the triplet of poems celebrating the cultural rituals used to punctuate the natural rhythms of life. Ringing changes on the traditional nursery-rhyme refrain, "ding dong bell," the tolling bells of "Ding a Ding," like those of "Sing Me a Song," remind the reader of time's passage and life's fruition. In "Ding a Ding," Rossetti again employs paired stanzas to contrast joy and sorrow, but here she balances a wedding against a funeral. The next poem dramatizes the substance of the first stanza of "Ding a Ding":

> A ring upon her finger,
>   Walks the bride,
> With the bridegroom tall and handsome
>   At her side. [90]

Less obviously but no less surely Rossetti takes up the burden of the second stanza of "Ding a Ding" in the poem that follows "A Ring upon Her Finger." In spite of the cheerfulness of "Ferry Me Across the Water, Do, Boatman, Do" (91), the image of paid passage across the water suggests for the adult reader, if not the child, Charon's duties on the Styx—a subject that the poet had addressed just as whimsically, if more pointedly, in "Charon," published posthumously in *New Poems* (1896).

In keeping with the progressive arrangement of the volume, this triplet of lyrics on weddings and funerals ushers in a series that features childish wives and husbands. Cora Kaplan, speaking of the poet's reliance on synecdoche and metonymy, asserts that her verses generally "attempt to escape immediate or specific social determination" (61). Rossetti's grown-up singsongs, however, conduct an interrogation of the way marriage, the most intimate of cultural institutions, affects gender. The tensions consequent upon her mediation of patriarchal constructions of femininity are further complicated by her personal ambivalence on the subject of woman's position. Curiously, even though her own desire "to attain to the character of a humble orthodox Xtian" made it impossible for her to "aim at 'women's rights'" (Bell 111–12), her respect for motherhood compelled her to argue in favor of married women's suffrage. As she wrote to Augusta Webster, "If anything ever does sweep away the barrier of sex, and make the female not a giantess or a heroine but at once and full grown a hero and giant, it is that mighty maternal love which makes little birds and little beasts as well as little women matches for very big adversaries" (Bell 112). The heroic stature that Rossetti granted to mothers may account for the pathos of the shortest of the rhymes in *Sing-Song:* "Motherless baby and babyless mother,/Bring them together to love one another" (125). Her conservatism notwithstanding, she did not see maternity as the exclusive province of the married woman. In this respect, the couplet anticipates her later effort to claim the gratifications of motherhood for the single woman. "The childless who make themselves nursing mothers of Christ's little ones are," she observes in *The Face of the Deep,* "true mothers in Israel" (312).

Convinced that motherhood enlarged womanhood, Rossetti also believed that wifehood involved some diminishment. Because of the nature of Eve's "sentence," the "satisfaction" of woman's desire in marriage "must depend not on herself but on one stronger than she, who might grant or might deny" (*Face of the Deep* 312). Accordingly, when she treats feminine desire and dependence in her marital singsongs, dissatisfaction rivals satisfaction as her theme. Although the actors in these diminutive lyrics are themselves wee and little, Rossetti provides acute insight into larger issues relating to the generational and sexual dynamics of the family. "I Have a Little Husband" (104), for instance, poignantly renders a wife's emotional dependence. Restricted to the sphere of home and hearth, she must, like the adult Minnie, await her roving husband's return for the fulfillment of her desire. On the other hand, "Wee Wee Husband" (103) represents women's economic dependence in light of a two-stanza debate between husband and wife. The accompanying illustration of Punch and Judy actuates the element of conflict latent in the poem. Recapitulating the end-rhymes of "Wee Wee Husband," "What Does the Bee Do?" again dramatizes the domestic economy of marriage: husbands and fathers "bring home money," wives and mothers "lay out the money," and babies "eat up the honey" (108). Astonishing in its restrained simplicity, the poem aligns women and children as consumers of wealth against men (and bees) as producers of wealth. Such shrewd perceptions were not lost on contemporary reviewers. Citing "If I Were a Queen"

(33), situated earlier in the sequence, one reader observes that it contains "perhaps a bit of satire . . . and a wise word on woman's wrongs" (review of *Sing-Song, Scribner's Monthly* 629). Another notes that this lyric possesses "a touch of hidden wisdom which the babies will find when they come to talk over the woman's-rights question" (review of *Sing-Song, Nation* 295). Because the innocuous impersonality of nursery rhyme encouraged Rossetti to engage the cultural determinants of behavior and belief rather more directly than she was otherwise wont, her juvenile lyrics on adult relationships are especially susceptible to ironic reading.

Among the lyrics on domestic relationships, Rossetti includes a few on old women and several on dolls that also address nineteenth-century constructions of femininity. Honored with gifts of food, "the dear old lady in the lane" (105) and Grandmamma in "A Peach for Brothers, One for Each" (115) command the lyric speaker's admiration. By contrast, the speakers of the doll poems barely repress their resentment of girlhood. In "I Have a Poll Parrot" (109) and "All the Bells Were Ringing" (102), torn and broken dolls may signal the necessary growth of the individual beyond childish toys. But although Molly in "All the Bells Were Ringing" mourns the loss of her plaything, the speaker's attitude communicates hostility rather than nostalgia. Anticipating Aunt's asperity in *Speaking Likenesses,* these poems register Rossetti's resistance to the ideology of feminine dependence insofar as it relegates women to what the social historian Carol Dyhouse calls "a permanently 'adolescent' state" (118).

"I Caught a Little Ladybird" (101) not only clarifies this resistance but illuminates the positioning of the doll poems among those on marriage. A conventional emblem of girlhood, the doll becomes a displaced metonym for Victorian womanhood in the course of the lyric.

> I caught a little ladybird
>   That flies far away;
> I caught a little lady wife
>   That is both staid and gay.
>
> Come back, my scarlet ladybird,
>   Back from far away;
> I weary of my dolly wife,
>   My wife that cannot play.

> She's such a senseless wooden thing
>   She stares the livelong day;
> Her wig of gold is stiff and cold
>   And cannot change to grey.
>
> [*Complete Poems* 2:44]

Added in the 1893 edition, the last two stanzas bespeak the continuing care that Rossetti lavished on her nursery rhymes to elucidate her meaning and refine the structural integrity of the poetic sequence. Her additions to "I Caught a Little Ladybird" move the poem from a charming reprise of a traditional nursery rhyme ("Ladybird, Ladybird, Fly Away Home") toward a species of cultural criticism, for in her reflection on the dolly wife, she comments ironically on Victorian women's consignment to perpetual childhood. More sardonic than "If I Were a Queen," the revised "I Caught a Little Ladybird" is likewise a women's rights poem. Its speaker prefers the freedom of the ladybird, who travels afar like the sailor in "I Have a Little Husband," to the insensibility of the dolly wife, who, moreover, lacks not only vitality but consciousness. Endorsing the lively play of thought and action above physical prettiness, Rossetti captures the doll's deficiencies in the stare that paradoxically persists through the livelong day and in the artificial wig of gold that cannot change to grey. Conveying the hint of a sneer in the sibilance of the ninth and tenth lines, she subverts a feminine ideal that militates against change and growth.

Having followed the child from infancy to maturity, Rossetti implies generative and cyclical renewal by again featuring babies in her final lyrics. Having also taken the reader from dawn to dusk, she closes the cycle with several poems on the moon, the archetype of change. Amid these nighttime lyrics, however, she also includes one on daytime. In one of the recursive moments in the book, this reflection on what the sun, apparently omniscient, might tell of joy and sorrow allows the poet to begin her final recapitulations and bring her readers to an enlarged awareness.

> If the sun could tell us half
>   That he hears and sees,
> Sometimes he would make us laugh,
>   Sometimes he would make us cry:

> Think of all the birds that make
>   Homes among the trees;
> Think of cruel boys who take
>   Birds that cannot fly.   [121]

The last four lines balance the first four lines and restate the double play between what is heard and what is seen and between what provokes laughter and what provokes tears, while the rhymes of the second and sixth lines and the fourth and final lines formally bind the two parts of the poem. The lyric is one of a pair, for Rossetti speculates in the next lyric, "If the Moon Came from Heaven" (122), about what the moon might impart. She encourages readers to think twice in "If the Sun Could Tell Us Half," but she now says wonderingly, "Only think." Because the moon "peep[s] by night/ And do[es] not peep by day," her tale is necessarily not just conjectural but partial. On second thought, the sun, which Rossetti figures as the moon's masculine complement, can also tell only half a tale even if he tells all he knows. What is important, however, is not what the sun or moon might know but what the reader might think. Inasmuch as "If the Moon Came from Heaven" completes "If the Sun Could Tell Us Half," meaning resides in the reader's capacity to comprehend the sequential relation between the two poems and to reconcile into inclusive wholeness the antithetical positions represented by such pairs as day and night, joy and sorrow.

At the end of *Sing-Song,* Rossetti seeks to bring the reader round in time and in comprehension. Ever sensitive to the poet's design, Hughes takes up the idea of the temporal cycle in his illustrations, several of which include circles. In "If the Sun Could Tell Us Half," the circle of the sun reigns in the background of the illustration; in "If Stars Dropped Out of Heaven" (119), the darkened face of the earth encompasses the haloed angel; in "Is the Moon Tired? She Looks So Pale" (118), the crescent moon appears; and in "If the Moon Came from Heaven" and "O Lady Moon, Your Horns Point Toward the East" (123), the moon wanes further. For the triplet of lyrics beginning with "Motherless Baby and Babyless Mother," Hughes again incorporates circles in his designs: in the first, a Celtic cross is in the background, and mother and child unite over the grave in the foreground (125); in the second, a full circle encloses a child beside its mother's bed (126); and in the last of the poems on

Fig. 4. "Baby Lies So Fast Asleep": Hughes modifies the circle motif for his tableau of death. The blackness that overarches the dead child puts the snowdrop—a conventional emblem for hope—into clear relief.

death, a half circle frames the child who clasps "a snowdrop in her hand" (127). Harking back to the many poems of untimely loss at the beginning of the volume, lyrics such as "Motherless Baby and Babyless Mother" attempt to restore a harmony disrupted as early as "My Baby Has a Father and a Mother" (3) and "Our Little Baby Fell Asleep" (4). The latter precisely balances "Baby Lies So Fast Asleep," fourth from the end of the sequence (fig. 4). Because *sleep* stands euphemistically for death here, both of these lyrics conflate separate temporal movements in the sequence and afford further insight into Rossetti's sense of a cosmic moral order. As Roderick McGillis states, she "presents death as a positive aspect of life . . . by identifying death as one point in a larger pattern" (222) and as "an imaginative idea" (223). Death is not conclusion but part of a continuum; it is a rest and a beginning, a passage into new life.

At the juncture of carnal and spiritual existence, death and birth —apparent antonyms—are in fact synonyms. Although parts of *Sing-Song* seem morbid because they remind readers of the fragility of temporal existence, the volume as a whole offers the solace and reassurance of providential design. To the extent that Rossetti's design in *Sing-Song* seeks to capture this greater design, the volume exceeds the mathematical precision of 120 lyrics. Nevertheless, the poet provides a fitting end to the child's day in the two concluding lullabies. Of these, the last contains the fewest words and the tautest rhymes, moving through a kind of linguistic minimalism to the silence of closure. Notwithstanding this gesture to finality, "Lie A-Bed" (130) also challenges the ability to define an

Figs. 5 and 6. "Angels at the Foot" and "Lie A-Bed": Hughes's use of the same basic design for the first and final lyrics takes the reader visually from the end of *Sing-Song* to the beginning. The Victorian ideal of women as angels in the house may further explain the mirror resemblance between the mother of "Lie A-Bed" and the adult figure on the other side of the cradle in "Angels at the Foot."

end, for it looks forward "till daybreak," or the beginning of *Sing-Song* (figs. 5 and 6). And because Rossetti has so recently called attention to sleep as both temporal and eternal rest, the final lines, "Never wake:—/Baby, sleep," also resist single-minded approaches to closure. Meaning, like life, inheres in a generative rather than a conclusive order.

Once all is said in *Sing-Song*, Rossetti has proceeded through one diurnal cycle, one annual cycle, and one life cycle, establishing thereby a syntax that governs her development of reiterated motifs. Within each of the successive movements, scattered poems on birds and beasts, flora and fauna, wind and weather, provide thematic emblems. Although these repeated motifs contribute to the unity of the sequence, the meaning that Rossetti attaches to a particular image changes from rhyme to rhyme. Indeed, the multivalent associations mobilized and remobilized in such intertextual play might well suggest, as Steven Connor argues, that Rossetti treats "language as a game—an essentially closed, self-sustaining activity" and that nursery rhymes permit her "to indulge the expressivity of a language emptied of content" (440). By reinvoking motifs, she seems, however, not to divest language of content but to demonstrate how context invests language with meaning. By recontextualizing motifs, she explores the connotative possibilities of language and so challenges, albeit playfully, the intellectual and imaginative resources of her readers.

Rossetti's floral catalogs provide a prime example of the way the sequential placement of repeated motifs affects their meaning. Early in the volume "Hope Is Like a Harebell Trembling from Its Birth" represents the first of several floral poems. In looking forward to the treatment of the rose toward the center of the volume, this lyric is anticipatory, like springtime. Although "Harebells and sweet lilies show a thornless growth," still, "the rose with all its thorns excels them both" (17). But because the rose is less suitable as an emblem for childhood than the primroses that Minnie and Mattie and fat little May gather, it is rarely mentioned in the other spring lyrics. Once the volume moves toward high summer and toward adulthood, however, Rossetti makes it an emblem for feminine desirability. Personifying the rose as female, she privileges it within her floral catalogs. Even as the sequence passes into its autumnal phase, the rose who "tips her bending briar,/And half unfolds her glowing heart" remains the "lady of all beauty" (99). The thorny rose eclipses not only the apple tree and the corn but the lily as well.

> The lily has a smooth stalk,
>   Will never hurt your hand;
> But the rose upon her briar
>   Is lady of the land.   [99]

Later lyrics reverse the hierarchical relation established in the floral poems.

Omitting such qualifying conjunctions as *but* (17, 99) or *yet* (74), used in earlier inventories, the poet implies the superiority of the lily over the rose by giving it the position of final emphasis in one rhyme late in the sequence.

> The rose that blushes rosy red,
>   She must hang her head;
> The lily that blows spotless white,
>   She may stand upright.   [112]

Full-blown rather than half-blown, the rose cedes to the upright and spotless white lily. Uninterested in budding or blossoming woman-hood at this point in the volume, Rossetti now refrains from giving priority to the rose's beauty. Later still, the feminine rose is wholly repudiated: "A rose has thorns as well as honey,/I'll not have her for love or money" (116). Recalling "Wee Wee Husband" and "What Does the Bee Do?" the end-rhymes "honey" and "money" infect the rose with the taint of sexual and commercial exchange. The speaker instead responds to the needs of the approaching winter, choosing "holly, bold and jolly,/Honest, prickly, shining holly" (117).

As the floral poems suggest, Rossetti is far from capricious in the different meanings that she ascribes to her favorite images. Examining the significance of a specific image within the context of a specific moment, she explores the subtleties of poetic form and language and the semantic resonance of rhyme and rhythm, silence and sound, apposition and repetition. Similarly, her translations, additions, and revisions, like Hughes's illustrations, attest to the inexhaustible vitality of the poetic processes chronicled in *Sing-Song*. Because the accumulative on-come of successive rhymes posits a dialectic (as in "Sing Me a Song") between the discursive modes of song and tale, lyric and narrative, the progressive arrangement of *Sing-Song* provides a fertile matrix for readers, whatever their ages, to participate in these perpetually generative and abundantly worthwhile processes.

In respect to theme, form, and structure, *Sing-Song* does not differ substantially from Rossetti's verse for adults. Such adult pieces as "Winter Rain," "Winter: My Secret," "Another Spring," "Spring Quiet," "Spring," "A Summer Wish," "Summer," "Autumn," and "Autumn Violets" manifest the same preoccupation with temporal change. For her very slight singsongs, Rossetti does not neglect her craft but pares away all linguistic excrescence and works within the narrowest and most impersonal of lyric forms to distill a fullness of meaning. Like her nursery rhymes, the many poems simply entitled "Song" in *Goblin Market and Other Poems* (1862) and *The Prince's Progress and Other Poems* exhibit a technical range and dexterity, a suggestiveness of thought and feeling, belied by their physical smallness and verbal economy. Nursery rhyme as a genre thus provided the poet, already adept at polishing simplicity into subtlety, with a discipline to which she was accustomed. So although *Sing-Song* deliberately calls attention to its status as children's literature through allusions to "Hop-o'-my-thumb and little Jack Horner" (16) and adaptations of nursery rhyme refrains like "cock-a-doodle-doo" ("kookoorookoo") and "ding dong bell" ("ding a ding"), the poet carefully reworks her material in the composition of lyrics individually and collectively.

Notwithstanding the modesty of its claims as a nursery rhyme book, *Sing-Song* reveals the same self-conscious architectural refinement evident in Rossetti's volumes of adult verse. In fact, it anticipates the sequential movement of *A Pageant and Other Poems* (1881), which Rosenblum identifies as "a pivotal work" (149) in Rossetti's oeuvre. Beginning with two keynote poems, *Pageant* then proceeds through "The Months: A Pageant," a "drawing-room acting piece" written for the family of "one of the All Saints Sisters" (C. Rossetti, *Family Letters* 96). Using the calendar to place temporal experience within a ritualized form and order, the title poem reenacts the movement from winter through autumn dramatized in *Sing-Song* and anticipates the movement from early to later life in *Pageant* as a whole. The second movement in the volume includes several important sonnet sequences—namely, "Monna Innominata," "The Thread of Life" and "Later Life"—that Rossetti hoped would "claim attention" from mature readers (*Family Letters* 94). Insofar as "The Months" precedes a pageant of verse for adults, the 1881 volume reinscribes the sequence chronicled in *Sing-Song* as a generic, as well as a temporal, phenomenon and shows that the connection between Rossetti's verse for children and adults is fluid and processive. What Rosenblum says of her religious and secular poetry applies equally, therefore, to her work for children and adults: these two "canons" of verse possess an essential "sameness" in the approach taken to language and life (155).[11] But Rossetti's poetry, for all its sameness, reveals a startling expressive versatility and experiential intensity.

Childless, Christina Rossetti dedicated her rhymes "without permission to the baby who suggested them" (*Sing-Song,* v)—Charles Cayley's nephew—and rejoiced later when her brother William's children were "imbued with *Sing-Songs*" (*Family Letters* 74).

Although she thought herself "to be deficient in the nice motherly ways which win and ought to win a child's heart" (75), she imbued *Sing-Song* with the necessary poetic feeling to win not just children but adults. Indeed, because *Sing-Song* alternates, as Dante Gabriel Rossetti observes, "between the merest babyism and a sort of Blakish wisdom and tenderness" (2:797), the volume positions itself between two audiences. Although its semichildishness is certainly not unadapted for the innocent listener, its semisuggestiveness should commend itself to the notice of experienced readers. In *Sing-Song,* as in Rossetti's other volumes of verse, the poet's imposition of order on individual lyrics enhances their formal and thematic suggestiveness and contributes to the structural integrity of the collected works. Adapting her characteristic concerns to the technical constraints of nursery rhyme, she exploits the vigor and flexibility of a genre so familiar as to breed critical neglect, if not contempt. The product of animated wit and seasoned wisdom, *Sing-Song* demonstrates Rossetti's resilience as a poet. It belies, moreover, its own artless simplicity and contains many fine lyrics not unadapted for mature reflection.

Notes

1. In "Christina Rossetti and Poetic Sequence," Rosenblum follows the lead established by David A. Kent in two essays on the structural significance of *Verses.* In "W. M. Rossetti and the Editing of Christina Rossetti's Religious Poetry," Kent argues that Rossetti's brother's rearrangement of *Verses* in *The Poetical Works of Christina Georgina Rossetti* is responsible for its "reputation as a loose compilation devoid of significant structural meaning—the product, in short, of 'slavish copying' and no more" (21). In "Sequence and Meaning in Christina Rossetti's *Verses* (1893)," he demonstrates that the meaning of the volume as "spiritual pilgrimage" (261) inheres in the sequential order that Rossetti imposed on disparate poems collected from her devotional prose works.

2. Rosenblum calls *A Pageant and Other Poems* (1881) "Rossetti's third volume of new poems" (146).

3. With "some regret" (C. Rossetti, *Poetical Works* 489), William Rossetti refrained from dismembering the sequence and dispersing individual nursery rhymes among his sister's mature verse. Because, as Kent demonstrates, William had no such scruple with respect to *Verses* or indeed any of her other volumes, he must have appreciated the structural integrity of *Sing-Song.*

4. In "Christina Rossetti's *Sing-Song* and Nineteenth-Century Children's Poetry," Barbara Garlitz's failure to consider the relevance of arrangement to meaning could lead to misperception. For her, Rossetti "too often used stock themes, though, of course, her superior style, taste, and judgment greatly improved them" (542). But in overlooking the originality of *Sing-Song* as a cohesive sequence, Garlitz does not sufficiently distinguish the volume from the popular anthologies that she uses for comparison. Furthermore, her contention that "the nature poems have no moral"

(539) holds only insofar as they do not function as moral exempla; the poems are shaped by the morality informing the volume. Finally, although she rightly points out the moral and sentimental components of *Sing-Song*, Garlitz does not adequately treat its inherent playfulness and so loses the balance that Rossetti so carefully constructs.

5. Rossetti's addition of five more lyrics to the 1893 edition does not substantially alter the dynamic. She did, however, expand many lyrics. She supplemented "I Have a Little Husband" and "The Dear Old Lady in the Lane" each with an extra stanza, for example. These additions clarify the narrative dimensions of the original lyrics.

6. Unless otherwise noted, all citations to *Sing-Song* refer to the pagination of the Dover edition, a faithful and full republication of the volume as it first appeared in 1872.

7. William repeats her self-estimate in his "Memoir" for *The Poetical Works:* "Her habits of composition were entirely of the casual and spontaneous kind, from her earliest to her latest years" (lxviii). Inspiration "came to her (I take it) very easily, without her meditating a possible subject, and without her making any great difference in the first from the latest form of the verses which embodied it; but *some* difference, with a view to right and fine detail of execution, she did of course make when needful" (lxviii–lxix). But as Antony Harrison points out in the first chapter of *Christina Rossetti in Context*, she submitted her work to intensive revision. Like the revisions to "Maude Clare," "Song" and "The Bourne," which Harrison discusses (4–10), Rossetti's translation of the *Sing-Song* lyrics into Italian and her comments on the difficulties encountered in the process provide insight into her habits of composition. For *Ninna-Nanna*, she sought the help of "a better Italian" (*Family Letters* 77)— her cousin Teodorico Pietrocola-Rossetti. Appreciating his assistance, she nevertheless preferred her "own in case their Italian could pass muster,—and very likely it could not, which would make all the difference" (78).

8. Commenting on this passage from *Time Flies*, Steven Connor says that Rossetti "is remarkably dogmatic in her devotional works about such frivolity in language" (441). But as the following pun on *branded* suggests, she was not so dogmatic as to refrain from wordplay even while stating her reservations about it: "This connexion of fire with St. Blaise is not, it seems, accounted for: the fact however remains certain. A pun on his name of 'Blaise' has been suggested as the connecting link, but only to be branded as 'absurd' by at least one author of repute. Yet let us hope that this particular pun if baseless is also blameless" (*Time Flies* 26).

9. Colvin's comments on the adult reader complement Knoepflmacher's reflections on the adult writer in "Balancing of Child and Adult." Concentrating on the work of Margaret Gatty, Carroll, and Kipling, Knoepflmacher demonstrates that Victorian fantasists' conscious awareness of two classes of readers inspired them to exploit an ironic complexity inherent in "the simultaneous yet opposing demands of growth and arrest" (497).

10. The illustrations for *Sing-Song* caused Rossetti much consternation and delayed publication. Originally she approached her publisher, then F. S. Ellis, with a manuscript she had illustrated herself. At her later request, Alice Boyd was commissioned to execute the illustrations. The result was less than happy. However, Ellis's hesitation to publish *Sing-Song* after the lukewarm critical reception given to *Commonplace*, a volume of prose tales, provided Rossetti with a welcome way of avoiding offense to Boyd. Only after she had received her release from Ellis and turned to the publisher George Routledge and Sons did Hughes become her illustrator.

11. This sameness is most evident in "Goblin Market" precisely because it confounds generic distinctions. Although Rossetti did not write "Goblin Market" for children, the end of the poem constructs the experience of the poem as a tale about

childhood told to children, for Laura—the sister who falls prey to goblin tempta-
tions—"call[s] the little ones/And tell[s] them of her early prime,/Those pleasant
days long gone/Of not-returning time" (*Complete Poems* 1:25, ll. 548–51).

Works Cited

Bell, Mackenzie. *Christina Rossetti: A Biographical and Critical Study*. 1898. Reprint.
New York: Haskell House, 1971.

Colvin, Sidney. Review of *Sing-Song*, by Christina G. Rossetti; *The Princess and the
Goblin*, by George Macdonald; *Through the Looking-Glass*, by Lewis Carroll; *More
Nonsense*, by Edward Lear. *Academy* 3 (15 January 1872): 23–24.

Connor, Steven. "'Speaking Likenesses': Language and Repetition in Christina Rossetti's *Goblin Market*." *Victorian Poetry* 22.4 (Winter 1984): 439–48.

Dyhouse, Carol. *Girls Growing Up in Late Victorian and Edwardian England*. London:
Routledge and Kegan Paul, 1981.

Garlitz, Barbara. "Christina Rossetti's *Sing-Song* and Nineteenth-Century Children's
Poetry." *PMLA* 70 (1955): 539–43.

Harrison, Antony H. *Christina Rossetti in Context*. Chapel Hill: University of North
Carolina Press, 1988.

Kaplan, Cora. "The Indefinite Disclosed: Christina Rossetti and Emily Dickinson."
In *Women Writing and Writing About Women*, ed. Mary Jacobus. London: Croom
Helm, 1979.

Kent, David A. "Sequence and Meaning in Christina Rossetti's *Verses* (1893)." *Victorian Poetry* 17.3 (Autumn 1979): 259–64.

———. "W. M. Rossetti and the Editing of Christina Rossetti's Religious Poetry."
Pre-Raphaelite Review 1 (May 1978): 18–26.

Knoepflmacher, U. C. "Avenging Alice: Christina Rossetti and Lewis Carroll."
Nineteenth-Century Literature 41.3 (December 1986): 299–328.

———. "The Balancing of Child and Adult: An Approach to Victorian Fantasies
for Children." *Nineteenth-Century Fiction* 37.4 (March 1983): 497–530.

McGillis, Roderick. "Simple Surfaces: Christina Rossetti's Work for Children." In
The Achievement of Christina Rossetti, ed. David A. Kent. Ithaca: Cornell University
Press, 1987. 208–30.

Rosenblum, Dolores. "Christina Rossetti and Poetic Sequence." In *The Achievement
of Christina Rossetti*, ed. David A. Kent. Ithaca: Cornell University Press, 1987.
132–56.

Rossetti, Christina. *The Complete Poems of Christina Rossetti*. Ed. R. W. Crump. 3 vols.
Baton Rouge: Louisiana State University Press, 1979–90.

———. *The Face of the Deep: A Devotional Commentary on the Apocalypse*. 4th ed. London: Society for Promoting Christian Knowledge, 1902.

———. *The Family Letters of Christina Georgina Rossetti*. Ed. William Michael Rossetti.
1908. Reprint. New York: Haskell House, 1968.

———. *The Poetical Works of Christina Georgina Rossetti*. Ed. William Michael Rossetti.
London: Macmillan, 1904.

———. *Sing-Song: A Nursery Rhyme Book*. Illus. Arthur Hughes. 1872. Reprint. New
York: Dover, 1968.

———. *Speaking Likenesses*. London: Macmillan, 1874.

———. *Time Flies: A Reading Diary*. London: Society for Promoting Christian Knowledge, 1885.

Rossetti, Dante Gabriel. *Letters of Dante Gabriel Rossetti*. Ed. Oswald Doughty and
John Robert Wahl. 4 vols. Oxford: Clarendon, 1965.

Rossetti, William Michael, ed. *Rossetti Papers, 1862 to 1870*. London: Sands, 1903.

————. *Selected Letters of William Michael Rossetti.* Ed. Roger W. Peattie. University Park: Pennsylvania State University Press, 1990.

Ruskin, John. *The Works of John Ruskin.* Ed. E. T. Cook and Alexander Wedderburn. 39 vols. London: George Allen, 1903–12.

Review of *Sing-Song*, by Christina G. Rossetti. *Nation* 14 (2 May 1872): 294–95.

Review of *Sing-Song*, by Christina G. Rossetti. *Scribner's Monthly* 3 (1872): 629.

Taylor, R. Loring. Preface to the Garland edition of *Sing-Song, Speaking Likenesses, Goblin Market.* New York: Garland, 1976.

"We Don't Mind the Bumps": Reforming the Child's Body in Louisa May Alcott's "Cupid and Chow-chow"

Angela M. Estes and Kathleen Margaret Lant

Perhaps the most appalling aspect of Louisa May Alcott's most famous novel, *Little Women* (1868), is the consistent and unrelenting violence that Alcott (1832–88) perpetrates against her characters, against their aspirations, and against her own novel. In this beloved children's story, Alcott distorts and mangles her own narrative and refashions, even mutilates, the bodies of her fictional children. Because Jo—Alcott's favorite character—is far too willfully independent and intelligent to exist in the polite world of nineteenth-century American fiction, she must be reformed to meet the needs of Alcott's audience.

To preserve the decorum required of her and to offer her young readers a message that will not threaten their development into proper and acceptable "little women," Alcott not only disables Jo by metaphorically lobotomizing her and representing her as the mild-mannered Beth but also dismantles and reshapes her text into a story of courtship and marriage. This reshaped and reimagined narrative masks the real horror that lies at the center of *Little Women*—the mutilation and murder of young Jo (Estes and Lant 115–16).

Such atrocities were not, for Alcott, accomplished with impunity, for in her creative life she found herself conflicted about the violence that she committed upon such characters as Jo March. Loyal to the values of the domestic realm, venerated by the nineteenth-century American middle class, Alcott espoused standards for appropriate feminine behavior, but at the same time she felt compelled to depict independent women who would conform to Ralph Waldo Emerson's dicta concerning self-reliance and self-assertion. Her admiration for Emerson was great; she once wrote that "in his own [books] I have found the truest delight, the best inspiration

Children's Literature 22, ed. Francelia Butler, R. H. W. Dillard, and Elizabeth Lennox Keyser (Yale University Press, © 1994 Hollins College).

of my life" ("Reminiscences" 213). But her ambivalence toward his doctrines is clear in her discussion of her own characters:

> I think my natural ambition is for the lurid style. I indulge in gorgeous fancies and wish that I dared inscribe them upon my pages and set them before the public. . . . How should I dare to interfere with the proper grayness of old Concord? The dear old town has never known a startling hue since the redcoats were there. Far be it from me to inject an inharmonious color into the neutral tint. And my favorite characters! Suppose they went to cavorting at their own sweet will, to the infinite horror of dear Mr. Emerson, who never imagined a Concord person as walking off a plumb line stretched between two pearly clouds in the empyrean. [Pickett 107–8]

Alcott longed to create female characters who could express their own sweet will and live as exuberantly and independently as Emerson would have desired a man to live, but she felt strongly her duty to her impressionable readers. As if reaffirming her commitment to her child audience, to the propriety she claimed—but could not always practice—and to the pedagogical aim that she said she cherished as a children's writer, Alcott wrote to William Henry Venable in 1872 that she was grateful her stories were "considered worthy to be used for the instruction as well as the amusement of young people" (*Letters* 172).

In *Little Women*, then, Alcott resolved the conflict between duty to the female sphere and desire for independence in her characters with her assaults upon the body and brain of young Jo. In the same way, Alcott's approach to her children's stories is frequently violent and explosive. In "Fancy's Friend" (1882), for example, Fancy's young playmate—who threatens the Victorian values of Fancy's uncle—is literally dismantled and washed out to sea. Order is restored, but violence is the necessary precursor to that order. In the children's stories, then, perhaps because they are shorter than the children's novels and require a more compressed and speedy resolution to the tensions generated, Alcott resorts to violence against the body of the child, a violence characteristic of the most lurid of horror stories. She accomplishes her resolution of the conflicts inherent in her fiction through the refashioning and rearrangement of the child's body.

Because Alcott and her readers saw her as a guide to young

people, because those who read her works felt that she offered stories about appropriate behavior for the young, the social implications of her assaults upon the body of the child are significant. What exactly is Alcott accomplishing, what is she teaching, with these acts of violence? In a consideration of the place of literary study in the historian's craft, R. Gordon Kelly points out that children's stories in nineteenth-century America enable us to understand how children were shaped to become satisfactory members of their society. Such stories offer a paradigm of "the ways in which a group defines and symbolizes the principles of order thought to structure and sustain a given way of life" and may even "define, often quite directly, the limits of permissible behavior in certain circumstances and suggest typical and acceptable modes of reward and punishment" (154). Using Kelly's observations as an approach to the stories of Louisa May Alcott, Joy Marsella paraphrases Kelly, claiming that "one can examine children's literature to understand a body of knowledge that a group considers essential to its continued existence" (xxiv). Marsella goes on to assert that Alcott sought to fulfill a moral aim in writing for children: "Alcott intended that . . . [her stories] be interpreted as teaching stories. . . . Alcott wanted her readers to take away a lesson that would help them in their lives" (xxiii).

In examining "Cupid and Chow-chow," we would like to explore how Alcott renders the requirements of survival in a much darker way than Kelly or Marsella might imagine.[1] In attempting to offer a model of appropriate behavior to the child audience, Alcott finds herself conflicted by the character she creates—Chow-chow, a girl who, because of her energy and independence, cannot conform to the standards Alcott espouses. Alcott finds herself advocating decorous conduct for Chow-chow, conduct that must ultimately deprive her of what Alcott claims to cherish in her female characters— sweet will. What emerges from the ambivalent narrative is a harsh social criticism. Even as Alcott demonstrates how both young men and young women must behave to move successfully into adulthood as middle-class Americans of the nineteenth century, she undermines and critiques her own advice by showing how children who follow such advice must be perverted from their own energies and inclinations.

We will argue, then, that Alcott departs seriously from the aim of children's literature as expressed by Kelly and Marsella because of her deep ambivalence toward her own culture. While focusing on what children need to know to navigate the tides of adulthood, Alcott perhaps inadvertently lays bare in "Cupid and Chow-chow" the most pernicious tendencies of nineteenth-century American society—the imperative to marry and the practice of heterosexuality. In this story Alcott presents two children—one of each sex— and proceeds to perform the most diabolical acts of reshaping and reforming upon them so that they will fit comfortably into an emblematic marriage. She twists and turns the two youngsters so viciously in order to make them conform that it becomes clear that conformity demands too high a price: marriage is an inhumane and procrustean arrangement which threatens mental health and physical well-being.

"Cupid and Chow-chow" presents the story of two cousins, the title characters, who meet during an extended visit by Chow-chow's family to Cupid's family. Their relationship is, from the outset, stormy. Cupid is an excessively loving little boy who seems incapable of restraining his overt and aggressive demonstrations of affection. Chow-chow is a willful and feisty little girl who is devoted to pursuing her own interests, among them the suffragism she has learned from her mother. Chow-chow resists the persistent Cupid, and although they play together, Chow-chow's vehement rejection of Cupid ultimately causes him to be injured physically. Chow-chow remains intent, like her mother, on her suffragist activities until she is hurt when she falls from a platform during a fiery feminist speech. Throughout the story, the parents watch the children and comment upon their actions, using the children's relationship as a means of commenting upon their own. Cupid and Chow-chow battle constantly over the feminine behaviors that Cupid requires of Chow-chow. In spite of her resistance, Chow-chow eventually renounces her budding feminist sensibilities, and Alcott's tale concludes with a sweet and tender reconciliation between the two children. The story, thus, seems to end with the affirmation that tolerance, kindness, and mutual consideration are necessary for successful relationships between the sexes. And the resolution of the difficulties explored in "Cupid and Chow-chow" can be read, as well, as a caveat concerning the dangers of assertive, independent, and willful behavior on the part of women.

Most readers of "Cupid and Chow-chow" assume that in this story Alcott fulfills the educational and socializing impulses which Kelly and Marsella ascribe to children's literature while at the same time furthering her commitment to women's rights.[2] Seeking to explain Alcott's seemingly vicious parody of women's suffrage in the story ("woman's puckerage," as Chow-chow calls it, is ridiculed throughout the tale), Sarah Elbert asserts that Alcott does not abandon "her own commitment to the New England Woman Suffrage Association and to the *Woman's Journal* position within the woman's rights disputes" (237); in fact, Elbert observes, Alcott's depiction of a young feminist educates all to the necessities of a careful, thoughtful, and mutual approach to women's issues: "The outcome of this tale is a wiser understanding of woman's rights all around" (238). Elbert's argument seems persuasive, but she does not deal with Chow-chow's renunciation of her feminism at the end of the story.

Joy Marsella argues that Alcott consciously hoped to influence young readers to adopt reasonable and measured approaches to social problems, including the problem of female independence and assertiveness. She maintains that Alcott favored those attitudes which were least disruptive and most cooperative; of "Cupid and Chow-chow" she asserts, "This story, with its message directed at both parents and children, suggests the practical position that Alcott adopts in all of her stories. It is a position born of the belief that the best way to correct a situation or to prepare for change is to work within the traditional institutions" (99). In a far more radical reading, Elizabeth Keyser views "Cupid and Chow-chow" as a lesson on the necessity of redefining sexual roles, foregrounding "the story's concern with exploring women's sexual nature and men's sexual tyranny" (111). Keyser goes on to argue that the story ultimately reflects Alcott's conviction that young women must learn independence and young men restraint so that "far more radical reform" (121) is possible.

While we agree with Keyser that Alcott criticizes and questions the construction of gender in her culture, we disagree with those who see Alcott's story as offering lessons to young readers on successful accommodation to the demands of marriage. The violence that Alcott must perpetrate on the bodies and minds of her child protagonists makes it difficult to believe that Alcott is offering here a lesson on appropriate behavior. We argue that Alcott creates and investigates the emblematic relationship of Cupid and Chow-chow not to provide instruction on achieving successful relationships between the sexes—not even to reveal the need for a radical reform of marriage, as Keyser asserts—but rather to launch a devastating critique of the social construction of heterosexuality and the institution of marriage.

Alcott's attitude toward marriage, like her attitude toward Emerson's doctrines, was strongly ambivalent, and this ambivalence must be considered in any attempt to understand "Cupid and Chow-chow." Alcott consistently affirmed her belief in marriage as "life's best lesson" (*Letters* 108), but even this phrase reveals a certain negative attitude toward marriage; at its most successful it is a lesson, not a joy. In a letter to Moncure Daniel Conway, dated 18 February 1865, in which she discusses her novel *Moods*, Alcott makes clear her feeling that marriage can be a disaster but that—under the best of circumstances—it can offer the participants much: "[H]alf the misery of the world seems to come from unmated pairs trying to live their lie decorously to the end, & bringing children into the world to inherit the unhappiness & discord out of which they were born. . . . I [h]onor it [marriage] too much not to want to see it all it should be & to try to help others to prepare for it that they may find it life's best lesson not its heaviest burden" (108).

In "Happy Women," an essay published in the *New York Ledger* in 1868, nearer the publication date of "Cupid and Chow-chow" (1872), Alcott's serious reservations concerning marriage crystallize: "One of the trials of woman-kind is the fear of being an old maid. To escape this dreadful doom, young girls rush into matrimony with a recklessness which astonishes the beholder; never pausing to remember that the loss of liberty, happiness, and self-respect is poorly repaid by the barren honor of being 'Mrs.' instead of 'Miss' " (203). Alcott goes on to present the lives of four women who chose not to marry. She describes "M," who refuses marriage because "I dare not sell my liberty" (204), and "A," "a woman of a strongly individual type, who in the course of an unusually varied experience has seen so much of what a wise man has called 'the tragedy of modern married life,' that she is afraid to try it. Knowing that for one of a peculiar nature like herself such an experiment would be doubly hazardous, she has obeyed instinct and become a chronic old maid" (205). Alcott's message in "Happy Women" is that a woman's individuality, pride, liberty, and happiness are seriously threatened by marriage.

In contrast to the women described in "Happy Women," all three female characters in "Cupid and Chow-chow" submit to the loss of liberty, happiness, and self-respect of marriage, and their submission forms the deadly center of this story for children. Before Alcott makes clear the degree to which aggressive young Chow-chow must be reformed to accommodate herself to the institution of marriage, Alcott must unmask the realities of mid-nineteenth-century American marriage. Three heterosexual couples are presented in "Cupid and Chow-chow"—two adult couples (the parents) and young Cupid and Chow-chow. As the children's relationship develops, amid conflicts and outright physical fights, as the children move successfully toward forming a proper adult union, the parents of the children work out their own differences by observing the progress of the infant courtship: "After dinner, as the mammas sat sewing and the papas talking or reading in one room, the children played in the other, quite unconscious that they were affording both amusement and instruction to their elders" (699).

Even as the children grow into versions of their parents, it becomes clear that the personalities of each have been strongly shaped by their parents' personalities. Cupid is "a trifle vain . . . every mirror showed him a rosy face, with big blue eyes, smiling lips, white teeth, a cunning nose, and a dimple in the chin, not to mention the golden mane that hung about his neck" (690–91), and because his mother has nurtured his vanity, his sole motivation seems to be his need to be loved. Cupid tells Chow-chow, "I'm your cousin, and you *must* love me" (692). Cupid's mother, Mrs. Ellen, has created this "contented young peacock" (691) because she is a traditional and proper woman who knows and accepts her place in the domestic realm and in marriage. Mrs. Ellen lavishes affection upon her husband and upon her son, setting her in sharp contrast to Chow-chow's mother, a committed suffragist who has filled Chow-chow with her feminist zeal. Chow-chow's father describes his wife and daughter this way: "Her mother's ideas are peculiar, and she wants to bring Chow-chow up according to the new lights,—with contempt for dress and all frivolous pursuits; to make her hardy, independent, and quite above caring for such trifles as love, domestic life, or the feminine accomplishments we used to find so charming" (693).

As the story progresses, the conflicts between Cupid and Chow-chow reflect the conflicts generated by the relationships between their own parents. Cupid's parents watch the drama unfold with sympathy and with concern, but they never seem particularly troubled by what goes on in this archetypal clash between masculine privilege and feminine assertion. Chow-chow's parents, however, observe with more interest, for their relationship suffers discord brought about by Mrs. Susan's feminism. What the children do together—moving toward each other, moving apart, resolving their disagreements—mirrors the marriages of both sets of adults. Marsella observes that when Cupid and Chow-chow "play house," they "role-play the normal sequence of their parents' day, a foil which allows Alcott to discuss adult roles and relationships in the guise of children's play" (97).

But both marriages have a sinister aspect, which Marsella does not note, perhaps because it is not as apparent as the overt similarities between parents and children. If the scene of playing house represents the normal sequence of their parents' lives and relationships, something is deeply wrong with those relationships. Here, hidden in an apparently inconsequential scene, sequestered within the child's play of the story, Alcott secures her most devastating view of marriage. In fact, she focuses our attention on this scene of playing house in a powerful yet subtle manner. Structurally it is as if the story were arranged in concentric circles: We, as readers, situate ourselves in the outermost circle and watch the parents. The parents, in the next circle, watch Cupid and Chow-chow, who are situated within a circle more deeply embedded in the story. Finally, Cupid and Chow-chow, playing themselves in their mock marriage, inhabit the very center of the telescoping structure. Alcott, thus, forcefully calls our attention to this narrative moment, fixing our gaze on this telling tableau.

As Alcott portrays the fledgling relationship between Cupid and Chow-chow, she informs us that "the couple" has nine children, and when Chow-chow, now "married," sends her husband off to work, "Mrs. C. bestirred herself at home in a most energetic manner, spanking her nine dolls until their cries rent the air, rattling her dishes with perilous activity" (700). When Chow-chow decides that she must attend a Puckerage meeting, Cupid asks to accompany her, but she replies, "No, you can't! Papa *never* goes; he says they are all gabble and nonsense, and mamma says his club is all smoke and slang, and they *never* go together" (701).

Instead, Cupid spends his evening at "the club" and somehow forgets to return "home"; in fact, he discovers that—according to Chow-chow—he has "been out all night." When he finally does return, Chow-chow is furious and denies Cupid his share of the pie she has been saving for him. When he demands some, Chow-chow says no and Cupid responds angrily:

> This ruffled him, and he told madam she was a bad wife, and he wouldn't love her if she did not instantly give him his share of the little pie. . . . Mrs. C. sternly refused, and locked up the pie, declaring that she hated housekeeping and wouldn't live with him any more, which threat she made good by quitting the house, vowing not to speak to him again that day, but to play alone, free and happy. [701]

Abandoned by his "wife," Cupid seeks to maintain himself and his enormous brood, but the effort proves too much for him: "The deserted husband sat down among his infants with despair in his soul, while the spirited wife, in an immense bonnet, pranced about the room, waving the key of the pie-closet and rejoicing in her freedom. Yes, it was truly pathetic to see poor Mr. Cupid's efforts at housekeeping and baby-tending; for, feeling that they had a double claim upon him now, he tried to do his duty by his children." Cupid's solution to his inability to sustain his role as both father and mother is to murder—at least in his imagination—his excessively large family: "[H]e soon gave it up, piled them all into one bed, and covered them with a black cloth, saying mournfully, 'I'll play they all died of mumps, then I can sell the house and go away.'" He proceeds then to bury "the dead infants . . . under the sofa" (701).

What exactly are we to make of this marriage if it reflects the realities of the parents' unions? As a metaphorical representative of the American wife, a wife who is a feminist, a mother, and a partner, Chow-chow embodies complexities that the surface of the story obscures. In the first place, it is clear that domestic violence is rampant in the household. Alcott offers no explanation for Chow-chow's severe punishment of her children, but a thoughtful consideration of the position of the nineteenth-century middle-class wife might provide abundant answers. Although many women had more leisure and more time to read and to think, their restriction to the domestic realm may have seemed stifling. The troubled marriage between Cupid and Chow-chow seems to have filled Chow-chow with an uncontainable fury; her desire for meaningful activity—Chow-chow wants to lecture, to lead others, to organize for women—has been impeded, and this situation has made her resent her children: "[H]er dolls lay unheeded in corners after a few attempts at dressing and nursing had ended in *ennui*" (699). Her beatings of the dolls may reflect her frustration.

Second, Cupid finds nine children too many to care for, so Chow-chow, too, must find them burdensome, especially when we consider her commitment to Puckerage and the time that activity must involve. Clearly the issue of birth control is being raised here, and Alcott seems to imply that a happy family may be a smaller, more successfully managed family. Finally, the murder of the children by their father is chilling as well. Infanticide as a means of ridding oneself of unwanted and unexpected children and as a strategy for dealing with poverty or the inability to care for children would not have been unknown to Alcott. As Sara Evans writes in her history of American women, "Accounts of abortions and infanticide, frequent in the newspapers and court records of the early nineteenth century, attest to the close relationship between notions of motherhood and real social conditions" (85).

If we read "Cupid and Chow-chow" metaphorically and note the dynamics within the emblematic family, we realize that Alcott has serious reservations about uncontrolled childbearing and about the relationship between husband and wife. A significant point that most readers have ignored is that Cupid and Chow-chow begin their marriage with financial difficulties—"Cupid's finances were in a bad state"—and Chow-chow is concerned: "I shan't marry a poor boy" (698). As Evans points out, nineteenth-century American women without sufficient financial resources found their families larger and much more burdensome than did those women whose families were more prosperous: "[M]any poorer women . . . continued to see motherhood as a condition of extreme jeopardy at worst, and extreme hardship at best" (85).[3]

The sexual fidelity of the parents is called into question here, too, for the story seems to imply that both fathers may have spent nights away from home. We suspect that Chow-chow's father has, because Chow-chow is aware that such things happen and is quick to accuse Cupid of this disloyalty. Cupid, because of the "cosey" picture of marriage that his papa and mama present, expresses "great surprise" at Chow-chow's accusation; even he, however, is fully aware of the gravity of the charge that he had been out all night. He responds immediately by becoming defensive, blaming Chow-chow for the situation and calling her a "bad wife" (701). The hint of marital infidelity is clear in both relationships since both children are fully aware of the ramifications and seriousness of staying out all night. And the resolution of the conflict over marital fidelity is telling as well: Chow-chow deprives Cupid of his conjugal pleasure, the pie, as punishment.

Alcott is not simply offering a feminist diatribe against unequal marriage, marriage which must be reshaped to be workable, nor is she deferring to those who support marriage wholeheartedly. Instead, she has delineated marriage as an institution that—as it is constructed for middle-class American men and women—has potentially devastating consequences. As practiced in "Cupid and Chow-chow," marriage is frequently corrupt and dehumanizing; it may, under less than ideal circumstances, be replete with violence, infidelity, frustration, and mistrust. What is especially curious about Alcott's story, however, is that she offers no solution to the problems of marriage but, rather, launches a full-scale attack on the institution by demonstrating that the only people suited for marriage are those who can be entirely reshaped so that they may exist within this arid and violent institution. Just as Chow-chow's dolls incur injury so that they may quell their young mother's anger, just as they must be reshaped and patched together "with chalk and ink, and plasters of paper stuck all over their faces" (701) to continue as members of this infant family, so Cupid and Chow-chow must rearrange their essential selves, must reform their bodies and their minds so that they may enter the heterosexual realm.

As the emblem of masculinity in Alcott's metaphorical marriage, Cupid, whom Alcott terms "a regular little god of love" (690), represents erotic passion and—for the woman of the nineteenth century—all the problems that erotic, heterosexual love entails: unwanted pregnancy, sexually transmitted diseases, death in childbirth, sole responsibility for offspring (who may fall ill or die), and the insistent demands of a woman's ruling master, her husband. In fact, Cupid is consistently characterized in sexual terms: he is beautiful and loving, he is affectionate and demonstrative, and he is even quite aggressive about his advances toward his young cousin.[4] At their first meeting he insists that she kiss him, love him, defer to him—as any husband of his time would do: "He *must* get at her. So the instant Aunt Susan let him go he ran after the truant, quite panting with eagerness and all aglow with amiable intentions." When Chow-chow rejects his advances, Cupid insists, "Don't be frightened. I'm Cupid. I must kiss you. I truly must. I always do when people come, and I like you very much" (691). He declares himself to Chow-chow confidently, the implication being that no woman of any sense would resist the demands of physical passion, and Chow-chow's resistance so vexes him that he forces himself upon her physically, kissing her repeatedly: "[H]aving begun, Cupid did not know when to leave off" (691).[5]

Alcott thus places the responsibility for all problems with sexuality upon the male and demonstrates that Cupid's own emblem of masculine sexuality must be dismantled for his relationship with Chow-chow to endure. For Cupid and Chow-chow to marry, to fulfill the promise of their relationship as heterosexuals, Cupid must be rendered impotent. Provoked by Cupid's vanity and motivated by a "desire to improve her race" (694), Chow-chow taunts Cupid and forces him to allow her to cut his "yellow hair . . . falling in long, curling love-locks" (690). Chow-chow's assaults to Cupid's body continue as she figuratively castrates him.[6] Challenging him to place his finger in the workings of a hay-cutting machine, she promptly disables him: "Cupid laid his plump forefinger between two wheels, bent on proving his courage at all costs. Chow-chow gave a brisk turn to the handle, slipped in doing so, and brought the whole weight of the cruel cogs on the tender little finger, crushing the top quite flat" (696). By the end of the story Cupid is so successfully reformed that he learns not to make physical or emotional demands upon Chow-chow which she cannot accommodate. In fact, Cupid's reformation—or deformation—is so successful that "the little hand . . . might never be whole and strong again" (696); that is, his sexuality shall, in all likelihood, never be restored. In Alcott's indictment of marriage, it is clear that one of her chief targets is the dangerous sexual arrangement that victimizes woman, and to surmount the problems of this arrangement, the source of sexual pressure and tension must be removed. Alcott considers marriage—especially in the inevitability of sexuality and pregnancy—dangerous for women; for that reason, she imagines that the heterosexual marriage will work safely for women only if sex is completely eradicated.

Chow-chow presents a different aspect of Alcott's bitter denunciation of marriage. If Cupid must be unsexed for marriage to work, if he must be deprived of his desire, his potency, and his strength, Chow-chow must be deprived of the qualities that render her an inappropriate candidate for marriage as well. Chow-chow must submit to the same sort of psychic violation and physical reformation with which Alcott handles the irrepressible Jo in *Little Women*. Because it is clear, both from Cupid and Chow-chow's relationship and from the relationship of Chow-chow's mother and father, that feminists—self-reliant, thinking, and assertive women—do not make good wives, Alcott concludes that to be married, a woman must be metaphorically lobotomized.

Alcott does not criticize feminism here but rather demonstrates with a heavy irony that marriage is a corrupt arrangement because an independent woman cannot exist within its confines: significantly, Chow-chow's head, the seat of her knowledge and will, must be violently rearranged, receiving a blow—resulting in a "purple lump" (703)—that seems to reorient her to her family and to her young lover. Chow-chow—delivering a women's Puckerage lecture —is thrown from a heavy piece of furniture and badly bruised. Her response is to repudiate her nascent feminism and to cling to her mother, the feminist Mrs. Susan, in a moment that seems to reestablish the vital family unit. As Chow-chow renounces her cause, so does her mother, and both seem to have undergone complete mental transformation to do so.

The metaphorical assaults to Chow-chow's body continue unabated, for, by the end of the story, Chow-chow has so lost the feisty spirit which caused her to hold herself aloof from Cupid's embraces that she is now ready to succumb to Cupid completely. The pie, which Chow-chow has tauntingly withheld from Cupid, is now to be divided "zackly in halves," as Cupid insists "with masculine justice" (704). This scene is not, however, evidence of the couple's happy and egalitarian resolution of their conflicts; their romance is not "sealed by sharing a pie" (Elbert 238). Rather, the pie has been from the beginning of the story associated with Chow-chow's sexuality and thus her body. In fact, Chow-chow has consistently been associated in Cupid's mind with an edible treat—physical pleasure: "Her very name was pleasing to him, for it suggested Indian sweetmeats" (691). The attack on the pie is frighteningly aggressive; Cupid produces a "jack-knife," cuts the pie in half, and together they consume the treat: "[T]hey devoured the little bone of contention." In this "childish ceremony," Cupid and Chow-chow have consummated their marriage by cannibalizing Chow-chow's very body "until the last crumb vanished" (704).

In the final scenes, all three heterosexual couples are united, but both Cupid and Chow-chow have undergone both psychic and physical reformation to accommodate themselves to their new relationship. Chow-chow "penitently" renounces her suffragist platform in cloying babytalk—"I'm not going to have any flatporm; I'm going to be good and play with Coopy, if he'll let me"—while Cupid stands "near with a torn jacket and a bruise on the already wounded hand" (703), as if the physical rearrangement that he has thus far endured has been insufficient to ensure his permanent alteration. Chow-chow then acquiesces to Cupid—even her hair is radically altered—but Cupid is very careful to keep his embraces chaste and cool: "[Cupid's] ready and eloquent forgiveness touched Chow-chow's heart, and the lofty top-knot went down upon Cupid's shoulder as if the little fortress lowered its colors in token of entire surrender. Cupid's only sign of triumph was a gentle pat on the wild, black head" (704). The problematic sexuality of this relationship is foregrounded by Alcott's use of sexually evocative language. Chow-chow's eyes are "shy" and "wet" (703), signaling both her sexual innocence and her sexual readiness. And her entire being is a "fortress," a virginal stronghold that has now yielded in "entire surrender" (704).

As Cupid and Chow-chow resolve their differences, so do Mr. George and Mrs. Susan, and Alcott concludes the story with a forecast of marital happiness, which seems heavily ironic, given her portrayal of domestic violence and disharmony and her own physical abuse of her characters. As Cupid and Chow-chow agree to be friends "and never quarrel any more . . . Mr. George's eyes made the same proposal, and his wife answered it as tenderly as Chow-chow did Cupid. Not a word was said, for grown people do not ''fess' and forgive with the sweet frankness of children; but both felt that the future would be happier than the past, thanks to the lesson they had learned from the little romance of Cupid and Chow-chow" (704).

Clearly this happy view of marriage does not withstand an examination of Alcott's story with respect to the child's body and its metaphorical significance. Alcott's assaults on the bodies of the children in "Cupid and Chow-chow" reveal that the institution of marriage can be maintained and perpetuated only by men and women whose very being has been radically altered. By the end of the story, Cupid and Chow-chow, along with their adult counterparts, can look forward to a "future . . . happier than the past" only because they have been physically dismembered and metaphorically lobotomized into suitably marriageable versions of themselves. Alcott has—as her audience expects—written a story that offers the young a lesson on how to navigate the difficulties of their own culture, how to create a successful marriage. The triumph at the end of the story, however, is undercut by the fact that we watch Cupid and Chow-chow march happily off into the future of marriage as if into the land of the living dead, declaring proudly, "[W]e don't mind the bumps" (704).

Notes

This essay is taken from our book *Their Own Sweet Will: Resistance and Relationship in the Works of Louisa May Alcott,* forthcoming from the University of Tennessee Press. A version of the essay was read in the Children's Literature Section of the Modern Language Association Conference, 1992. Our work on "Cupid and Chow-chow" was supported in part by a research grant from the Children's Literature Association.

1. The story first appeared in *Hearth and Home* 4.20–21 (18 and 25 May 1872). Later it was collected in *Cupid and Chow-chow, etc., Aunt Jo's Scrap-Bag,* vol. 3 (Boston: Roberts Brothers, 1874); see Marsella 150. References are to the Booss edition of 1982.

2. The notable exception is Eugenia Kaledin, who finds "Cupid and Chow-chow" to be an unabashed example of Alcott's "self-denial," a betrayal of her own commitment to the suffrage movement: "[T]he polemical force of 'Cupid and Chow-chow' is such that we put it down feeling no ambiguity. It is clearly an outspokenly hostile argument against the Woman's Suffrage Movement, a group Alcott had identified with throughout her life" (256).

3. Alcott's concern over birth control and the family structure may have been fueled by her commitment to the reformist zeal of her father, Bronson Alcott, who had led his family to live in the utopian community of Fruitlands. Several of the utopian communities which sprang up during the early part of the nineteenth century began, as Evans puts it, "to experiment with new forms of sexual relations which challenged the male/female, public/private dichotomy" (77). Evans points out that many such communities were concerned with birth control and management of masculine sexuality (78). In fact, one reason Fruitlands itself may have failed was that the more radical participants convinced Bronson Alcott that celibacy was necessary to the utopian community (Showalter xiv).

4. We follow Elizabeth Keyser here in her reading of Cupid as "a diminutive version of Eros" (117).

5. Keyser calls this act a metaphorical rape (111).

6. Keyser, too, finds this a scene of "symbolic castration" that indicates Alcott's concern with "men's sexual tyranny" (111–14). Keyser argues that men's need to prove themselves ultimately undermines masculine sexuality because it "actually unmans them—or prompts women to try to do so" (114). We, however, argue that Alcott is not concerned here with establishing a potentially equal sexual relationship between men and women—with, in Keyser's terms, restraining masculine sexuality and exploring feminine sexuality (111). Alcott foregrounds the potentially negative effects of sexuality on women's lives and indicates that masculine sexuality must be eradicated for even the dark version of marriage she foreshadows here between Cupid and Chow-chow to be accomplished.

Works Cited

Alcott, Louisa May. "Cupid and Chow-chow." In *Works of Louisa May Alcott,* ed. Claire Booss. 1873. Reprint. New York: Avenel, 1982.

———. "Happy Women." In *Alternative Alcott,* ed. Elaine Showalter. New Brunswick: Rutgers University Press, 1988.

———. *Little Women, or Meg, Jo, Beth and Amy.* 1868. Reprint. Boston: Little, Brown, 1968.

———. "Reminiscences of Ralph Waldo Emerson." *Youth's Companion* 55.21 (25 May 1882): 213–14.

———. *The Selected Letters of Louisa May Alcott.* Ed. Joel Myerson and Daniel Shealy with Madeleine B. Stern. Boston: Little, Brown, 1987.

Elbert, Sarah. *A Hunger for Home: Louisa May Alcott's Place in American Culture.* New Brunswick: Rutgers University Press, 1987.

Estes, Angela M., and Kathleen Margaret Lant. "Dismembering the Text: The Horror of Louisa May Alcott's *Little Women.*" *Children's Literature* 17 (1989): 98–123.

Evans, Sara M. *Born for Liberty: A History of Women in America.* New York: Free Press, 1989.

Kaledin, Eugenia. "Louisa May Alcott: Success and the Sorrow of Self-Denial." *Women's Studies* 5 (1978): 251–63.

Kelly, R. Gordon. "Literature and the Historian." *American Quarterly* 26 (May 1974): 141–59.

Keyser, Elizabeth. "'Playing Puckerage': Alcott's Plot in 'Cupid and Chow-chow.'" *Children's Literature* 14 (1986): 105–22.

Marsella, Joy A. *The Promise of Destiny: Children and Women in the Short Stories of Louisa May Alcott.* Westport, Conn.: Greenwood, 1983.

Pickett, LaSalle Corbell. "Louisa May Alcott." In *Across My Path: Memories of People I Have Known.* Freeport, N.Y.: Books for Libraries, 1970.

Showalter, Elaine, ed. Introduction to *Alternative Alcott.* By Louisa May Alcott. New Brunswick: Rutgers University Press, 1988.

The Inner Family of The Wind in the Willows

Bonnie Gaarden

> When all is said the boastful, unstable Toad, the hospitable Water Rat, the shy, wise, childlike Badger, and the Mole with his pleasant habit of brave boyish impulse, are neither animals nor men, but are types of that deeper humanity which sways us all. [Richard Middleton, circa 1908, quoted in Green 258]

As I began to read criticism of *The Wind in the Willows,* I found myself disconcerted to see the main characters frequently described as "bachelors." The small but emphatic voice of my childhood reading insisted that these characters were like nothing so pedestrian as adult human males; they were the Rat, the Mole, the Toad, and the Badger—ageless, timeless, genderless. Certainly, as the critics say, the book is rich in literary and social satire, and it gains a great deal of power in its evocation of a pastoral golden age; certainly the main characters resemble Kenneth Grahame's friends as well as aspects of his own personality. But none of this can account for the delight I took in the novel at nine. It seems to me that Grahame's story appeals to all ages because it illustrates at least two dynamics intimately familiar at all ages: family relationships and psychological growth.

That the four main characters are neither plain-and-simple animals nor disguised humans is indicated by their unique presentation in the text. In *The Wind in the Willows* there are many rabbits and field mice, any number of swallows, and hordes of weasels and stoats, but only one Water Rat, one Mole, one Toad, and one Badger, whose species names and personal names are the same. Like the original, hermaphroditic Adam of alchemy, they include all Ratness, Moleness, and so forth, in their own singular selves, standing out from the more ordinary multitudes of other animals like Platonic forms. Appropriately, as Lois Kuznets has noted, these characters display "feminine" as well as "masculine" characteristics ("Whither Blows" 176, 179): they feed one another, nurture and

Children's Literature 22, ed. Francelia Butler, R. H. W. Dillard, and Elizabeth Lennox Keyser (Yale University Press, © 1994 Hollins College).

support one another, and foster among themselves a cosy domesticity. In this context, Grahame's refusal to so much as name any female animal until the very last page of the book does not obliterate the feminine. Rather, it circumvents the reader's habit of classifying individuals primarily by sex,[1] and leads us to differentiate, instead, by species.

But having created four unique and autonomous characters of differing species, Grahame proceeds to set up distinctly familial roles and relationships among them.[2] Badger and Rat are mature, parental characters. Initiated in their world's ways, they are insiders of River Bank society who can manage the Wild Wood; they are protectors, rescuers, teachers, and directors of Toad and Mole. Toad and Mole are child figures, uninitiated outsiders, the learners and seekers of the book. Mole is a novice on the River Bank, and Toad, although he has inherited a grand house and important social station, has yet to grow into either. Yet these characters do not simply fill family roles. Their autonomy, uniqueness, and gender inclusivity allow us to experience them as psychic entities that inhabit everyone's soul.

Badger, for instance, is the father. He is biggest, potentially dangerous ("Nobody interferes with *him*. They'd better not" [10]), often gruff and authoritative. When present, he is in charge; he scolds Toad in the name of Toad's father (213–15) and "paternally" pats the other characters on the head (60). He is the final rescuer: "When people were in any fix they mostly went to Badger, or else Badger got to know of it somehow" (68). He alone of the main characters is never seized by violent emotion, never tempted to leave home.

But Badger is not only a father figure. He also resembles the organizing center of the psyche, the "inner guiding factor" that Jungians call the Self. Some individuals experience the Self as an inner source of wisdom, which the Naskapi Indians call the Great Man (Von Franz, "Process" 163), and Badger enjoys "great man" status in his community. He lives in an underground labyrinth in "the heart," "the very middle," of the Wild Wood (10, 40). Both the labyrinth and the wood are common symbols of the unconscious (Jung "Approaching" 76; Von Franz, *Fairytales* 93). That Badger lives in the center of the wood reflects the key position the Self holds in the unconscious, as the "greatest power in the psyche" (Von Franz, "Process" 234). The unconscious contains, and is partly shaped by, past cultural traditions (Von Franz, *Fairytales* 52), so it is fitting that

Badger's labyrinth winds its way through the ruins of an ancient city and that Badger is the only character who demonstrates any awareness of history (72–73).

Badger is elusive; he cannot be socially called on or invited, but must be caught as he slips along a hedgerow at dawn or dusk, or "hunted up in his own house in the middle of the wood, which was a serious undertaking" (98). The Self, too, is not casually available but can be encountered only after much developmental work. Just as Badger "simply hates society" (14) and can be found only by those willing to leave the beaten track, the Self demands that we differentiate ourselves from the collective. Just as Badger is a director and a rescuer, the Self directs the psyche toward expansion and maturity (Von Franz, "Process" 163, 207, 237).[3]

Rat, in contrast, is motherly. He, too, is a rescuer, saving both Mole and Toad from immersions in the River (17–18, 199), finding Mole in the Wild Wood, and chaperoning Toad through his misadventures in the gypsy cart. But where Badger is authoritative, Rat is empathetic and nurturing; he adopts Mole into his home and teaches him to swim and to row; he skillfully steers Mole through the emotional crisis of "Dulce Domum" and is so worried when Toad fakes a physical collapse that, suspicion giving way to concern, he runs to fetch a doctor (107–8); he hates "disappointing people" even to indulge his own inclinations (29), and disciplining Toad makes him feel "like a brute" (236). Where Badger, like the traditional father, is often not available, Rat, like the traditional mother, is always at hand. And unlike Badger, Rat is emotionally vulnerable, as shown in his susceptibility to wanderlust in "Wayfarers All."

Rat thus personifies those psychic aspects traditionally conceived as feminine. He is associated with water, a feminine symbol. In many ways he functions like a man's anima, or "inner woman." As the anima is an initiator into spiritual life, or "soul guide" (Von Franz, "Process" 193; *Fairytales* 67), so Rat leads Mole to Pan and interprets the song of the panpipes. As the anima enables the "flow of life" in the psyche (Von Franz, *Fairytales* 68), so Rat enables Mole's new life on the river.[4] As the anima emphasizes relatedness, so Rat introduces Mole into community. The anima also mediates between the ego and the Self (Von Franz, "Process" 195), and we notice that it is Rat who brings Mole and Toad into contact with Badger, finding Badger's door when he and Mole need shelter (53–55) and instigating Badger's involvement in the troubles of Toad (64). Artistic creativity and sensitivity to nature are anima characteristics (Von Franz, "Process" 186), and Rat is a nature poet, celebrating the joys of river life in verse and song.

Mole is the good child of the story, his steady growth and maturation contrasting with Toad's erratic career.[5] In the first third of the book he depends on Rat for physical rescue and emotional support. In the next few chapters we see him becoming less dependent as he joins the attempt to reclaim Toad and participates in the rescue of Portly the Otter and in the spiritual revelation of Pan Island.

A turning point occurs in "Wayfarers All," in which Mole is able to recognize Rat's "possession" and take both aggressive (174) and empathic (175) action to help his friend recover. From then on we see Mole more in the company and under the direction of Badger than of Rat as the animals undertake the liberation of Toad Hall. This sequence parallels the development of a child, who first learns basic skills of self-care and cooperation within the family from her "mothers" (male or female) and then moves into the outside world, the realm of the "fathers," where she must master skills of defense and aggression.

Like any child, Mole has fits of impatience in which he overestimates his capacities: when he seizes the oars from Rat (17) and when he takes off by himself into the Wild Wood (43). But he learns from these failures. By acknowledging his limitations (19, 76) he ultimately transcends them, learning how to swim and row (21) and winning the competence and confidence needed to "stroll" through the Wild Wood (240–41).

In Mole, the developing-child character, we can see the healthy "growing edge" of the ego, full of wonder, easily pleased, eager to learn. In a typical path to psychic maturity, after integrating the anima or animus, an individual may develop a conscious awareness of the Self (Von Franz, "Process" 207–8). Thus Mole, after finding a mentor in Rat, also discovers a strong affinity with Badger based on their common love of being underground. According to Jungian analyst Marie Louise von Franz, the ego is a "mirror image" of the Self (*Fairytales* 43) and, in optimum psychic health, obeys the Self's promptings and guidance—hence Mole's functioning, in the last third of the book, as a sort of Badger, Junior. Badger's disquisition to a "heartily assenting" Mole about underground as home can be read as a lecture in praise of the goal of all psychic development, the stable inner life that results from "living from one's center" and that enables one's soul to remain intact despite outer circumstances. "There's no security, or peace and tranquillity, except underground. And then, if your ideas get larger and you want to expand—why, a dig and a scrape, and there you are! If you feel your house is a bit too big, you stop up a hole or two, and there you are again! No builders, no tradesmen, no remarks passed on you by fellows looking over your wall, and, above all, *no weather*" (70–71).

Rat's riverbank dwelling, Badger observes, is liable to floods (as demonstrated psychologically in "Wayfarers All"), and Toad is most exposed of all, vulnerable to blown-off tiles, sinking and cracking walls, broken windows, draughty rooms—all of which reflect the unstable Toad's tendency to be blown from boisterous exuberance to utter despair at every puff of circumstance.[6]

Toad is the bad child—not morally bad, just rawly unsocialized. Toad, who is said to have been modeled partly on Grahame's young son, Alastair (Green 269, 282), is like a "natural" child in his total self-centeredness, inability to consider others (see Sale 183), and lust to be the center of attention. He is driven by uncontrolled, self-glorifying impulses, moving restlessly from one fad to another, searching for external props to complete himself. Ultimately, he is questing for an inflated and all-powerful sense of himself: "Toad at his best and highest, Toad the terror . . . before whom all others must give way or be smitten into nothingness and everlasting night" (113). He is struggling to realize, in other words, the very young child's fantasies of omnipotence. Unlike Mole, Toad seems incapable of learning from disaster. Unchastened by imprisonment, danger, and disgrace, he describes his adventure into the Wide World as "fun" in which he came off rather well (200–202), and no catastrophe long suppresses his penchant for conceited songs.

Toad, whom Peter Green calls "the Id personified" (282), represents the ego's primitive impulses, that juvenile wildness that most people learn to govern but few entirely outgrow. He is our primal self-centeredness, love of speed and admiration, lust to sweep everything down in the wave of our magnificent onset. As such, he arouses the same sheepish amusement as the inflated "moi" of Sesame Street's Miss Piggy. As Mole grows by assimilating Rat and Badger, Toad remains immature in resisting them. Toad's rebellion against Badger's gruff authoritarianism resembles the ego's "hardening" against the guidance of the Self.[7] Such hardening produces *hubris* (Henderson 123) and various neuroses (Von Franz, *Fairytales*

43–44), and, appropriately, Toad behaves like a manic-depressive (Green 282–84) with hubris as his leading characteristic.[8]

Recognizing the differences between the characters' roles helps us, I think, to understand a recognized ambiguity in the novel: Grahame's attitudes about home as opposed to adventure, or doing one's duty as opposed to breaking away. Green, among others, demonstrates that both poles attracted Grahame, generating a powerful inner conflict that may have largely produced his impulse to write (53). Many critics have seen this inner conflict reflected in the novel. Where Mole's departure from home is treated positively, Rat's attempt at a similar departure is forcibly aborted, and Toad's adventure into the Wide World seems disapproved by the author, as well as the other characters.[9] If we read the story as a tale of psychic growth, however, these differences can be accounted for by differences between the characters and their developmental stages.

Mole's movement away from and back to his old home is part of his maturation. He leaves his dark underground burrow for a new and exciting community, but when he smells his old home on a winter walk, he is overcome with nostalgic longing and takes Rat to visit it. There, before he goes to sleep, he looks over the "familiar and friendly things which had long been unconsciously a part of him" and "saw clearly how plain and simple—how narrow, even—it all was; but clearly, too, how much it all meant to him. . . . He did not at all want to abandon the new life and its splendid spaces. . . . But it was good to think he had this to come back to, this place which was all his own . . . and could always be counted upon for the same simple welcome" (96).

Mole has genuinely outgrown his little "cellarage" to become an inhabitant of the "upper world," but he continues to love, remember, and occasionally yearn for his old burrow. The return is an integrating experience; he will move back to his new, expanded field of endeavor and accomplishment with greater wholeness because of this renewed acquaintance with his past and with his private resources after this reconnecting with, and reaffirmation of, his own underground.

Water Rat also moves away from and back to his home. Sarah Gilead has pointed out the similarities between Ratty's impulse toward the Ocean and Mole's emergence from burrow to River Bank: both impulses occur in response to a seasonal "call" (spring growth and autumnal migration), both animals find a potential mentor and are fascinated by his stories, both share an initiatory picnic with the mentor, which is followed by an invitation ("Undoing" 153–54). But there are also profound differences between Rat and Mole and their respective experiences. From the beginning of the story, Rat is presented as a more mature figure than Mole, with a developed identity, expertise, and commitments, which all center on the River. He is the River's poetic genius and personification.[10] It is Rat who first hears the panpipes, and he, not Mole, can understand the words in the music, suggesting not only a spiritual sensitivity but also his close attunement to the rural god.

There is also a difference in the quality of the excitement and fascination involved in these experiences. Mole's departure from Mole End is emotionally simple, full of the delight of fresh air after stale, escape from boring routine, sights and sounds and company after "the seclusion of the cellarage" (1–2). He is "spellbound" by the River like a small child trotting after a story-spinning elder (3), but there is never a hint that this sort of spell alters his normal consciousness. On the other hand, Rat's fascination with the stories of Sea Rat suggests hypnosis.

[The Sea Rat] filled his glass with the red and glowing vintage of the South, and, leaning towards the Water Rat, compelled his gaze and held him, body and soul, while he talked. Those eyes were . . . foam-streaked grey-green . . . in the glass shone a hot ruby. . . . The twin lights, the shifting grey and the steadfast red, mastered the Water Rat and held him bound, fascinated, powerless. The quiet world outside their rays receded far away and ceased to be. . . . Lastly, in his waking dream it seemed to [Water Rat] that the Adventurer had risen to his feet, but was still speaking, still holding him fast with his sea-grey eyes (171–72).

The Sea Rat, after issuing his invitation, leaves Water Rat "paralyzed and staring." Then Ratty "mechanically" returns home to pack, moving "like a sleep-walker," and, when addressed by Mole, responds in a "dreamy monotone." Most alarming to Mole, Rat's eyes are no longer "clear and dark and brown" (175) but "glazed and set and turned a streaked and shifting grey—not his friend's eyes, but the eyes of some other animal!" (174). As we know, but Mole does not, these are the eyes of the Sea Rat.

This fascination seems less like the liberating attraction of healthy

growth and more like psychic possession, resembling Toad's reaction to motorcars (see Kuznets, *Kenneth Grahame* 108). When Toad
is first "possessed" by that attraction, he, like the bewitched Rat,
speaks in a "dreamy monotone" (37). Both animals are said to
be "mastered" "body and soul" by "passion" and plunged into a
"waking dream" in which normal reality recedes (112). In this state,
both animals react to the blocking of their goals with physical struggle, then emotional paroxysm, and, finally, depression and apathy
(104–5, 174–75). We can see that although Rat's impulse away from
home parallels Mole's circumstantially, it parallels Toad's "strange
seizure" emotionally (see Gilead, "Undoing" 154). We might read
Grahame here, not as alternately celebrating and warning against
impulse, but as suggesting that all impulses are not equal and that
a movement which at one stage of development amounts to healthy
growth may, at another, do psychic damage. In short, whereas Mole
appears to be appropriately exercising the omnipotentiality of adolescence, Rat's more advanced development and deeper commitments make continuity the healthier choice.

It is frequently said that Rat "sublimates" his desire to roam in
his poetry, like his creator, who worked out his own adventure-duty
conflict in his writing. The sensitivities—to description, to seasonal
change, to emotional currents "in the air" (154)—that make Rat
a poet also render him liable to emotional possession. We might
think of Rat's movement from and back home as the product of runaway inspiration. In its strength and possessive aspect, Rat's seizure
resembles what Jungians call an anima mood, which is often associated with "wishful fantasy" and "destructive illusions" (Von Franz,
"Process" 187, 190). (The classic symbols of this dark anima aspect
are the Sirens, and we may note certain similarities in Ulysses' way
of dealing with the temptation they presented and Mole's treatment of the bewitched Rat.) [11] The constructive response to anima-
inspired fantasies, interestingly, is to concretize them in artistic creation, so that they add to the growth of the inner life, instead of
luring the victim ever deeper into the sea (Von Franz, "Process"
195). Whereas Mole's experience leads to personal growth, Rat's
experience fuels his art.

Toad leaves home to escape the restraint that his friends place
on his self-destructive behavior and finds, not freedom, but literal
imprisonment, as well as "enslavement" to his impulses (see Mendelson 135). Mole moves away from his old home toward maturation,

but Toad, in leaving, is running away from maturation, and Toad's possession is not, like Rat's, a brief aberration of a mature sensitivity and creative imagination but a headlong plunge into juvenile wildness.[12]

The retaking of Toad Hall, when all four animals come together, amply illustrates the familial and the psychological dynamics at work in this story. Rat's motherly role is contrasted to Badger's fatherly one. While Mole and Badger are out scouting the enemy position, Rat pulls Toad out of the River, feeds him, dries him, dresses him, and scolds him. Rat's fussiness during the arming scene is comically, stereotypically maternal in contrast to Badger's calm nonchalance.

> The Badger sat in the arm-chair, reading the paper, and not concerning himself in the slightest about what was going to happen that very evening. The Rat, on the other hand, was running round the room busily, with his arms full of weapons of every kind, distributing them in four little heaps on the floor. . . .
>
> When it began to grow dark, the Rat . . . stood each of them up alongside of his little heap, and proceeded to dress them up for the coming expedition. . . . The Badger laughed good-humoredly and said, "All right, Ratty! It amuses you and it doesn't hurt me. I'm going to do all I've got to do with this here stick." But the Rat only said, "*Please,* Badger! You know I shouldn't like you to blame me afterwards and say I had forgotten *anything!*" [217, 223–24]

Naturally enough, it is Rat who ends up babysitting during the expedition after Badger has threatened to send Toad back for his disruptive bumbling: "The procession moved on; only this time the Rat brought up the rear, with a firm grip on the shoulder of Toad" (225). And Rat is not set to oversee the weasel prisoners because he is "a poet" (230). Being a poet might mean being too sensitive, emotional, or imaginative, but any characteristic that one can fit into this context is almost certainly "feminine."

The good child–bad child contrast between Toad and Mole also emerges. Mole's increasing maturity and responsibility are demonstrated when he acts on his own initiative to plant disinformation among the stoat sentries (218–21) and when, in the skirmish, he effectively functions as Badger's major assistant (228–31). But whereas Mole is enormously useful, Toad is a nuisance, falling into the River, lagging behind, causing upset and confusion (224–25). Mole's ruse with the sentries earns Badger's resounding praise and some invidious comparison ("Mole, . . . I perceive you have more sense in your little finger than some other animals have in the whole of their fat bodies"), which makes Toad "simply wild with jealousy" (221). After the battle, Toad feels "rather hurt" that Badger does not compliment him as Badger has the Mole, but he "put[s] all his jealousy from him" to thank Mole for his efforts, thus finally earning much-desired paternal approval from Badger ("There spoke my brave Toad!" [229–31]). And when Toad writes "disgraceful" dinner invitations, which must be "confiscated" by Rat, "the good Mole" is set to "filling up plain, simple invitation cards" (237).

Viewed psychologically, the task facing the animals in this section is the reclamation and integration of the disruptive, self-destructive Toad. First they try to convert him, but neither rational argument nor appeals to his better nature have any lasting effect (101–2; 201–2). Then they attempt forcible restraint, but Toad escapes, steals a motorcar, and is jailed; the vacated Toad Hall is soon teeming with weasels and stoats—much less desirable neighbors than Toady! It is a psychological commonplace that trying to control unruly impulses by direct repression will only foster an even more unruly neurosis.

Ultimately, the animals gain access to Toad Hall through an underground tunnel that leads from the riverbank into Toad's pantry. Their passage suggests birth as irresistibly as Mole's original "breakout" into the upper world, and indeed, that underground journey introduces a new stage of life for the four friends. To this point, their efforts with Toad have led to more trouble. When they enter the tunnel, Toad is still a liability; his "nervous terrors" and inability to pay attention threaten to sabotage the whole expedition (224–25). All this changes, however, when Toad finally faces something that makes a true impression on him—his own caricature. The Chief Weasel, presiding over a banquet and mocking Toad in a "little song" sung in a "high, squeaky voice," hits Toad where it genuinely hurts, sending him into the fray "frenzied with excitement and injured pride" (227).

We see Toad enlisted into effective combat against Toadishness ("he went straight for the Chief Weasel" [227]) because, of all things, he cannot bear to be mocked. Knowing people will laugh will keep even an immodest person from seizing the spotlight; pride will do the job as well. Rat and Badger finish the reclamation project by showing that they have learned how to manage Toad, not by argument and not by force, but by understanding, anticipating, and outmaneuvering him. When they intercept his egotistical dinner invitations and announce that at this dinner there will be no speeches or songs, "Toad saw that he was trapped. They understood him, they saw through him, they had got ahead of him" (235). Toad's concession—"you are right, I know, and I am wrong"—and his assurance that "you will never have cause to blush for me again" (236) might indicate he has realized, as most children do, that flaunting an inflated ego draws ridicule, not admiration, and that his old self-promoting ways have, in fact, made him the "laughing-stock" of the stoats and weasels (237).

But notice that, for all the friends' trumpeted determination to produce a "converted Toad" (99), Toad is merely "altered" (240). There is no converting Toad, and even if "Toad's Last Little Song" were not written to make that very point, Grahame admitted as much when asked what resulted from Toad's good resolutions: "Of course Toad never really reformed; he was by nature incapable of it" (Green 248). What Toad *has* learned is how to use conventional behavior to gain Toadish satisfactions, becoming to all of his dinner guests "an object of absorbing interest" and confounding Rat and Badger with a superb performance of humility and modesty (239; see Mendelson 142). Our Toads will always be alert to such satisfaction and always be singing their conceited songs in the bedroom of our fantasy, but with self-awareness and strategy we can confine their displays, and Grahame, at least, seems to think that this is quite enough.[13] Indeed, what is most refreshingly pagan about *The Wind in the Willows* is Grahame's refusal to demonize Toady.

Toadishness has traditionally been demonized in Western culture. Notice, for example, that for Milton's Satan (who once appears "squat like a toad, close at the ear of Eve") the Toadish qualities of self-centeredness, inflation, the failure of decent feeling, and the refusal of appropriate behavior inexorably lead to hatred, cosmic alienation, self-disgust, malicious destruction, and impotence (*Paradise Lost* IV.800). If the Toad is truly so poisonous, our only hope is to uproot him wholesale from the personality: stomp him, strangle him, starve him, or at least, as Grahame's hysterical motorists demand, "Bind him, chain him, drag him to the nearest police-station! Down with the desperate and dangerous Toad!" (195).

But Grahame's Toad, properly understood, disciplined, and even appreciated, becomes one of the Four Heroes, a valued member of the final "quaternio" of characters that represents psychic wholeness (Von Franz, "Process" 214, 230). And Toad's flight from home, though so different from Rat's or Mole's, ultimately leads, like theirs, to good: his own integration and the taming of the Wild Wood, which symbolizes that expansion of consciousness in which psychic growth consists. A formerly inaccessible complex, which at unpredictable intervals leapt out of the unconscious to create havoc in feelings and behavior, now becomes conscious and thus subject to exploration and management.

In the last two paragraphs of the book, Grahame emphasizes the mythic stature that his "four Heroes" have achieved by introducing the first and only complete biological family in the story to laud and memorialize them.

> The mother-weasels would bring their young ones to the mouths of their holes and say, pointing, "Look, baby! There goes the great Mr. Toad! And that's the gallant Water Rat, a terrible fighter, walking along o' him! And yonder comes the famous Mr. Mole, of whom you so often have heard your father tell!" But when their infants were fractious . . . they would quiet them by telling them how, if they didn't hush, . . . the terrible grey Badger would up and get them. This was a base libel on Badger, . . . but it never failed to have its full effect.

With the weasels, for the first time in the novel, we enter "normal" family life. And there we discover the four friends as archetypes looming above that life, as receivers of veneration and dispensers of chastisement.

So, at the conclusion of our wise fairy story, Grahame's family of singular, androgynous animals are revealed as demigods of myth, or (what amounts to the same thing) as "types of that deeper humanity which sways us all."

Notes

1. Even in chapter 7 when Mole and Rat are discussing Otter's anxiety about the missing Portly, Grahame buries Mrs. Otter in collective nouns: "The Otters have hunted everywhere, and they've asked every animal" (119).

2. Peter Hunt suggests also that the animals form a family group, with Badger the father, Rat the brother, Mole the child-as-conformist, Toad the child-as-rebel (115).

3. The stasis of Badger's character, which makes him an appropriate symbol of

social convention, the entrenched power of the upper class, or ancient tradition, also fits him to represent Jung's Self, the psychic "centre" in which the "beginnings of our whole psychic life seem to be inextricably rooted," and toward which "all our highest and ultimate purposes seem to be striving" (*Two Essays* 250).

4. Lois Kuznets has noted that the "unceasing flow of the River" depicts life and is "the most available and general center of [imaginative] inspiration in the book" ("Toad Hall" 117–18). The Water Rat is a personification of the River and so shares these anima functions.

5. Hunt comments that the novel is, in part, Mole's bildungsroman, tracing his development "from outsider to insider, from child to adult, from lower class to middle class" (116).

6. Kuznets sees the locations of the animals' dwellings as composing a sort of character scale, from Badger's stick-in-the-mud stability to Mole's "grounded" development to Rat's openness to poetic inspiration (River floods!) to Toad's flightiness ("Toad Hall" 121–22).

7. In Jungian thought, the unconscious compensates for imbalances in conscious attitudes. Thus, as Toad grows more wild and heedless, Rat and especially Badger (anima and Self) grow more censorious and controlling.

8. Grahame has emphasized Toad's psychic primitiveness in choosing Toad's species. Of the four main characters, he is a reptile among mammals, yet only Toad lives in a house, is enraptured with machines, and directly associates with people. The character least biologically or emotionally sophisticated, in other words, is the most overtly human—a sly dig at that notion of human superiority that Grahame ridicules more overtly in *Pagan Papers* and *The Golden Age*. Toad's character seems to illustrate what both Grahame and Jung considered the characteristic problem of modernity, that is, the failure of humanity's grounding in nature and instinct.

9. Gilead concludes that the story that begins by celebrating the flouting of convention in favor of impulse ends with the animals linked in a stolid front of bourgeois respectability ("Grahame's *Wind*" 36); the end of the book, particularly chapter 9, "deconstructs" the pleasure-seeking idyll proffered at the beginning ("Undoing" 156). Mendelson, on the other hand, sees Grahame setting up a dialectic between adventure and home throughout the story but finally synthesizing the two poles in the form of adventure *for* home, or "helping," as the friends become warriors in defense of Toad Hall (141–42).

10. Rat and the River, appearing at the same time in the novel, are both "sleek, sinuous, full-bodied animal[s]" who fascinate Mole with "the best stories in the world" (3) and become his "newfound friend[s]" (20). When Rat is away from the River, he thinks about it "all the time" (31) and seems "really to be afraid that the river would run away if he wasn't there to look after it" (74).

11. Kuznets observes that "Mole must assist Rat in figuratively tying himself to the mast of his everyday life, as Ulysses did to his boatmates in order not to heed the Siren call" (*Kenneth Grahame* 110).

12. Christopher Clausen characterizes Toad's departure in similar terms.

13. Compare Kuznets's comment that Grahame's treatment of Toad suggests that "childish impulses are natural and recurrent and need not be repressed altogether" ("Toad Hall" 126). Both Mole and Rat occasionally fall prey to Toadish impulses (Rat's possession by wanderlust, Mole's overreaching in grabbing Rat's oars and in venturing alone into the Wild Wood), but they manage these impulses and are not dominated by them.

Works Cited

Clausen, Christopher. "Home and Away in Children's Literature." *Children's Literature* 10 (1982): 141–51.
Gilead, Sarah. "Grahame's *The Wind in the Willows.*" *Explicator* 46 (1987): 33–36.
———. "The Undoing of the Idyll in *The Wind in the Willows.*" *Children's Literature* 16 (1988): 145–58.
Grahame, Kenneth. *The Wind in the Willows.* New York: Scribner's, 1953.
Green, Peter. *Kenneth Grahame: A Biography.* Cleveland: World, 1959.
Henderson, Joseph L. "Ancient Myths and Modern Man." In Jung, *Man* 95–156.
Hunt, Peter. "Necessary Misreadings: Directions in Narrative Theory for Children's Literature." *Studies in the Literary Imagination* 18 (Fall 1985): 107–21.
Jung, Carl G. "Approaching the Unconscious." In Jung, *Man* 1–94.
———, ed. *Man and His Symbols.* New York: Dell, 1964.
———. *Two Essays on Analytical Psychology.* Trans. R. F. C. Hull. New York: World, 1953.
Kuznets, Lois. *Kenneth Grahame.* Boston: Twayne, 1987.
———. "Kenneth Grahame and Father Nature, or Whither Blows *The Wind in the Willows?*" *Children's Literature* 16 (1988): 175–81.
———. "Toad Hall Revisited." *Children's Literature* 7 (1977): 115–28.
Mendelson, Michael. "*The Wind in the Willows* and the Plotting of Contrast." *Children's Literature* 16 (1988): 127–43.
Sale, Roger. *Fairy Tales and After: From Snow White to E. B. White.* Cambridge: Harvard University Press, 1978.
Von Franz, Marie Louise. *An Introduction to the Interpretation of Fairytales.* Dallas: Spring, 1970.
———. "The Process of Individuation." In Jung, *Man* 157–254.

Response to "The Inner Family"
Cynthia Marshall

Bonnie Gaarden's essay on *The Wind in the Willows* is quite perceptive. Grahame's characters are treated with intimacy and compassion, so the essay contributes its own vitality to that of the river world. By setting into play the separate critical dynamics of family relationships and psychological development, Gaarden offers a potentially illuminating approach to the book. These dynamics apply to most children's literature, and particularly to a work so potentially revisionary in its rendition of interpersonal relationships as this one.

The conception of what the critical dynamics might offer, however, seems theoretically flawed and unnecessarily limited. The model of the nuclear family employed here is heavily inflected by gender, and the vaguely Eriksonian model of psychological development makes unacknowledged assumptions about gender, age, and class. It would have been helpful, I think, to use explicit formulations of family structure and ego psychology, rather than presenting these two very general but no less historically placed schema as though they were manifest in all times and places. The author may believe that the models are appropriate to Grahame as an early twentieth-century author, but the claim that Grahame's characters are "ageless, timeless, genderless" is belied by the attempt to assign them gendered roles within the familial and psychological schemes. Although the author claims that the characters represent "psychic entities that inhabit everyone's soul" and that the text "circumvents" classification by gender, the argument in effect reinscribes traditional, highly gendered, social-familial roles: the authoritative father, the nurturing mother, the maturing and the unsocialized (male) children.

This reductiveness is unfortunate, because the potential exists to create produc-tive dialogue between the familial and developmental schemas. Why, for instance, does Badger correspond to both father and the Self? Is the ideal self of Grahame's conception an authoritative, patriarchal figure? And what might we learn from the dual equation of Rat with a mother figure and with a poet? Does Grahame consider inspiration, or even authorship, to be a feminine trait? I wish Gaarden had consid-ered such questions more fully, for examining the interplay between its two sets of terms would have enriched "The Inner Family." Offering a sustained critical per-spective on those terms would have prevented the implication that nuclear families and autonomous selves are universal concepts.

One last comment—the reference to Milton's Toad nicely makes the point about the demonization of Toadishness, although here, too, Gaarden has an opportunity to complicate the analysis productively. When Satan appears "squat like a toad, close at the ear of Eve," the motif is sexual seduction, and if the parallel holds, the sexual implications of Grahame's Toad could also be considered.

Response to Cynthia Marshall
Bonnie Gaarden

A model must be invoked to be discussed. I do see culturally specific (though not necessarily nuclear) family roles operating in Grahame's text, but my point is that the text, even as it refers to the traditional roles, cuts the traditionally assumed link between common familial activities (nurturing, guiding, developing, rebelling) and gender—age, too, for that matter, though I did not make that point in the essay. My reading assigns familial and psychological functions to the characters but di-vorces those functions from gender. Perhaps the point would have been clearer had I used gender-neutral terms (Rat the Nurturer? Badger the Director?), rather than the unavoidably gender-linked mother and father.

I do not know what to make of the assertion that the maturing and unsocialized children represented by Mole and Toad are necessarily male. In my view, the puta-tive maleness of all the animal characters is nullified by their singularity and by the lack of female animal characters, and so the four main characters are, in effect, gen-derless or androgynous. Certainly Toad and Mole display characteristics culturally labeled feminine and masculine. In fact, toads in myth, fairy tale, and folklore are usually female, as well as regressive. Some cultures use them to represent the uterus.

Also, I do draw explicit relations between the (Jungian) developmental and the familial models, albeit without much reference to Grahame's personal psychology. Badger corresponds to both father and Self because, as a guide-director, he fits both the Western patriarchal concept of the father and Jung's idea of the Self as the Wise Elder of the personality. (In another cultural context, Badger might correspond to grandmother or uncle, rather than father, but he would still resemble Jung's Self.) In being both poet and nurturer, Rat evokes Jung's anima (those characteristics repressed by Western males as inappropriate to the culturally supported mascu-line role), which is formed on the mother-image and carries the artistically creative (birth-giving) function. The schemes are related by Jung's (and others') notion of the personality as complex and intra-active, the "inner family" of the title. No one could credibly imply that this historically placed concept is universal, but it does provide a "sustained critical perspective."

And I do think the parallel between Satan-as-Toad and Grahame's Toad holds: if Toady embodies the id, or "juvenile wildness," his(?) sexual implications are not far to seek. Even more directly, however, the squatting Satan impregnates Eve with the very essence of the Toadish: "Vain hopes, vain aims, inordinate desires/Blown up with high conceits ingend'ring pride" (IV.808–9).

Bodies and Pleasures in The Wind in the Willows

Cynthia Marshall

Although Kenneth Grahame originally objected to *The Wind in the Willows* being illustrated (Green 285), the text has since proved a site of much visual activity. From the coy early sketches of Ernest H. Shepard to Arthur Rackham's fantastic watercolors, illustrators have gloried in the imaginative possibilities of Grahame's text. Yet as Elaine Showalter notes of the numerous illustrations of Ophelia from Shakespeare's *Hamlet*, a visual tradition growing alongside a literary text can signal an absence in the text itself. Ophelia, lacking agency and development within the play, inspires attempts to complete her character, to fill in Shakespeare's bare sketch (Showalter 78). So, too, with *The Wind in the Willows*. I think illustrators are inspired not simply by the local charm of small animals in the English countryside but by a particular lacuna—an absence of consistent, direct reference to their physical characteristics.

For those who are not visual artists, other forms of accommodation may be necessary. Grahame's purpose was to trace a world of innocent delights and thereby to encourage children's identification with animals whose small bodies and large egos match their own. Yet today we have to wonder how innocent this prepubescent vision of the physical self is, particularly given Grahame's note to his publisher that the work was "clear of the clash of sex" (Ellmann xvii; Kuznets 175).[1] How effective can such a clearing be, and what are its costs? Here I will explore the relation between Grahame's evasion of mimetic fixity and the ideological marking in the text with regard to gender. I am concerned with both the poetics and the morality of representation—the access that it affords to readerly pleasure and the violence that it does to the represented object. After considering some purposes and effects of the absence of bodies from *The Wind in the Willows*, I will turn to the way in which the repressed—the clash of sex—returns, specifically in Grahame's portrayal of Toad in the guise of the washerwoman. Finally I will suggest how,

Children's Literature 22, ed. Francelia Butler, R. H. W. Dillard, and Elizabeth Lennox Keyser (Yale University Press, © 1994 Hollins College).

by treating gender as a role rather than a stable reality, *The Wind in the Willows* unsettles some of its own misogynistic violence.

Although this essay focuses closely on Grahame's text, the argument that I pursue has implications for the study of children's fantasy literature in general. I will suggest limitations in the model of feminist interpretation—empiricist, liberal feminism—that has recently dominated in the field. Such a model, while useful in identifying overt forms of sexism, assumes a rigorous gender opposition that does not regularly appear in imaginative literature for children. In the final section of this essay I will suggest how a poststructural form of feminism, one that resists the notion of (two) fixed genders, is more appropriate and helpful in analyzing works like *The Wind in the Willows*. A delight of classic children's fantasy is the creation of a realm where possibilities are multiple rather than exclusive. Kenneth Grahame strives for such freedom in his images of gendered behavior, hence his work imagines a world of multigendered possibility, even though it remains historically connected to a misogynistic society.

Pleasures Without Bodies

The world represented in *The Wind in the Willows* is one of multitudinous pleasures. From the early moments of Mole's glad animal pleasure in spring sunlight and a first glimpse of the river, Kenneth Grahame's text continually evokes the delights of the flesh—the simple, creaturely satisfactions of good food, welcome rest, comfortable shelter. Bodily as these experiences are, however, they are curiously detached from any sustained representation of the physical bodies of the central characters. Originally written for the author's young son, who was nearly blind from birth, *The Wind in the Willows* offers an unusual and compelling example of a children's text that does not privilege the visual senses.[2] Grahame relies on other sensory media, more fluid and less prone to iconolatry, to establish the experiences of his characters. The occasional reference to a forepaw or to Rat's swimming abilities or to Mole's propensity for underground lodgings scarcely interrupts an abiding understanding that these characters are not animals in any firm mimetic sense, for readers can share their experiential world—a world of buttered toast and comfortable house-slippers. Grahame's failure, or refusal, to represent their animal bodies thus seems to be in the service of establishing greater involvement on the part of Alastair Grahame, the original audience; such involvement breaks down the sense of character as other produced by more exotic portrayals.

Indeed, so successfully does Grahame effect the bond between readers and characters on the basis of shared pleasures that on those rare occasions when the beastly status of a character does receive explicit mention, we feel our own senses expanding to encompass the experience. When the Mole, passing through unfamiliar countryside, suddenly senses that he is near his former home, Grahame writes: "We others, who have long lost the more subtle of the physical senses, have not even proper terms to express an animal's inter-communications with his surroundings, living or otherwise, and have only the word 'smell,' for instance, to include the whole range of delicate thrills which murmur in the nose of the animal night and day, summoning, warning, inciting, repelling" (88). Reminding us of the greater perceptual powers of certain lower animals, Grahame establishes our differences through what we have lost in the evolutionary climb. Yet because most of us can, like Mole, recognize the sensation of home, even though we lack the vocabulary to speak of such awarenesses, the effect here is simultaneously to evoke and to elide a reader's difference from those others with their delicate thrills.

A larger sense of doubleness or undecidability marks the size and animal status of the characters. Toad is large enough to drive a human-sized automobile; Mole captures the old gray horse from the paddock and strolls along the high road "by the horse's head, talking to him" (49). At once beast and human, small and large, the characters move easily between radically discontinuous positions, partaking of the delights available to all and the troubles germane to none. The animal characters are undifferentiated, unrestrained—and so is the pleasure they enjoy and share with readers —a kind of *jouissance*. To fix their bodies through direct description would effect a limit, would ground experience to the world of logical causation and spatial possibility. An author who employs representation, writes Roland Barthes, "imposes on the reader the final state of matter, what cannot be transcended, withdrawn" (45). Grahame instead titillates with the textual evocation of pleasures without bodies.

Rat, Mole, and Badger move through a seasonal cycle of delight free from dissipation, in a comraderie free from contingency. The few responsibilities that shape their adventures are those of fellow feeling. The search by Rat and Mole for Little Portly, the missing young otter, offers a telling example both of their emotional bonds and of the way the text treats physicality. Nothing of crisis or even fear marks this search; instead, a mild shared anxiety—"Little Portly is missing again; and you know what a lot his father thinks of him, though he never says much about it" (117)—inspires Rat and Mole to spend the summer evening on the river. Doing so evinces their communal ties with Otter and suggests an easy sense of shared responsibility for the youngsters of the animal kingdom, although no sacrifice is involved in following these values; as Rat remarks, "It's not the sort of night for bed anyhow; and daybreak is not so very far off" (119). Their search upstream to the weir occasions a transcendent experience for Mole and Rat. They enter a "holy place" where they glimpse the "august Presence" of the "Friend and Helper" (123, 124), apparently Pan himself, the protector of small animals, including Little Portly. Yet no sooner have they reclaimed Portly than the vision fades into oblivion: "For this is the last best gift that the kindly demi-god is careful to bestow on those to whom he has revealed himself in their helping: the gift of forgetfulness. Lest the awful remembrance should remain and grow, and overshadow mirth and pleasure, and the great haunting memory should spoil all the after-lives of little animals helped out of difficulties, in order that they should be happy and light-hearted as before" (125). Knowledge of the demigod, once encrypted in consciousness, might spoil a perfect, and perfectly heedless, pleasure. So all trace of transcendence fades and with it all awareness, save for a vague melancholy sense that nature shows "less of richness and blaze of colour than they seemed to remember seeing quite recently somewhere—they wondered where" (126).

In portraying these animals mindlessly present before their god, Grahame's myth of preconscious access to divinity recalls Words-worth's address to the child "untouched by solemn thought," who "liest in Abraham's bosom all the year;/And worshipp'st at the Temple's inner shrine,/God being with thee when we know it not" (ll. 10, 12–14). What is posited in each case is an ultimate freedom—knowledge of divinity without the guiltiness of knowledge, without a sense of one's own godlessness. Innocence, figured as an inability to make distinctions, is preserved by wiping away the traces of difference between nature and the supernatural.

The episode with Little Portly contains another aspect of Grahame's strategy of effacing difference: although Rat refers to the Otter family as "they," specific concern for the missing child is repeatedly ascribed to the father alone. At this juncture a reader may notice the absence of female figures from *The Wind in the Willows*. The major characters and their god are all male; it is a boyhood fantasy of eternal school holiday with chums. Except for the brief mention of a mother hedgehog who has foolishly sent her children (sons, of course) to school in a snowstorm, the animal community of *The Wind in the Willows* contains no mention of the "other" sex. And only when Toad lands in prison and escapes in the guise of a washerwoman do human females enter the story. The exclusion of females from the preferred community is not explicitly mentioned, and we might suppose that Grahame aims nostalgically at producing the worldview of a child to whom sex is inconsequential. Yet the assumption that childhood is totally innocent of sex speaks strongly of denial, for children in modern societies are confronted with gender difference in toddlerhood. Even in societies in which young children are not themselves "breeched" according to sex (as in early modern Europe, when infants of both sexes were clothed in dresses until the age of five or six), gender-based variations in adult social roles are visible. There is no developmental period clear of the clash of sex, and so we can only conclude that Grahame writes from the view of (and arguably for the readership of) a male who finds *women* inconsequential. *The Wind in the Willows* exhibits one version of the homosocial economy that Eve Kosofsky Sedgwick has described as so central to the European literary canon (17). Emotional bonds in Grahame's fantasy are strictly "between men," and their exclusivity carries misogynistic overtones. While ostensibly dismissing sex, Grahame embraces sexism.

Thus an interpretive crux rests in Grahame's remark about rendering the book clear of the clash of sex: Does sex necessitate conflict? Can the clash be eliminated only by erasing gendered difference? And does the erasure of difference inevitably mean the erasure of women? Proponents of traditional liberal feminism, based on oppositional constructions of gender, fix on the lack of any woman's part in the story. Lois Kuznets has examined the role

given those women—human females—who do appear, and concluded that "women remain, forever, the Other in *The Wind in the
Willows*" (179). Kuznets's feminism takes us the helpful first step
toward understanding the function of gender in *The Wind in the
Willows*, but the textual effects of representation go unexamined in
her account.

Representation is necessarily a result of difference. Its metaphysical action turns on the crucial dialectic of absence and presence,
for the object that is represented must exist at some remove from
the representation. By framing and re-presenting, representation
appropriates its object, assuming toward it the stance of author,
shaper, god. If Grahame for the most part avoids these effects
by leveling differences between his animal subjects and human
readers, the episode in which Toad plays the washerwoman re-
activates the violence of representation, though with some peculiar twists in the ideological machinery. The image of Toad in the
washerwoman's clothes offers what has otherwise been absent from
the text: a visually realized and highly gendered body. But what
exactly does Toad-as-washerwoman represent?

"The Very Image of Her"

A reader might imaginatively assent to Toad's unlikely escapades in
inns and automobiles and to his ensuing experiences with magis-
trates and judges, but the washerwoman episode foregrounds the
issue of a small amphibian passing as a human, making this the crisis
point for any consideration of bodily representation in the text.
Whatever adjustments of size or scale have guided our visions of
Toad previously are disrupted by the far more explicit necessity of
fitting his toad-sized body into a washerwoman's clothes. Not only
the giggling admiration of the jailer's daughter for the completed
disguise—"You're the very image of her" (136)—but the ease with
which Toad passes the series of prison warders challenge a reader
to visualize Toad, to embody him specifically as a washerwoman.
The humor becomes more charged if we consider that the washerwoman is also being implicitly described as a toad.

Although the text otherwise has largely avoided the issue of em-
bodiment, physicality is bestowed on the washerwoman with a sudden, spotlighted effect. In the simplest sense, plot considerations
guide this choice: the jailer's daughter—"a pleasant wench and

good-hearted" (131)—plans Toad's escape, and the washerwoman provides the means to accomplish it. Yet the association between femininity and material limits demands attention. When the problems of physical existence emerge, when Toad's freedom is limited and his creaturely happiness is distressed, Grahame, as male authors typically do in Western culture, anchors these difficulties to a female body. The problematic material body has traditionally been feminine; "female figures . . . have incarnated men's ambivalence not only toward female sexuality but toward their own (male) physicality" (Gilbert and Gubar 12). By including three women in the tale of Toad's escape—the jailer's daughter, the washerwoman, and the bargewoman—Grahame evokes in a child who identifies with Toad a claustrophobic sense of the enormity of female figures.[3] Toad would have no occasion for converse with these women had he not been imprisoned, and keeping them comfortably at bay is a palpable delight of his return to bachelor existence. All our sympathy and involvement, even our readerly condescension and ridicule, are tied up with Toad. The washerwoman is not a character worthy of defending; she figures merely as an image to be exploited, a disguise to take advantage of; she exists in the text as a physical body without agency and without many pleasures, either.

Considerations of class compound the evident misogyny of Grahame's portrayals of the three women in the tale.[4] Toad shouts to the bargewoman who has penetrated his disguise: "You common, low *fat* barge-woman! . . . don't you dare to talk to your betters like that!" (170). When the jailer's daughter first mentions her aunt, Toad comforts her: "There, there, . . . never mind; think no more about it. *I* have several aunts who *ought* to be washerwomen" (134). "Washerwoman" functions pejoratively for Toad, as the social expression of personal lowliness. If the washerwoman's response to "the sight of certain gold sovereigns" is not enough to teach him more of the economic grounds of her existence, his own experience at the train station certainly does. Reaching into his pocket for money, he finds only folds of the cotton gown, "the strange uncanny thing that seemed to hold his hands," and realizes that he has left his waistcoat with money, keys, watch, pocketbook, "all that makes life worth living" (138), back in the jail cell. The apparatus of wealthy, self-directed existence coincides here with the apparatus of masculinity, so that two sets of terms are contrasted: on the one hand, Toad's easy assumption of being male, wealthy, and powerful; on the other, his realization of the washerwoman's struggle as female, poor, and powerless. The uncanny thing that confronts Toad, and by implication the reader, is gender difference, with its social and economic implications.

Gender Trouble

Read with an eye for gendered oppositions, *The Wind in the Willows* appears extremely misogynistic. Grahame effaces the feminine from his picture of pleasurable existence, imagining a life of bachelor charm seen from the standpoint of a nine-year-old boy of some means. Grahame vents spleen at the female sex through the realized vision of the toady washerwoman and through offhand remarks like Rat's chiding of Toad for making an ass of himself by being "ignominiously flung into the water—by a woman, too!" (185). To be a woman in this text is to lack not only means and power but even identity, for Toad can readily assume the washerwoman's role. Yet the issue of identity versus role playing may suggest that *The Wind in the Willows* qualifies its own misogyny with a fairly fluid, even theatrical, notion of gender construction. A poststructural notion of identity can suggest why Grahame thought it possible to eliminate the clash of sex without denying differences utterly.

The washerwoman episode shows how far Grahame is from a belief in fixed and immutable identity. Toad quickly learns that playing the part of the washerwoman is not simply a matter of donning her clothes. He must use speech and mannerisms to convince the various warders he passes that he is the washerwoman. And "he was soon agreeably surprised to find how easy everything was made for him. . . . Even when he hesitated, uncertain as to the right turning to take, he found himself helped out of his difficulty by the warder at the next gate, anxious to be off to his tea, summoning him to come along sharp and not keep him waiting there all night" (136–37). Toad experiences the social structuring of identity, the extent to which the washerwoman's behaviors are conditioned by those around her. Ordinarily the most irascible of creatures, Toad yet manages, as the washerwoman, to endure the insulting humor of the guards and to hold his temper. He begs and wheedles a place on the train, agreeing to wash shirts in return for the favor. He launches into a lengthy narrative of family troubles to win the bargewoman's sympathies. Confronted by the harsh requirements of life as a washerwoman, Toad responds by adopting what would doubtless be some of her own developed characteristics.

The sense here is that the washerwoman plays a role no less than Toad does, and part of the freeing humor of the episode is its subversion of the idea of fixed human identity. If the washerwoman's role is susceptible to Toad's adoption, something of the obverse is also true: Toad's character remains perpetually bound up with that of "the lady he was forced to represent" (137). As in the case of Falstaff forced into disguise as the old woman of Brainford (*The Merry Wives of Windsor*, 4.2) or with cross-gender impersonation more generally, readers are challenged to see some ground or basis for the crossover—some evidence that the character's gendering is ambiguous or unstable and hence liable to (temporary) alteration. Toad's emotional excesses make him a candidate for female impersonation. Not only does his bipolar disposition (alternating extremes of mania and depression) suggest the lability of his personality, but such displays of extreme emotion as Toad is given to are themselves culturally marked as feminine. Trying to imagine the stolid Badger in the washerwoman's clothes instead of Toad, for instance, suggests that some point of access, some shared boundary, is necessary to render transvestism believable and therefore socially disruptive and potentially comic. But Toad is not the only animal to wear the washerwoman's dress.

Whereas Toad's hysteria codes a feminine element to his personality, Mole's domesticity and his nurturant capacities (and perhaps his lack of confidence) grant him access to the washerwoman's role. Mole's late donning of the dress for an espionage mission against the stoats and weasels has important implications for issues of gender and representation. Mole's use of the costume is distinctly and intentionally appropriative; he presents his actions as playful ("I've been having such fun!" [197]), yet his disruption of the enemies' plans accomplishes a heroic purpose. Whereas Toad's disguise seemed a matter of exigency, Mole's reiteration of the role renders it less stable, more playful, and thus breaks down the strict gender barriers that structured the original act of transvestism. Mole's experience in the dress is parodic. The dress enters circulation as an object of exchange, rather than continuing to betoken gendered opposition.

This unsettling of prescribed gender roles requires consideration, even though it would be a mistake to overlook the extent to which *The Wind in the Willows* functions as a homosocial and intermittently misogynistic text. Kuznets is correct in noting that the "attractive androgyny of nurturing males [in the story] is one that can postulate no similar androgyny for females" (179), but she underestimates the subversive effects of any challenge to the established codes of gender behavior. Judith Butler's notion of gender as performance is particularly apposite to the washerwoman incidents in *The Wind in the Willows,* for Butler emphasizes the way parody loosens a claim to essential truth: "The parodic repetition of gender exposes . . . the illusion of gender identity. . . . As the effects of a subtle and politically enforced performativity, gender is an 'act,' as it were, that is open to splittings, self-parody, self-criticism, and those hyperbolic exhibitions of 'the natural' that, in their very exaggeration, reveal its fundamentally phantasmatic status" (146–47). Grahame's multiple uses of the washerwoman's role de-naturalize gender, transforming it from identity to social ruse. That only this particular role is so thoroughly open to parody may nevertheless suggest that Grahame has naturalized masculinity and allowed only fragmentary masks of feminine gender. I would argue, however, that Grahame's refusal to represent or describe the bodies of his animal characters renders them more than, and occasionally other than, their physical selves. Instead of seeing identity as determined in an essential sense by either the body or by cultural expectations, Grahame's text highlights the theatrical quality of the gendered self. Such a performative emphasis disrupts the gap between subject and object that ordinarily provides the field for representation, and offers instead an ongoing series of playful possibilities.

With regard to gender we find, then, a specific instance of Green's observation that "there is no *stability* in Grahame's dream-world and no incongruity" (286). A polarized construction of gender can scarcely be maintained without stability, and so Grahame partially deconstructs his own misogynistic system in the text. Where an essentialist feminism would reinscribe oppositions traced by gender, a poststructuralist model encompasses the freedom that Grahame gestures toward, although the fictional tale remains constrained by its historical moorings.

Notes

1. Peter Green renders this "*clean* of the clash of sex" (197, emphasis mine).
2. Green discusses the fact that "the animals are not conceived in visual terms" and

Grahame's response to "this problem": "When asked specifically (apropos the escape on the railway train) whether Toad was life-size or train-size, he answered that he was both and neither: the Toad was train-size, the train was Toad-size, and therefore there could be no illustrations." Green expresses disdain for visual representation, which "pins down Grahame's imagination to a single static concept" (285).

3. Another example is Mole's threatening attempt to keep Toad securely at home by reminding him of those "weeks in hospital, being ordered about by female nurses" (107).

4. Peter Hunt has examined traces of class conflict in *The Wind in the Willows*. Hunt's interesting essay focuses, like my own, on an absence in the text: Hunt notes Grahame's avoidance of class dialogue where it might be expected to appear. Although he notes the class snobbery in Toad's exchanges with the washerwoman and the bargewoman, he does not consider the interplay of class and gender.

Works Cited

Barthes, Roland. *The Pleasure of the Text*. Trans. Richard Miller. New York: FSG-Noonday, 1975.
Butler, Judith. *Gender Trouble: Feminism and the Subversion of Identity*. New York: Routledge, 1990.
Ellmann, Mary. Introduction to *The Wind in the Willows*. Grahame ix–xix.
Gilbert, Sandra M., and Susan Gubar. *The Madwoman in the Attic: The Woman Writer and the Nineteenth-Century Literary Imagination*. New Haven: Yale University Press, 1979.
Grahame, Kenneth. *The Wind in the Willows*. New York: New American Library–Signet, 1969.
Green, Peter. *Kenneth Grahame: A Biography*. New York: World, 1959.
Hunt, Peter. "Dialogue and Dialectic: Language and Class in *The Wind in the Willows*." *Children's Literature* 16 (1988): 159–68.
Kuznets, Lois R. "Kenneth Grahame and Father Nature, or Whither Blows *The Wind in the Willows*?" *Children's Literature* 16 (1988): 175–81.
Sedgwick, Eve Kosofsky. *Between Men: English Literature and Male Homosocial Desire*. New York: Columbia University Press, 1985.
Showalter, Elaine. "Representing Ophelia: Women, Madness, and the Responsibilities of Feminist Criticism." In *Shakespeare and the Question of Theory*, ed. Patricia Parker and Geoffrey Hartman. New York: Methuen, 1985.
Wordsworth, William. "It Is a Beauteous Evening, Calm and Free." In *The Poetical Works of William Wordsworth*, ed. Thomas Hutchinson. London: Oxford University Press, 1917.

Response to "Bodies and Pleasures"
Bonnie Gaarden

Cynthia Marshall's observations about the effects of Grahame's "evasion of mimetic fixity"—that it helps break down the boundaries between reader and characters and that, combined with the episodes of washerwoman impersonation, it emphasizes gender as a role—strike me as excellent. I wish I had thought of them.

The fluidity of gender in the novel is an important point in my own reading. Given fluidity and given that the lack of visual representation makes it easy for a reader to identify with these "undetermined" characters, we might postulate also that the novel could help young readers experience their own inner complexity, their ability to identify with more than one social, familial, or gender role. A reader can imaginatively become not only the "motherly" Rat offering hospitality but the "outsider" Mole accepting it, and so on. I remember, as a child, reading the scenes in which Badger lectures Toad and experiencing the patriarchal (or schoolmarmish) pleasure of scolding (*I* am the boss and *you* are out of line) together with the rebel's pleasure of defiance (So you're the boss—*so what? Poop poop!*).

One point of difference occurs in our evaluations of Grahame's exclusion of female animals from his pastoral paradise. Given Grahame's cultural milieu and personal history, I would not doubt his misogyny for a minute, but this seems to me one of those texts that is wiser than its author. I think the presentation of what is, in effect, a one-gendered *animal* world, in which the same characters who cook and clean and nurture one another also have adventures with swords and pistols, constitutes yet another effacement of difference, freeing "masculine" and "feminine" behaviors from their cultural pigeonholes and allowing them to be experienced as the inner possibilities—and therefore the individual choices—of all.

Clothed in Nature or Nature Clothed: Dress as Metaphor in the Illustrations of Beatrix Potter and C. M. Barker

Carole Scott

The tales of Beatrix Potter and Cicely Mary Barker's Flower Fairy series first graced the bookshelves of multitudes of middle-class nurseries during the early twentieth century. Remarkable for the brilliance of their illustrations as well as the liveliness of their texts, the books share a distinctive perspective on the intertwining of human life and the natural environment. The intense love for and delight in animals and flowers projected by the author-illustrators bestowed on generations of children a sense of oneness with nature that extolled life in all forms and drew no critical line between them. Potter and Barker both used the metaphor of clothing, expressed in vivid drawings as well as in the text, to merge the human world with that of animals and plants. While they shared the perception that dress may dramatize the point at which the natural and the human worlds touch, and indicate the perceived relation between the two, Potter and Barker visualized this understanding in very different ways. Where Barker pictures humanlike fairies dressed in fashions created from flowers and leaves, coverings derived from the natural world, Potter reverses the dynamic, picturing animals who wear people's clothes, clothes that represent the various classes and levels of sophistication found in human societies. This reversal of approach mirrors a significant contrast in the visions of life that inspire the works, particularly with respect to the role of the social environment in supporting or repressing children's natural feelings and impulses.

Both Barker and Potter were enthusiastic observers of nature, obsessed with making careful, detailed representations of what they saw. Both were influenced by and reflect the Pre-Raphaelite concern with what Potter expresses as the "somewhat niggling but absolutely genuine admiration for copying natural detail" (Hobbs 15).

Children's Literature 22, ed. Francelia Butler, R. H. W. Dillard, and Elizabeth Lennox Keyser (Yale University Press, © 1994 Hollins College).

Potter was encouraged in her work by one of the founders of the Pre-Raphaelite movement, family friend John Everett Millais, who commented that "plenty of people can *draw,* but you . . . have observation" (Potter, *Journal* 418). Keen powers of observation and a precise botanical or anatomical correctness characterize the illustrations of both writers, and no matter how nature is represented it is never compromised; their passion for exactness expresses a deference to natural forms.

Barker's drawings depict cultivated and wild flowers alike, valuing all of nature's variety. The artist used her sketches to create the most fantastical wardrobe of flower-inspired clothing for the children pictured in her Flower Fairy series, merging botanical accuracy with an imaginative sense of dress drawn from fashions of many eras and from theatrical costumes. Potter, too, used both natural and artistic sources for her drawings; her sketches and paintings include painstaking studies of her animal pets and a scientific portfolio of fungi illustrations prepared for the scientists at Kew Gardens. All exemplify a care and an objective perceptivity akin to Barker's. Potter's interest in clothing and costume is also evident in the well-chosen and carefully designed dress worn by her animal characters. She made many excursions to London art museums and found the historical costume collections at the Victoria and Albert Museum fascinating, on at least one occasion requesting that period clothing be removed from the display case so that she might make accurate sketches (Linder 118). The subject of this particular sketch was an Elizabethan coat embroidered with flowers, which she later included in *The Tailor of Gloucester*— an interesting example of the complex interweaving of nature and art where nature represented in one art form is transmuted into yet another.

The author-illustrators share a sense of the significance of clothing; besides its practical or aesthetic aspects, it communicates to both adults and children important, often subliminal or barely recognizable, messages about who they are, who they would like to be, how others view them, and what is expected of them. "Dress is not trivial. It is a necessary form of communication, particularly in urban society, and we use it all the time to convey unspoken signals to those around us. Sometimes judged immoral, it is also a system of coded moral precepts: the way we dress conforms to a whole range of moral and social customs and attitudes, and often, even today, we flout sartorial conventions at our peril" (Wilson and Taylor 11). Parents, who represent the social world, control their children's wardrobes and thus their earliest images of themselves, first seen as reflections in the mirror. As children grow, they may be encouraged in self-expression and self-identity or restricted in the development of a sense of self by parents who either allow them or forbid them to choose what they want to wear. Dressing up is such a popular game because, by changing their appearance, children can explore various selves and various options for future roles in the world.

The images of natural dress that Barker presents stimulate children's notions of how they might look and how they would feel dressed in such attire. An examination of her Flower Fairy costumes quickly reveals the eye of a designer and tailor. Flowers are used not only conceptually to provide color and line for the clothes but often as the basic raw materials from which the costumes are crafted. The flowers inspire design in three important ways: the hues of nature are reflected in the color and color variegation of the costumes; aspects of texture and form are translated into imaginative fabrics that give a tactile sense of plant material and fiber; and the leaves, petals, and other parts are disassembled and, their original shapes still recognizable, transformed into pattern pieces from which the clothing is created. This inspired translation stimulates a fresh perception and sharpens the reader's observation, so that a common plant takes on new character, and a less familiar one is more readily remembered.

Color is the simplest aspect to explore. The Cherry Tree Fairy's green shorts and red shirt and cap, like the Tansy Fairy's yellow dress and green jacket, borrow their colors in a straightforward manner. More complexity may be found in the polka dots of the Foxglove Fairy's pants, which mirror the spotted design inside the trumpet-shaped flower, and in the figured fabrics echoing berries and flowers from which the Sloe and Forget-Me-Not fairies' clothes are made. Most sophisticated are the slashed knickerbockers of the Dandelion Fairy, which capture the play of light across the dandelion flower, revealing the golden top and green underside of each slender filament.

Using flowers as fabric leads beyond color to shape and texture, whose variations reveal endless inventiveness. In the most straightforward case, the Flower Fairy just slips inside the whole flower. By

Fig. 1. The Fuchsia Fairy, from Barker, *A Flower Fairy Alphabet.* Copyright 1934, 1990, by the Estate of Cecily Mary Barker.

inverting a daisy, the pink and white petals become a tutu-like skirt, while the green calyx forms the bodice; the Fuchsia Fairy's dress uses the same formulation, with the bell becoming the skirt, the darker sepals the top, and the stamens the decoration at the hemline (fig. 1). Many hats are made this way: a flower bud, a berry, a seed pod, is opened and fit to the head as hat, hood, or crown. In more complex designs, Barker disassembles the plants to create entirely new costumes. She may strip off stalks to make stockings. She may fashion a hat and a purse of leaves, as she does with the Wayfaring Tree and Beechnut fairies, or create a tunic in which each original petal shape is still visible, as she does for the Periwinkle Fairy.

Like an accomplished dressmaker, she selects her fabrics carefully and with imagination, cutting the puffy part from the Canterbury bell and transforming it into knickerbockers, making a large fringed collar out of a marigold, choosing berries for jewels, and mounting the wings of sycamore seeds as fairy wings. The tailoring can become even more intricate. The tongue-shaped bottom of the heartsease flower becomes the skirt of the tunic, while the top part of the blossom is cut apart, turned upside down, and made into a bolero. For the Narcissus Fairy the ring inside the flower edges the neckline, armholes, and waist; and the costume of the Travellers' Joy Fairy uses the frilly inside petals as an underslip, with larger petals serving as an overskirt for a subtle two-texture, two-color contrast. The Gaillardia Fairy's costume exemplifies a number of these strategies: his tunic is layered, using the orange flower petals for the top and the spiky green sepals for the two lower tiers; the shoulder decorations are crafted from an opening bud, using both its slender sepals and the incipient flower, and the boots, made from leaves, have tops that echo the shapes on the shoulders; and his collar is made of the fuzzy brown ring around the center of the flower (fig. 2).

Barker may replicate the fabric finish, dressing the Willow Catkin Fairy in the furry material of an unopened pussy willow bud, and the Dogwood Fairy in doublet and shoes made of the shiny brown covering of the nut. Or she may exploit textures for dramatic touches: the bristly outside sepals make armorlike epaulets and a mail shirt for the Cornflower Fairy; thistles, Knapweed's armored waistcoat; and a berrylike fabric the waistcoat that the Blackberry Fairy wears.

Barker also portrays nature copying and enhancing itself. The Fuchsia Fairy's stance imitates the flowers that hang beside her; the Willow Tree Fairy bends like the leaves of her tree and the Laburnum Fairy like her blossoms; and the tendrils of the Gaillardia Fairy's hair echo the contours and the colors of his flower. The Ash Tree Fairy looks not only like the leaves but like a butterfly mimicking the leaves, and the Dogwood Fairy, wrapped within its leaves, is reminiscent of the caterpillar that forms its cocoon from them. These costumes represent the various kinds of camouflage that nature extends.

The drawings are stunningly sensuous, for the readers feel, taste, and smell the textures and fragrances, soft, sharp, silken, luscious. By taking each flower, fruit, nut, and leaf to pieces, Barker re-arranges the readers' perceptions, wakening the memory and the senses; and by re-creating the parts as clothing for the children in the pictures, she suggests a whole body contact that envelops the child in the natural covering. This sense of partaking in nature, of

Fig. 2. The Gaillardia Fairy, from Barker, *Flower Fairies of the Garden*. Copyright 1944, 1990, by the Estate of Cecily Mary Barker.

slipping inside and becoming the plant, is magnified by the identification of the child-reader with the character of the Flower Fairy. For just as the child takes on the shape of the flower or plant, so the plant expresses a human personality. Are the children flowers, or are the flowers children? Barker matches her perception of the flower with a human child's personality, so that each flower takes on unique human features and can even invite the child to "come to me and play with me . . . spend the whole long day with me." Thus the dandelion, an ineradicable plant, becomes a rambunctious and irrepressible boy in an Elizabethan costume who reminds us of Shakespeare's Puck:

> Gay and naughty in the garden;
> Pull me up—I grow again,
> Asking neither leave nor pardon.   [*Spring*]

The blackberry, whose delicious berries tempt children but whose thorns can hurt them, is somewhat malicious:

> I'll tear your dress, and cling, and tease,
> And scratch your hands and arms and knees.
>
> I'll stain your fingers and your face,
> And then I'll laugh at your disgrace.   [*Autumn*]

The Nasturtium Fairy is happy and fun loving, the Willow peaceful and retiring, Robin's Pincushion irrepressible, Nightshade solemn. Not only are the flowers' individual characters expressed as human personalities to which the children can relate, but the visual metaphor of flower-inspired dress may even suggest to the imaginative child that by dressing up in similar fashion he or she could enter into and become a part of this fanciful pastoral world.

For Barker the flowers are treasure houses of sartorial possibilities from which everyday dress or gala costume may be formed, complete with accessories. In this, the influence of the art nouveau movement is evident. Barker is not the first illustrator to represent flowers as human beings, nor the first to create dresses from blossoms. Walter Crane's *Flora's Feast* (1889), his most successful flower book, doubtless provided inspiration for her, but his flowers are not drawn with accuracy, and the figures are inserted haphazardly into flowers with little sense of fit. His lily of the valley ladies are loosely wrapped in a large leaf that hangs like neither leaf nor cloth and must be held up with one hand, and the tiger lily woman, like her tigers, simply erupts from her flower. The daffodil comes closer to Barker's vision but again lacks the truthful perceptivity and craft that give sensuous immediacy to Barker's work.

Barker does not subjugate nature to design as do contemporary artists of the arts and crafts movement, like William Morris and Charles Ricketts. Her pictures exquisitely balance the real and the fantastic and are closer in spirit to the jewelry of René Lalique (1860–1945), which broke with the tradition of stiff Victorian ornamentation, pioneering the blending of plants, animals, and the human face and body into the highly charged sinuousness that characterizes art nouveau. His glorification of the natural world is expressed in both subject and materials; no distinction is made between valuable and ordinary materials, and subjects are chosen from the human, animal, and plant kingdoms. His delicate portrayals of bees and dragonflies, sycamore seeds, raspberry fruit and leaves, wasps, beetles and water nymphs, human figures and faces, wisteria and poppies, are rendered in diamonds, sapphires, glass, enamels, bone, and horn, intricately intertwined, and made to be worn on women's hands, around their necks and waists, and twisted into their hair. Although Barker's work may not match the innovative brilliance and high artistry of Lalique's, nature drives her sense of craft as it does his.

Whereas Barker takes pleasure in nature-inspired dress, for Potter clothes are usually a matter of anxiety and are often downright constricting or hostile to life. While Barker's fairies seem to delight in the ways they can express themselves through the exquisite creations that they wear, most of Potter's creatures are simply covering themselves and might, like Peter Rabbit, wear red pocket handkerchiefs if their own clothes are not available. *The Tale of Mrs. Tiggy-Winkle,* for example, focuses entirely on the routine of keeping clothes clean. Here human chores are extended into the animal world: sheep have to send their grubby coats to be washed, and hens have to worry about dirty stockings with holes in them. Mrs. Tiggy-Winkle labors over Cock Robin's scarlet waistcoat, Tabby Kitten's mittens, and Tom Titmouse's "little dicky shirt-fronts," which have to be starched, and she exclaims over the results of Jenny Wren's party: a "damask table-cloth . . . stained with currant wine! It's very bad to wash!" To keep her clothes clean, Lucy, the human child, must wear a pinafore; but this practical garment is adorned with frills that must be ironed and goffered. The incessant round of producing the clean clothes necessary for keeping up appearances is a losing battle; Mrs. Tiggy-Winkle's voluminous clothes—cap, print gown, petticoat, and apron—cannot cover her hedgehog prickles, which stick right through; and Lucy and the animals are always losing things. Instead of reflecting harmony and pleasure, the clothes become the focus of the tension provoked by moving away from what is natural toward what is contrived—the discontents of civilization.

The weight of civilization is pictured as even more onerous in other incidents; Tom and his sisters in *The Tale of Tom Kitten,* for example, are dressed in "elegant uncomfortable clothes" that prevent the kittens from walking naturally, trip them up, lose their buttons, and fall off. The fragility of the civilization that they represent is exquisitely pictured in Tom, who "was all in pieces when he reached the top of the wall. Moppet and Mittens tried to pull him together; his hat fell off, and the rest of his buttons burst" (fig. 3). It is a relief when the Puddle-Ducks carry the clothes off to a watery grave,

Fig. 3. Tom Kitten: "Several buttons burst off. His mother sewed them on again," from Potter, *The Tale of Tom Kitten.* Copyright 1907, 1987, by Frederick Warne & Co.

even though their action is inspired by a ridiculous vanity. We are reminded of Tom's imprisonment in his tight clothes when he is, in a later story, tied up with string and covered—clothed—in pastry, ready to be cooked and eaten by the hungry rats, Samuel and Anna Maria Whiskers. The sense of being trapped and suffocated inside the wrong covering makes an ironic comment on his earlier experience.

Another example may be found when Peter Rabbit escapes from Mr. McGregor and certain death by casting off his shoes, which impede his running, and by wriggling out of his blue coat with brass buttons, which entraps him in a gooseberry net. As he sheds his shoes and coat, Peter becomes increasingly rabbitlike, running on all fours instead of just his hind legs, thus evading Mr. McGregor's sieve. Similarly the kittens, having lost their clothes to the Puddle-Ducks, have a wonderful time mocking their mother's clothes when they are shut upstairs in disgrace. The sense of freedom that all feel when they lose their clothing is marred by the knowledge that what they have done is reprehensible and that their mothers will not be pleased. Whether lost accidentally or accidentally on purpose, the freedom is short-lived and tinged with guilt; just as Adam and Eve covered their shame with fig leaves, so the animals, even though they have "dear little fur coats of their own," must, like human children, submit to being covered. Potter's message to children suggests that clothes, and the social self they represent, are imprisoning; they mar and hide the real, natural self, rather than provide a means to express it.

In Potter's time most middle- and upper-class women were unfortunate enough to be victims of the corset, which, in producing the fashionable hourglass figure, crushed the flexible lower ribs, permanently altering their shape, and constricted the lungs and vital organs, sometimes endangering health but certainly causing great discomfort (Kunzle chapter 4). Layers of clothing and the bustle further impeded natural movement and diminished comfort. Because their bodies were constricted, women blushed easily, fainted at the slightest provocation, and had dainty appetites. Unlike their working-class sisters, "ladies" were perceived as fragile; they needed to be taken care of and shielded from the harshness of the world.

Beatrix Potter's life exemplifies this vision of woman. As with many girls of her time and class, much of her young life was spent cloistered in the nursery with her governess for company. During summers in the country she was free to roam around, but otherwise her major contact with the natural world was through her pets, the originals of many of her characters, whom she drew obsessively. She wrote of "the irresistible desire to copy any beautiful object which strikes the eye. Why cannot one be content to look at it? I cannot rest, I must draw" (106). But when she attempted to make a place for herself in the world by means of her scientifically accurate botanical drawings, she was received with scorn, her work devalued and treated without seriousness simply because of her gender (Lane 46–47). It is logical that in her books she should depict this distortion and imprisonment of natural expression by means of clothing, the socially determined declaration of who one is required to be.

Through visits to the art galleries and her family's friendship with the painter Millais, Potter cannot have failed to see the images of women that the Pre-Raphaelites presented, images that had a significant, though not immediate, impact on the world of fashion.

Dante Gabriel Rossetti's pictures of contemporary women do not present them in the distorting and uncomfortable Victorian dress, dependent upon corsets, crinolines, and bustles, but show the new, simple "aesthetic dress," whose flowing lines with unfitted sleeves and loose waists offered a recognition of the human form and a comfort and ease of movement denied to most Victorian ladies.[1] Although acceptable in paintings and in certain advanced circles, the clothes, tied in popular thought to political issues of emancipation and moral issues of sexual freedom, were not embraced by the world at large for many years; "to wear a loose-waisted, corsetless ensemble was to court social disapproval. So intimately were dress and morals related that loose clothing was perceived as an infallible signal of moral looseness" (Wilson and Taylor 31). Potter was subjected to these sentiments, and photographs of the young Beatrix picture her properly and restrictively attired.

Barker, born in 1895 (thirty years after Potter), was not imprisoned in a corset but wore dresses contoured to the female body and offering a freedom of movement that reflected a similar freedom from the kinds of social repression that Potter endured. Because of poor health, Barker was, like Potter, educated by a governess at home in London, going away to the country for summer holidays. Also like Potter, she was largely self-taught, and began drawing at an early age. But children, not animals, were her favorite subjects, and her family life was pleasant and companionable. Many of her Flower Fairies are based on portraits of children attending her sister's nursery school, and her relationships with them were based on ongoing human contact. In contrast, Potter's contact with her former governess's children, for whom she first wrote her stories, was characterized by occasional visits and letters.

While the Pre-Raphaelite influence was important to both artists, for Barker (who particularly admired Millais and Burne-Jones) its religious dimension was of special significance, and her work includes illustrations for devotional books and designs for church windows and murals. The sense of serenity and harmony with nature pervades both her religious and her secular work, and the children that feature prominently in both are generally carefree and joyful.

The physical and social straitjackets that inhibited Potter's self-realization gave way when she grew older and asserted the financial independence earned with her successful children's books.[2] Her

later marriage and life as a farmer in a small village permitted
her to escape the fashionable clothes and behavioral restrictions
to which she had been subjected, and allowed her to find a place
where she was actively engaged with the natural world in a practical
way. In her books, mostly written before she achieved this state, the
tension between what is natural and what is proper is thoroughly
explored, as is the blurry dividing line between human beings and
animals. Whereas Barker's elflike children merge happily with the
beautiful natural world that surrounds them and whose unique-
nesses they express, Potter's darker vision permeates the stories she
weaves; the lives of her animals are balanced between a natural
and a human environment, both of which provoke anxiety. Where
Barker's world is sunshiny and celebratory, Potter's is shadowed
and conflicted.

For Potter clothes are what people must learn to wear as they
grow up and go out into the world. The Flopsy Bunnies are too
little to need them; Tom Kitten and his sisters have to wear them
only on special occasions; Pigling Bland and Alexander are dressed
when they leave home; the Country-Mouse, who wears no clothes
at all, is contrasted with the Town-Mouse, who has several outfits:
an overcoat and a bowler hat, jackets and waistcoats of different
colors, and "long tails and white neckties." When people take on
clothes, they take on the restrictions and anxieties of society and
the burdens of being grown up. And clothes make life complicated:
Alexander would not have lost his papers if there had been no
pockets to put them in, and Jemima Puddle-Duck surely would not
have been taken in by the fox if she had seen him without the suit
that made her think he was a gentleman.

Although in some notable instances Potter reveals a delight in
clothes similar to Barker's, in general the different attitudes toward
dress represent the attitude to life that pervades the stories. Barker
dresses children in petals and berries so that they may recognize
and feel a kinship with flowers and plants, seeing themselves as part
of, rather than distinct from, the natural world and as a reflection
of the same beauty and individuality, but Potter attires her animals
in people's clothes, blurring the distinction between the animal and
human realms so that children may perceive the relation between
animal and human nature and more readily recognize what is natural and what is not in human character and society.

Echoes of the wider world tend to pass through a historical or theatrical medium before they reach the realm of Barker's Flower Fairies. The Dogwood Fairy tells of being a warrior "When, long ago,/Arrows of Dogwood/Flew from the Bow," and the Mountain Ash Fairy of witchcraft in times past; both of these representations are bookish and storylike. The patriotic Wild Rose Fairy, who lauds her native land, singing "'England, England, England' all day long," is surely more suited to a theatrical piece than real life, as is the Nightshade Fairy, who warns children against eating the poisonous berries and is dressed in an exotic, Oriental style. The Cornflower Fairy with her somewhat military tunic is also wearing a costume rather than ordinary clothes. There is often a hint of artifice in the almost self-conscious sense of craft and aesthetic emphasis with which Barker presents nature.

Similarly, when social position and relationship are represented among the Flower Fairies, they usually derive from wordplay on their names and are not always expressed in their clothing. Queen of the Meadow and Kingcup may "reign in springtime pomp" with "kingfisher-courtiers" and apprehend "trespass[ers] on royal ground," but they are clothed like the other fairies. Although Mallow, nicknamed Rags-and-Tatters, is appropriately dressed as a poor roadside peddler selling cheeses, Ragged Robin, the "tattered piper," is in disguise, for, we are told, he is really a princeling. Again we are aware of a kind of pastoral fantasy world where emotion is distanced and harsh reality does not intrude; the poverty, like the regal trappings, is more representational than actual. Equally pictorial are Lily of the Valley kneeling with her bells in prayer and Jasmine, as sensuous as her heavy scent, wearing a filmy garment that looks like a nightdress and that has slipped down, uncovering her to the waist on one side; both images carry a sense of graphic art rather than human experience. Although the human world is allowed to touch, even intrude into, Barker's natural paradise, it does not disrupt the mood of harmony that she portrays. In contrast, Potter's human and animal worlds can exist separately or as one intertwined community, and in both forms there is danger, fear, and death.

Potter's characters usually wear clothes recognizable from the human world, even if some are a little out of date. Other than the period clothes in *The Tailor of Gloucester* and Jeremy Fisher and friends' Regency outfits, most of the clothing portrayed would have been worn by people who lived in the country during the time that she farmed or a generation or two before then. Although their clothes are not fashionable, some of the characters are very well turned out: the gentlemanly and caddish fox in *The Tale of Jemima Puddle-Duck* wears tailored plus fours and a scarlet waistcoat, Miss Ribby changes from her blue and white dress with white apron and red and white shawl to a frilled and trimmed lavender gown with lace shawl, and Mrs. Tittlemouse wears a ruched pink overdress, tied up with a pink ribbon, to cover her blue underskirt.

The question raised by Barker's work, "Are the children flowers, or are the flowers children?" has a parallel in Potter's, for her animals merge their own natures so aptly with the behavior and personalities of children that we wonder whether her animals have become children or vice versa. Potter disliked drawing human figures and had no talent for it; the correspondence with her publishers over her attempts to improve the drawing of Lucy in Mrs. Tiggy-Winkle's kitchen details her frustration, and her rare human figures often have their backs to us.[3] The presence of the children in *The Tale of Two Bad Mice* is suggested by the two dolls, Lucinda and Jane, with their stiff bodies and their plaster food, which is lovely to look at but inedible, as Tom Thumb and Hunca Munca discover. Where human beings and animals coexist, the people are almost always adults; the only child featured in any of the stories is Lucy. The other glimpses are of the farm boy who appears in one picture in *Jemima Puddle-Duck* but is not mentioned in the story, the back view of two little girls, also not mentioned, in *Ginger and Pickles,* and some children included in the market scenes in *Little Pig Robinson.* Almost all of the children in her tales are not human beings but animals.

Even though the animals draw on the actions and emotions characteristic of human children—the kittens in *Tom Kitten* dress up in their mother's clothes, for example, and Miss Moppett tries to deceive the mouse by hiding her head in a duster (and later tying him up in it)—their animalness is never compromised. Their behavior is what we would expect: rabbits sneak into people's gardens and eat the vegetables, mice chew things to pieces and make nests out of them, cats toss their prey into the air and play with them, foxes hunt geese and eat birds and eggs. Potter manages to translate their essence into completely appropriate human parallels: foxes are cunning, geese stupid, kittens playful, rats vicious. Aesop's fables may have presented some similar types, but Potter moves beyond the typical to create real, recognizable characters. She does this through the words they speak and, most evocatively, through the illustrations, where she achieves an exquisite balance between the vitality of the animal body and the poignancy of human emotion. The dress that the animals wear is especially important in dramatizing this balance and fostering empathy in the child reader.

In *The Tale of Peter Rabbit,* Peter lies trapped in the gooseberry net. He is still dressed in his "blue jacket with brass buttons, quite new," but his rabbit nature is predominant, for he looks close to lifeless, like a dead animal, his body lying heavily, his eyes closed, having "g[iven] himself up for lost." While his body relapses into animalness his coat holds him in a human dilemma, and in the next illustration, escaping from coat, net, and Mr. McGregor's sieve, Peter looks once more like generic rabbit, for both he and the reader are for the moment lost in the purely animal emotion of escape. But when he eventually eludes both Mr. McGregor and his cat and finds the door to freedom locked, the illustration again reflects the very human emotion expressed in the text: Peter cries not only because the door is locked but also because the mouse is unable to tell him how to get out. Peter stands on one foot, the other resting upon it; the angle of his head and ears, the paw resting on the door, the other held to his mouth—all communicate human feeling, although the shape of the animal is perfectly lifelike. As Anne Hobbs so succinctly says, "The body language is half human, the bodies are not." In fact, she notes that this particular picture is "a sly reflection" of Anna Lea Merritt's "Love Locked Out," a visual and evocative reference for contemporary readers (22, 23).

Another example might be drawn from the fox in *Jemima Puddle-Duck,* whose sophistication is represented not only by his country gentleman's plus fours but also by the newspaper, which he uses partially to conceal himself, just as his clothes conceal his true nature. When he shows Jemima into the tumbledown shed filled with the feathers of earlier victims, he turns back to wink at the reader, tapping his nose to suggest complicity in the secret that poor Jemima is too gullible to understand. Miss Moppett's peeking through the hole in the duster is also a gesture more human than animal, as is Mr. Bunny's striding home triumphantly with his booty of vegetables in *Benjamin Bunny,* Mr. Jackson's complacent thumb-twiddling as he blows thistledown seed all over Mrs. Tittlemouse's clean room, and Hunca Munca's rocking her baby next to the stolen cradle in *The Tale of Two Bad Mice.*

The tension between the animal and human characteristics depicted in Potter's illustrations is expressed in a variety of examples: there are well-dressed animals with fully developed human characteristics, there are animals who are not dressed and look quite ordinary—such as Kep, the collie who routs Jemima's fox, in the illustration where Jemima is telling him "the whole story"—and there are those most delicately poised between the two extremes. When Mrs. Tittlemouse falls asleep in her rocking chair from sheer exhaustion, she is curled up exactly the way a mouse lies when it is asleep, and her striped dress and apron and rocking chair balance but do not negate her animal character. Readers can recognize both her mouseness and her human feelings of emotional and physical exhaustion with no sense of contradiction, just as we sense Mrs. Flopsy Bunny's anxieties when she cannot find her children; the particular rigidity of the ears and neck and the way the head is held, the tense stillness of the body, the diminutive figure of the rabbit in the extensive landscape, all convey her emotion, even as the animal is accurately depicted against a realistic country background. The blue pinafore worn by the rabbit serves to link the animal body with the human emotion. These poignant illustrations express the "anxiety, vulnerability and pathos [that] are implicit in the attitudes of her animals" (Hobbs 23), even while their surroundings may seem serene and sunlit.

Potter's stories fascinate because they blend the human and animal spheres at so many levels. Sometimes we find animals and people sharing the same society; at others the animals create a society of their own, patterned after the human one. In *Pigling Bland* the human narrator discusses in a friendly fashion with Aunt Pettitoes the manners and appetites of the piglets, and Pigling and Alexander must carry the correct travel papers for their journey; when Alexander misplaces his, he is escorted home by the human Policeman. In *Ginger and Pickles,* in contrast, the animals have created their own economic society and no human beings may be found. *The Tale of Benjamin Bunny* depicts both societies, human and animal, coexisting on separate planes; Mrs. Rabbit runs her own store for her fellow creatures, while the McGregors see the rabbits as destructive intruders from another sphere with no individual personalities.

The shared world often lacks real equality—Pigling and Pig-wig are viewed as potential bacon by farmer Piperson, for example—but so does the purely animal world, where Mr. Tod steals the

Flopsy Bunnies for his dinner. Tabitha Twitchit is appalled when Samuel and Anna Maria try to cook Tom Kitten but thinks nothing of baking mouse pie. Hierarchy exists in all of Potter's created worlds: Mrs. Tittlemouse views pests from the insect kingdom with a hostility similar to that with which Mr. McGregor regards the rabbits. Potter sees harmony and discord in animal and human nature alike; she does not romanticize.

The demarcation of class and hierarchy, which is frequently expressed in mannered behavior and in elegance of dress, is balanced against this blurring of the lines between the animal and human kingdoms. Potter's ambivalence about the dictates of proper society, a society whose power she both sought and resented, is expressed in the clothing that she gives her animals; sometimes dress is the mark of social class, which can be empowering and restrictive, sometimes it is just a simple covering. In all cases, however, it remains separate from the person and can be put off and on as occasion demands; clothing is not at all, as for Barker's Flower Fairies, an expression of an essential and distinctive part of the individual but is, rather, the expression of a social self that may be at odds with the real. The real self may be disguised by or imprisoned under a fancy covering, as with the fox who sweet-talks Jemima, Mrs. Tiggy-Winkle, whose prickles poke through her clothes, and Tom Kitten, whose energies first his mother and then the rats unsuccessfully try to encase. But if there is friction between the real self and the social, the real self will prevail, the social unravel.

Potter has written one book, her favorite, in which she departs completely from this negative approach to clothing. Unlike her other works, *The Tailor of Gloucester* is a romance set in a misty Elizabethan past. Potter, unlike in her other works, deliberately sets each picture in a frame, sharply delineating the borders of the illustration. Having set the boundaries of time and space, she is free to weave a fairy tale that centers on clothes. Like Barker, she pictures with delight the garments that the Tailor is making for the Mayor's wedding, "a coat of cherry-colored corded silk embroidered with pansies and roses, and a cream colored satin waistcoat—trimmed with gauze and green worsted chenille" (Potter, *Tailor* 10), and lovingly details the construction: "There were twelve pieces for the coat and four pieces for the waistcoat; and there were pocket flaps and cuffs, and buttons all in order. For the lining of the coat there was fine yellow taffeta; and for the button-holes of the waistcoat there was cherry-colored twist" (13–14).

The fabrics and thread from which the wedding coat and waist-coat are made—silk, satin, and worsted (from silkworms and from sheep)—come from natural sources, and their relation to nature is enhanced by the pansies and roses embroidered on the silken coat and the poppies and cornflowers on the waistcoat, so that the bride-groom reflects both the animal and the plant worlds in his garb. The manufacture of the garments involves a working relationship between the human tailor, his cat, and the mice who do most of the needlework, reiterating the harmony between human beings and the other animals that inhabit the earth. The exquisite clothes that the mice make for themselves—the embroidered, beribboned, and frilled dresses and bonnets, for example—once again blur the dividing line between people and animals, but the laughter at the human vanity thus mirrored is kind—not cynical, as it was with the Puddle-Ducks.

Potter, like Barker, not only focuses her attention on the par-ticulars of the natural fabrics she describes but also highlights the flower-inspired embroidery, especially the intricate sense of design and artisanship. Although Barker confines her materials to plants—her Flower Fairies' shoes are made not of leather but of burnished, glossy nutskins—she and Potter in this story both celebrate human-kind's artful expression of natural life. Both clothe their characters in the beauties of nature, acknowledging their interdependence and their involvement.

The initial inclusion of many songs in *The Tailor of Gloucester*, later omitted because they interfered with the shape and the pace of the story, is also of interest (Linder 117). The story expresses jubilation throughout (it originally included intoxicated mice, also cut at the editor's suggestion) and depicts a bright world closer to Barker's vision, unclouded for the most part by Potter's darker side. This mood of celebration, found when she escapes from her own time and plunges into another era, is expressed as Barker expresses it, by exulting in the creation of clothing.

Dressmakers are powerful artists who create people's outer selves, reflecting, enhancing, or concealing the inner person. Their realm, like other aspects of human civilization, involves "pleasure and dan-ger, conformity and the breaking of taboos" (Wilson and Taylor 12). Victorian dress—and all the social repression that it commu-nicates—shaped Potter's self-concept and its expression in her art, and her tales depict the ambivalence characteristic of fashion in an age of conflict. Where Potter's art represents her struggle for self-

realization and freedom in a restrictive society, Barker's creations
depict her aesthetic and sensuous vision of a harmonious world
where nature and human nature are in concert.

Yet Barker's books, though enchanting and timeless in their detail and rich in botanical lore, portray a fantasy world that is sentimental rather than real; the charming texts may be instructive,
descriptive, or emotive, but they do not challenge the reader to
confront deeper issues, and the messages often remain superficial.
Potter's life, more earthbound and more conflicted, is expressed
in stories that reveal fears, anxieties, and disharmonies. Her tales
have great psychological staying power, for they depict the eternal
conflicts and anxieties that concern most children, and confront the
perils involved in surviving, both physically and emotionally, in a
dangerous world.

Notes

1. See, e.g., Rossetti's portraits of Elizabeth Siddall and Janey Morris and his
photograph of Janey Morris taken in 1867.
2. Potter's journals, written in a secret code that she thought no one could unravel,
further testify to the need to express an identity whose natural impulses had to be
hidden, a private self known by no one else. Although the thoughts and emotions expressed seem perfectly proper, the desire for concealment suggests the constriction
of Victorian life.
3. "I am not good—or trained—in drawing human figures. They are a terrible
bother to me when I have perforce to bring them into the pictures for my own little
stories" (Lane 132–33).

Works Cited

Barker, Cicely Mary. *Flower Fairies of the Autumn.* London: Warne, 1990.
———. *Flower Fairies of the Garden.* London: Warne, 1990.
———. *Flower Fairies of the Spring.* London: Warne, 1990.
———. *Flower Fairies of the Summer.* London: Warne, 1990.
———. *Flower Fairies of the Trees.* London: Warne, 1990.
———. *Flower Fairies of the Wayside.* London: Warne, 1990.
———. *Flower Fairies of the Winter.* London: Warne, 1990.
———. *A Flower Fairy Alphabet.* London: Warne, 1990.
Hobbs, Anne Stevenson. *Beatrix Potter's Art.* New York: Viking Penguin, 1989.
Kunzle, David. *Fashion and Fetishism.* Totowa, N.J.: Rowman and Littlefield, 1982.
Lane, Margaret. *The Magic Years of Beatrix Potter.* London: Warne, 1978.
Linder, Leslie. *A History of the Writings of Beatrix Potter.* London: Warne, 1971.
Potter, Beatrix. *The Journal of Beatrix Potter from 1881 to 1897.* London: Warne, 1966.
———. *The Tailor of Gloucester.* London: Warne, 1989.
———. *The Tale of Benjamin Bunny.* London: Warne, 1989.
———. *The Tale of Ginger and Pickles.* London: Warne, 1989.
———. *The Tale of Jemima Puddle-Duck.* London: Warne, 1989.

————. *The Tale of Jeremy Fisher.* London: Warne, 1989.
————. *The Tale of Johnny Town-Mouse.* London: Warne, 1989.
————. *The Tale of Little Pig Robinson.* London: Warne, 1989.
————. *The Tale of Miss Moppett.* London: Warne, 1989.
————. *The Tale of Mrs. Tiggy-Winkle.* London: Warne, 1989.
————. *The Tale of Mrs. Tittlemouse.* London: Warne, 1989.
————. *The Tale of Mr. Tod.* London: Warne, 1989.
————. *The Tale of Peter Rabbit.* London: Warne, 1989.
————. *The Tale of Pigling Bland.* London: Warne, 1989.
————. *The Tale of Samuel Whiskers.* London: Warne, 1989.
————. *The Tale of the Flopsy Bunnies.* London: Warne, 1989.
————. *The Tale of the Pie and the Patty Pan.* London: Warne, 1989.
————. *The Tale of Tom Kitten.* London: Warne, 1989.
————. *The Tale of Two Bad Mice.* London: Warne, 1989.
Wilson, Elizabeth, and Lou Taylor. *Through the Looking Glass: A History of Dress from 1860 to the Present Day.* London: BBC Books, 1989.

Heroic Ideology and the Children's Beowulf

Anna Smol

Viewed by British and American writers as the story of an exemplary hero who could teach boys the virtues of their race, the Anglo-Saxon poem *Beowulf* became children's literature at the turn of the century, when it was retold in numerous adaptations. *Beowulf* accommodated well the prevailing heroic ideology evident in books such as those by G. A. Henty or boys' magazines such as *Chums* that propounded an image of an Anglo-Saxon hero as a muscular good sport unafraid of staring down the enemy in a heroic last stand (MacDonald). Such stories were designed to inspire imitation; the American writer and editor Hamilton Wright Mabie expresses a common view when he states in his introduction to *Heroes Every Child Should Know:* "The possibilities of the heroic are in almost all men. Stories of the heroes have often made other men strong and brave and true in the face of great perils and tasks, and this book is put forth in the faith that it will not only pass on the fame of the heroes of the past but help make heroes in the present" (xviii). The belief that one could make heroes in the present, that one could see in the hero the potential existing in every man and boy, characterizes these early retellings of the Beowulf story.

The choice of a model in Beowulf, "this grand primitive hero who embodies the ideal of English heroism" (Ebbutt 1), owes much to the interests of nineteenth-century scholars and general readers. The earliest retellings of *Beowulf* appeared after John Mitchell Kemble's edition in 1833 and translation into modern English in 1837 (Greenfield and Robinson 126, 130). Often included in anthologies of medieval stories with introductions outlining current theories of epic, myth, or race, these versions are difficult to categorize as exclusively for either adults or young readers; more likely, they would have appealed to the kind of broad audience Hélène A. Guerber imagines for her 1916 volume of epic stories designed "for the use of young students or of the busy general reader" (*Book* 6). By the early decades of the twentieth century, how-

Children's Literature 22, ed. Francelia Butler, R. H. W. Dillard, and Elizabeth Lennox Keyser (Yale University Press, © 1994 Hollins College).

ever, we also find retellings proclaiming children as their intended readers, such as Henrietta E. Marshall's *Stories of Beowulf, Told to the Children* (1908); Thomas Cartwright's *Brave Beowulf* in the Every Child's Library series (1908); and John Harrington Cox's *Beowulf: The Anglo-Saxon Epic, Translated and Adapted for School Use* (1910). These adaptations illustrate Zohar Shavit's theory that the canonized children's literary "system" accepts certain stories and conventions only after they have been approved for adults. In the case of *Beowulf*, the romantic, nationalistic emphasis of nineteenth-century medieval scholarship, popularized in the early translations, provides the foundation for an idealization of this hero in children's stories that has not often been challenged.[1]

Influenced by the nationalistic aims of nineteenth-century philology, first German and then English scholars idealized a pure Teutonic hero not yet corrupted by more refined, effeminate Latin, French, and Christian influences.[2] The mid-nineteenth-century German scholar J. P. E. Greverus writes: "In *Beowulf* . . . the ancient Germanic national character stands rough, but pure in its colossal Nordic pagan magnificence, perhaps superficially tainted here and there with Christian dogma, but fundamentally the ancient manful pagan world sound to the core" (Stanley 34).

The conviction that Beowulf illustrates a national character soon pervaded the views of children's writers as well. The 1910 retelling by M. I. Ebbutt, reprinted and available in children's bookstores in 1987, states: "The figure which meets us as we enter on the study of Heroes of the British Race is one which appeals to us in a very special way, since he is the one hero in whose legend we may see the ideals of our English forefathers before they left their Continental home to settle in this island. . . . Beowulf stands for all that is best in manhood in an age of strife" (1). Ebbutt even envisages this exemplar of the Anglo-Saxon race as the stereotypical Aryan, a handsome young boy "with fair locks and gallant bearing" in whom "wise men might have seen the promise of great strength in his powerful sinews and his mighty hands, and the signs of great force of character in the glance of his clear blue eyes" (6).

With the story of Beowulf, then, writers such as Ebbutt believed that children could learn about the perceived origins of their race and nation. We find this motivation in not only English but also American writers, some of whom saw the foundations of their cultural institutions and what came to be seen as their superior racial qualities in the Anglo-Saxons (Horsman). Certainly, the number of versions of *Beowulf* printed in the United States proclaiming themselves for children or for school use testifies to the American interest in the poem for educational purposes. Thomas Cartwright, the author of *Brave Beowulf*, published in New York in 1908, tells the reader of his story: "If you read it carefully, you will learn from it much about the manners and customs of the Anglo-Saxons, before they crossed the seas and came into Britain. This story should be read, then, as an interesting first book of Anglo-Saxon history" (ii).

Cartwright exemplifies the nineteenth-century view of the poem as an archaeological and historical source document, but this perception frequently coexisted with a romanticized treatment of the subject. Guerber begins her 1910 collection with the statement: "If there is a phrase in our tongue which connotes the atmosphere of romance it is that of 'the Middle Ages'" (Guerber, *Myths* xi), and Ebbutt elaborates on the appeal of medieval literature for its reader: "Down all the dimly lighted pathways of mediaeval literature mystical figures beckon him in every direction; fairies, goblins, witches, knights and ladies and giants entice him" (i), and Cox, in his 1910 version "for School Use" tells us that "this translation of the fine old tale of Beowulf makes available for children of the elementary schools the one masterpiece depicting—and contemporary with—the dawn of that picturesque era, the age of chivalry" (preface). It was possible to see in *Beowulf*, then, an opportunity for entertainment, as well as instruction, in a story "told in such beautiful words that they thrill us with delight and make us feel as if those old days were fresh and living" (Marshall viii).

The interest in re-creating those old days stems from a romantic belief in the value of a natural, unrefined literary tradition preserved by illiterate bards or, as Guerber would have it, written "in rude alliterative verse, rhyme not being known in England before the date of the Norman Conquest" (Guerber, *Myths* 1). An explanation of the primitive origins of Anglo-Saxon culture, with its underlying assumption of progress, is made by Thomas J. Shahan in 1901 in *A Book of Famous Myths and Legends*, part of the Young Folks' Library series: "Ages ago, when the world was young, people did not know as much of nature and its secrets as we do now. Moreover, they did not have the art of writing, or if known to them, it was used only by a few, and its value for handing down the facts of history was not clearly understood" (xv). Shahan continues: "The study of the old beliefs, old customs, old memories that have thus floated down among the simple, remote and unlearned peoples of the world reveals much history that would else be unknown" (xix). Nine years later, Ebbutt describes the Anglo-Saxons similarly as uncivilized but with a certain kind of nobility: "Perhaps there was little of spiritual insight in the minds of these Angles and Saxons, little love of beauty, little care for the amenities of life; but they had a sturdy loyalty, an uprightness, a brave disregard of death in the cause of duty, which we can still recognise in modern Englishmen" (vii).

These children's versions reflect the views of romantic historians who, as Allen Frantzen points out, "linked past and present in the paradigm of parent-child relationships, in which the present was the fulfillment—the adult form—of the past" (64). The Anglo-Saxons, those simple, remote, and unlearned peoples, were viewed in relation to sophisticated, modern, and learned English-speaking peoples as children are to adults. From here it is easy to slide into the belief that the literature of these cultural primitives is appropriate to those usually taken to be the simple and unlearned always in our midst—children.

Beowulf, then, is the original English role model, and the view of nineteenth-century scholars that the Christian references in the poem were later corruptions does not deter retellers of the story who have a moral point in mind. For example, almost all the adaptations that I have seen omit reference to a passage in the Old English poem known as the Song of Creation, a paraphrase of the opening of Genesis.[3] Many of the adaptations prefer not to translate the Old English word *wyrd* as "fate," which is ambivalent enough to accommodate a Christian sense; instead, translators such as Donald MacKenzie often leave the word as *Wyrd,* so that readers can imagine a Germanic goddess at work: "It shall be as Wyrd decrees— Wyrd who measures out a man's life" (*World's Heritage* 18). Even if Beowulf is taken to be a pagan hero, however, he still can be cast in a saintly light, as in M. W. MacDowall's English version, which follows W. Wagner's German translation in inventing this picture of the hero after his battle with Grendel:

The rays of the rising sun streamed in at the window and lighted up his head as with a halo. His companions crowded

round him and greeted him with awe and reverence. Then he
fastened the trophy of his victory over the door of the hall, and,
having done this, he returned thanks to All-father for having
given him strength to withstand the monster. The warriors
knelt round him and joined him in his praise and thanksgiving.
[272–73]

The translator cannot help redeeming the noble heathen Beowulf
by making his pagan story as Christian as possible. And should the
poem prove uncomfortable at points, as when Beowulf's qualities
are summed up with a rather un-Christian emphasis on pride—
Beowulf was *lofgeornost*, "most eager for praise"—then the retellers
may alter the sense of the Old English.[4] For example, H. E. Marshall
states: "Of all rulers he was most worthy of praise" (114). Other
translators devise an alternative ending, such as the funeral scene,
which concludes Kate Milner Rabb's 1896 paraphrase, in which "the
Gothic folk lamented the death of their tender prince, their noble
king, Beowulf" (161), or H. A. Guerber's last sentence, describing
the funeral directions "piously carried out" by Beowulf's people,
who "had loved their brave king Beowulf, who had died to save
them from the fury of the dragon" (*Myths* 17).

The revisions point to some of the constraints that authors generally feel when writing for children. The *Beowulf* adaptors almost
always simplify the narrative order of the Old English poem, omitting its complex background of kin relationships or its suggestive
juxtapositions of scenes and speeches. What is left is a story that
brings into high relief the actions of Beowulf against three monstrous enemies, Grendel, Grendel's mother, and the dragon. The
focus on the hero and his actions accommodates the persuasive
and moral criteria often applied to children's literature. The hero
typically strikes a handsome, imposing figure and speaks in an
elevated, archaic style—Cox's version has Beowulf saying to the
Danish watch: "Be thou gracious in directing us. . . . Thou knowest
if it is true as we heard say, that among the Scyldings some mysterious persecutor manifests terrible enmity in the dark nights" (12).

Beowulf does not take on superhuman dimensions, however.
Ebbutt, for example, describes the fight with Grendel's mother as
"terrible and almost superhuman" (25). Readers can believe that
others might have the potential to imitate the hero, especially when

they look at the various illustrations of the monsters that he vanquishes. In Cartwright's *Brave Beowulf,* Grendel is barely taller than Beowulf, who is shown gripping him in an armlock, and in J. H. F. Bacon's illustrations for Ebbutt's edition, the dragon lying beside Beowulf looks about the size of an alligator.

Girls were occasionally invited to admire the actions of the hero—*Brave Beowulf,* for example, begins with a letter to "my dear Boys and Girls"—but the heroic ideal espoused in these versions excludes female participation. As Hamilton Mabie states: "To be some kind of a hero has been the ambition of spirited boys from the beginning of history" (xi). The reviewer who described Ebbutt's retelling as "an excellent book for boys" (*Book Review Digest* 120) was probably expressing typical expectations for this type of publication.

The exclusivity of this heroic ideal becomes most evident when we look at how the adaptors deal with the women in the Old English poem. In the middle section, after Beowulf's fight with Grendel and before his return to his homeland, we hear of several women cast in the role of "peace-weavers," women given in marriage to cement relations between two families. Among them is Hildeburh, who suffers the death of husband and son in a violent feud. Unlike the passive and silent Hildeburh, Queen Wealhtheow is a peace-weaver who tries to build defenses for her family through powerful speeches that alternately supplicate and command. Grendel's mother, on the other hand, speaks no language but only acts—and effectively—when she attacks the heroic society in revenge for her son's death, thus drawing Beowulf deeper into her feud with Hrothgar.[5]

Because the allusiveness of the work is usually downplayed in the adaptations, Hildeburh's story is rarely told. If mention is made of her, the point of view and import of her story, known as the Finnsburh digression, are altered from the Old English, where the focus is mainly on Hildeburh's grief at the loss of her husband and her son and the impossible position in which she is cast as peace-weaver between warring families (*Beowulf* ll. 1063–1159). Cox concentrates on the men in the story, omits Hildeburh's name, and mentions her being taken away only as a last affront to her husband, Finn, who thereby loses not only life but also chattel: "There was sung the deathless lay of the fight at Finnsburg, which told how Hnaef of the Scyldings was fated to fall in Frisian land, how Finn himself was

slain at his own home and his queen carried away" (34–35). The following rather painful verses from A. J. Church's version completely
delete Hildeburh from the story.

> To the Frisian land,
> With a chosen band,
> Brave sons of the Dane,
> O'er the ocean plain
> Did Hnaef of the race of the Scyldings go
> In the stress of battle Fate laid him low.   [24]

And M. I. Ebbutt converts the story into a jingoistic morality tale:
"The minstrels sang of the Fight in Finnsburg and the deeds of
Finn and Hnaef, of Hengest and Queen Hildeburh. Long was the
chant, and it roused the national pride of the Danes to hear of the
victory of their Danish forefathers over Finn of the Frisians" (19).

While Hildeburh is overlooked, Queen Wealhtheow usually appears, but a version, like Cartwright's, in which Wealhtheow's diplomatic speeches are reproduced is rare. Her appearance is often
summarized in one sentence, as in this version by MacKenzie: "A
great feast was held, and Queen Wealhtheow, wife of Hrothgar,
having given the golden cup to the king, carried it next to Beowulf,
to whom she gifted two golden armlets, a mantle, and a jewelled
collar" (*World's Heritage* 14). In other instances, she is conceived of
in more romantic than Anglo-Saxon terms; where the Old English
refers to Wealhtheow as a "gold"- and "ring-adorned queen," "a
noble woman," "excellent in mind," "wise in words," and "mindful
of proper procedures" (*Beowulf* ll. 613–41, 1162–68), many retellings picture her as a gracious, beautiful hostess. Ebbutt describes
her as "the fair and gracious Queen Wealhtheow" (14), who after
her cup-passing duties "went to sit beside her lord, where her gracious smile cheered the assembly" (15). Church imagines this scene:
"King Hrothgar himself came forth from his chamber, and the
Queen with him, and a bevy of fair ladies in gay apparel" (21). Cox
uses romantic terms to describe the queen's women as "a bevy of
maidens" (30). The emphasis on the queen's beauty and good influence, reminiscent of the Victorian "Angel in the House" propped
up by her "bevy," downplays her political role and fails to capture
the force of the epithet *ides,* which is applied to her twice (*Beowulf* ll.
620, 1168); the word is used in Old English poetry to describe, as
one critic puts it, "no ordinary woman" (Meaney 159) but a woman

who is exemplary or dangerous and who may even be related to the half-supernatural warrior-women Valkyries in Northern mythology (Damico, *"Beowulf"'s Wealhtheow*).

That leaves Grendel's mother, who arises from her mysterious home, attacks Beowulf, and is defeated by the hero in an action that seems to bear no relation to the concerns raised by the full portrayal of Hildeburh and Wealhtheow. The pared-down children's translations give us simply a monster-woman who must be eliminated as an enemy of the hero. Beowulf defines himself, not in opposition to someone who draws him into a revenge cycle such as we are made aware of in the stories of Hildeburh and Wealhtheow, but in opposition to someone or something completely foreign to him, someone who is by nature opposed to him—he destroys the female monster, the not-heroic.

MacDowall takes one approach to this section of the poem by exaggerating the monstrous qualities of Grendel's mother. Whereas the Old English poem states that she comes to Heorot and, in her haste to escape injury, grabs and kills one man, MacDowall provides us with this invented scene: "At midnight a great column of water rose in the midst of the sea, and out of it came a gigantic woman, whose face was as grey as her garments. Her eyes shone like coals of fire, her bristly hair stood up on end, and her long bony arms were stretched out as though in search for prey" (274). Upon entering the hall "she slew one warrior after another, in spite of their resistance, and slaked her thirst with their warm blood" (275). This monstrous woman is the victim of the hero's deed of bravery and strength, and that is all there is to her story.

Instead of exaggerating the enemy woman, some versions use the strategy of omission to highlight the hero's self-sufficiency.[6] Ebbutt, for example, does tell us that "the awful sea-woman flung Beowulf down on his back and stabbed at him with point and edge of her broad knife," but in the same sentence she states that Beowulf, "exerting his mighty force, overthrew her and sprang to his feet" (25). Guerber glosses over the fact that Grendel's mother sits on Beowulf: "Fast in her grip she clasped him, and strove to crush out his life," and she attributes the victory to the hero's equipment and physical strength: "Fortunately, however, the hero's armour was weapon-proof, and his muscles were so strong that before she could do him any harm he had freed himself from her grasp" (*Myths* 11). It is unusual for adaptations to mention, as the original poem stresses, that

Beowulf might have perished there if "holy God," "the wise Lord," "the Ruler of the skies," had not been controlling the fight and deciding its outcome (*Beowulf* ll. 1553–56). Ebbutt typically attributes the victory to Beowulf's strength and rage: "Dead the monster sank to the ground, and Beowulf, standing erect, saw at his feet the lifeless carcase of his foe" (26).

The heroic ideal formulated for young readers in these late nineteenth-century and especially early twentieth-century versions of *Beowulf* is not an isolated cultural phenomenon. Racial theories of Anglo-Saxon superiority over foreign peoples fueled British imperialism at the turn of the century. With the hero highlighted and simplified in his solitary fights against monstrous "Others," coming to his glorious end supported by his "chum" Wiglaf, Beowulf illustrates the qualities of strength and bravery that were being glorified for future soldiers of the Empire. One version of the story employs the typical contemporary discourse of war in stating that Beowulf "in spite of repeated disaster, always returned to the charge. His coolness and courage kept up the spirits of his men" (MacDowall 268).

The story was not without interest in the United States, either. There, as Reginald Horsman has explained, the same European, romantic views of the Anglo-Saxons as the source of exemplary racial qualities were adapted to justify American domestic and economic policies. Some of the British retellings of the *Beowulf* story, such as MacDowall's and Marshall's, were published simultaneously in England and the United States, and writers like Cartwright, Cox, and Shahan were published in America.

The extent to which these writers express an overt interest in racial theories of Anglo-Saxon superiority varies, but most of the retellers of the story for young people encourage pride in Anglo-Saxon origins and the importance of knowing something about the old poem. Rabb, in her 1896 Chicago edition, wrote of how she saw in epic poetry a repository of wisdom for those "feverish from the unrest of our time" (5); in an era in which rapid change had altered traditional certainties, *Beowulf* could be seen as a guide to and justification for behavior. Children's writers believed that they could "make heroes in the present."

Notes

I am grateful to Joanne Graham, librarian at Boys and Girls House, Toronto Public Library, for her generous assistance in making available to me many of the books discussed here. I would also like to acknowledge the financial support that I received in the form of a Mount Saint Vincent University Research Grant.

1. Charles Keeping and Kevin Crossley-Holland depart significantly from the usual heroic ideology presented to children in their 1982 illustrated *Beowulf*. See Mills for a discussion of the way Crossley-Holland's text and especially Keeping's illustrations undermine the image of heroism.

2. For further discussions of nineteenth-century Anglo-Saxon scholarship, see Stanley and relevant articles in Berkhout and Gatch. A survey of literary histories dealing with the Anglo-Saxon period is provided in Calder.

3. *Beowulf*, ll. 90–98. The standard scholarly edition of the poem was first edited by Fr. Klaeber in 1922; the third edition with supplements is still published today and is the version cited here. Klaeber provides a detailed introduction, including sections entitled "The Christian Coloring" and "Genesis of the Poem," as well as textual notes. See Klaeber 131 for his note on the Song of Creation.

4. George Clark summarizes the range of critical opinion on *lofgeornost* from Tolkien's negative reading of the word as a conclusion to a Christian tragedy to various rebuttals reading the word as heroic praise (chapter 1).

5. Several critics have recently explored the significance of the women in the poem. Overing examines the masculine economy of the poem, in which women such as Hildeburh and Wealhtheow expose the paradoxical demands of the heroic code. See the essays by Audrey Meaney and Helen Damico, which deal with Wealhtheow and Grendel's mother. Damico examines Wealhtheow in the context of warrior-women and valkyrie-brides in heroic literature in her book *"Beowulf"'s Wealhtheow and the Valkyrie Tradition*.

6. Perhaps the most awkward example of omission occurs in "Beowulf, the Brave Prince," by Clara E. Lynch, printed "With Ecclesiastical Approval" in Chicago in 1932. Lynch introduces "the second monster" with no mention of the revenge motive (presumably this would not have received ecclesiastical approval). Lynch does not admit that the monster is Grendel's mother, obviously too uncomfortable a fact. The first acknowledgment of the monster's gender springs upon the reader as suddenly as Grendel's mother does upon Beowulf: "The monster saw Beowulf coming, and lay waiting for him. As soon as he touched the bottom, she sprang upon him and seized him in her terrible claws" (273). This mysterious female is then called "monster" to the end of her story.

Works Cited

Anson, W. S. W. Introduction to MacDowall.

Berkhout, Carl T., and Milton McC. Gatch, eds. *Anglo-Saxon Scholarship: The First Three Centuries*. Boston: Hall, 1982.

Beowulf and the Fight at Finnsburg. Ed. Fr. Klaeber. 3rd ed. Lexington: Heath, 1950.

Book Review Digest. Minneapolis: Wilson, 1910.

Calder, Daniel G. "Histories and Surveys of Old English Literature: A Chronological Review." *Anglo-Saxon England* 10 (1981): 201–44.

Cartwright, Thomas J. *Brave Beowulf*. Every Child's Library series. New York: Dutton, 1908.

Church, A. J. *Heroes of Chivalry and Romance*. 6th ed. [1898.] Reprint. London: Seeley, 1918.

Clark, George. *Beowulf*. Twayne's English Authors series 477. Boston: Twayne, 1990.

Cox, John Harrington. *Beowulf: The Anglo-Saxon Epic, Translated and Adapted for School Use*. 1910. Reprint. Boston: Little, Brown, 1918.

Damico, Helen. *Beowulf's Wealhtheow and the Valkyrie Tradition*. Madison: University of Wisconsin Press, 1984.

Damico, Helen, and Alexandra Hennessey Olsen, eds. *New Readings on Women in Old English Literature*. Bloomington: Indiana University Press, 1990.

Ebbutt, M[aud] I[sabel]. *Hero-Myths and Legends of the British Race*. London: Harrap, 1910. Reprinted as *The British*. Myths and Legends series. London: Mystic Press, 1987.

Frantzen, Allen J. *Desire for Origins: New Language, Old English, and Teaching the Tradition*. New Brunswick: Rutgers University Press, 1990.

Greenfield, Stanley B., and Fred C. Robinson. *A Bibliography of Publications on Old English Literature to the End of 1972*. Toronto: University of Toronto Press, 1980.

Guerber, H[élène] A. *The Book of the Epic: The World's Great Epics Told in Story*. London: Harrap, 1916.

———. *Myths and Legends of the Middle Ages: Their Origin and Influence on Literature and Art*. London: Harrap, 1910.

Horsman, Reginald. *Race and Manifest Destiny: The Origins of American Racial Anglo-Saxonism*. Cambridge: Harvard University Press, 1981.

Keeping, Charles, and Kevin Crossley-Holland. *Beowulf*. Oxford: Oxford University Press, 1982.

Lynch, Clara E. "Beowulf, the Brave Prince." In *Cathedral Basic Readers*. Book 4. Chicago: Scott, 1932.

Mabie, Hamilton Wright, ed. *Heroes Every Child Should Know: Tales for Young People of the World's Heroes in All Ages*. Every Child Should Know series. Garden City: Doubleday, 1913.

MacDonald, Robert H. "Signs from the Imperial Quarter: Illustrations in *Chums*, 1892–1914." *Children's Literature* 16 (1988): 31–55.

MacDowall, M. W. *Epics and Romances of the Middle Ages*. Adapted from the work of W. Wagner; ed. W. S. W. Anson. 10th ed. 1882. Reprint. London: Routledge; New York: Dutton, 1917. Reprinted as *Epics and Romances of Our Northern Ancestors: Norse, Celt, and Teuton*. London: Norroena Society, 1907.

MacKenzie, Donald A. *Teutonic Myth and Legend*. Myth and Legend in Literature and Art series. London: Gresham, n.d.

———. *The World's Heritage of Epical, Heroic, and Romantic Literature*. Vol. 2. London: Gresham, 1919.

Marshall, H[enrietta] E. *Stories of Beowulf, Told to the Children*. Told to the Children series, ed. Louey Chisholm. London: Nelson; New York: Dutton, 1908.

Meaney, Audrey L. "The *Ides* of the Cotton Gnomic Poem." In Damico and Olsen 158–75.

Mills, Alice. "Two Versions of *Beowulf*." *Children's Literature in Education* 17 (1986): 75–87.

Overing, Gillian R. *Language, Sign, and Gender in* Beowulf. Carbondale: Southern Illinois University Press, 1990.

Rabb, Kate Milner. *National Epics*. Chicago: McClurg, 1896.

Shahan, Thomas J. *A Book of Famous Myths and Legends*. Vol. 6. Young Folks' Library series. Boston: Hall, 1901.

Shavit, Zohar. *Poetics of Children's Literature*. Georgia: University of Georgia Press, 1986.

Stanley, E. G. *The Search for Anglo-Saxon Paganism*. Cambridge: Brewer; Totowa, N.J.: Rowman, 1975.

The Secret Garden *"Misread"*: *The Broadway Musical as Creative Interpretation*

Phyllis Bixler

"What distinguishes the most important literature is its ability to engender new interpretations," Perry Nodelman has recently suggested (107), citing Frank Kermode's identification of such textual "openness" as a defining characteristic of what we call "classics" (44). By this measure, Frances Hodgson Burnett's *Secret Garden* (1911) is a "most important" classic. Few if any children's texts are more frequently discussed in papers at scholarly assemblies; few have been more often adapted in other media. A Metro-Goldwyn-Mayer film starring Margaret O'Brien was made in 1949; television films were produced for the British Broadcasting Company in 1975 and the American Columbia Broadcasting Company in 1987; and Warner Brothers released yet another version in 1993. In the last decade there have been at least four musical adaptations. Nona Sheppard and Helen Glavin turned the book into a children's opera, performed in England in 1991, and in that year an opera by Greg Plishka and David Ives was given its world premiere in Pennsylvania. The book has also been twice adapted for the musical theater, in Great Britain in 1983 and in America in 1991. Although the latter adaptation did not receive unalloyed critical praise, it was the musical production nominated for the most awards in the 1990–91 Broadway season. Marsha Norman received a Tony for her musical book, the producer Heidi Landesman won one for her set, and Daisy Eagan won another for her portrayal of Mary Lennox; Grammy-winner Lucy Simon composed the music, and Tony-nominee Susan H. Schulman directed the production. *The Secret Garden* ran successfully on Broadway from 5 April 1991 to 3 January 1993; beginning on 28 April 1992, a North American road tour was scheduled to run longer than its Broadway version.

Professional obligation more than personal desire drove me to Saint Louis to see the tour production in May 1992. The movie adaptations had seemed aesthetic lightweights compared to Bur-

Children's Literature 22, ed. Francelia Butler, R. H. W. Dillard, and Elizabeth Lennox Keyser (Yale University Press, © 1994 Hollins College).

nett's novel, and I considered my interest in *The Secret Garden* nearly exhausted by years of teaching it, writing about it, listening to papers and reading articles about it. Happily, only a few short scenes snapped me out of this smugness. Unlike the movie adaptations, whose power was largely borrowed from Burnett's original, the musical had an energy of its own. Set, staging, words, and music offered in different media the textural unity and complexity that had sustained my interest in the novel over the years. I felt the presence of a persuasive and provocative interpretation of the novel—persuasive because the musical was in important ways reading the book as I and other female readers and feminist critics had, provocative because the musical had found new openness in Burnett's text. Reminding myself that the playwright, composer, set designer, and director were all women, I affirmed my intuition that on some issues in some books we can indeed speak of communal female responses. Considering the deletions from and additions to Burnett's text, I recalled Harold Bloom's assertions that poets (and presumably musical theater creators) necessarily "misread" their precursors (or sources) in moving beyond them (14). Recalling reviews suggesting that the musical had distorted or eliminated some essence of Burnett's text (for example, see those by Frank Rich and David Richards), I mentally retorted that different readers find different essences, as I had at different times over the years, that reviewers and critics also misread, if usually less venturesomely, according to Bloom. Finally, comparing my enjoyment of the musical to my earlier pleasure in writing about *The Secret Garden* and in reading articles that taught me something new about it, I agreed with Bloom that critical essays, like poems—or musicals—are "creative" (43), adding to the text as much as zeroing in on some primary essence. What follows, therefore, is a misreading or "creative interpretation" (Bloom 43) of the musical *The Secret Garden*, as well as a commentary on the musical as a misreading or creative interpretation of Burnett's novel.[1]

Having introduced myself as a misreader, it is appropriate to provide more information about these primary creators of the musical as well as their collaborative process. Many interviews and other articles marked the opening of the musical, in part because the multimillion-dollar Broadway venture was headed by a team of women. Though ambivalent about this focus on their shared gender, the women described their collaboration as especially "comfort-

able," "caring," and "nurturing" (Watts 25, 70); these are mothering values stressed in Burnett's novel, of course, and the women
also spoke of their work as a kind of collective gardening (Watts
70; Simpson 21). That they had a very close collaboration is suggested also by the fact that often, in interviews, they individually
gave a question the same or very similar answer. They brought to
their teamwork a variety of professional and reading backgrounds,
however.

Turning *The Secret Garden* into a musical was originally the idea
of the producer and set designer, Landesman. A cast album for
the British musical—which she has appropriately labeled "a bad *My
Fair Lady*"—sent her back to Burnett's novel. Convinced that the
book contained a good musical, Landesman gave it to Norman—
Landesman had designed sets for two of Norman's plays. Landesman's interest in adapting a children's classic was not surprising,
for she had coproduced and done considerable creative work on
Broadway musical adaptations of Mark Twain, in *Big River* (1985),
and the Brothers Grimm, in *Into the Woods* (1987). Although *The
Secret Garden* had made little impression on her as a child, she
had loved *Alice in Wonderland* and E. Nesbit, as well as the later
Narnia series. Norman, however, was not an obvious choice to write
the script. Plays such as her Pulitzer Prize–winning *'night, Mother*
(1983), ending in a suicide, and *Getting Out* (1977), portraying a
young woman's first day out of prison, had earned her a reputation
as, in her words, "this queen of tragedy" (Mootz). She had not previously read *The Secret Garden* and in fact had read few children's
classics, having skipped from the missionary-adventure books that
her mother bought for her to her own choice of the Brontës and
Jane Austen. However, Norman had always wanted to work on a
musical, she had written an unproduced one on the Shakers, and
she was eager to work with Landesman again.

After working on *The Secret Garden* for four or five months, Landesman and Norman sent lyrics to six composers; Simon, they discovered, "knew *exactly* what the music should sound like" (Jones).
Unlike Landesman and Norman, Simon belonged to what they
would eventually call the Secret Garden Club (Simpson 20), composed of the many adults they met, usually female, who had a highly
personal, often proprietary, affection for Burnett's classic; Simon
had often reread *The Secret Garden*, as well as her other childhood
favorites, *The Wizard of Oz* and *Mary Poppins*, and she had been

working on a musical adaptation of the *Little House on the Prairie*. As Simon describes it, she "grew up in the heyday of American musical comedy. Arthur Schwartz was my parents' closest friend. I used to sit at the piano as a toddler and listen to his new songs" (Barbour). Simon also brought the team her experience in folk, rock, classical, and children's music; before her Grammy-winning albums for children, *In Harmony I* and *In Harmony II* (1980, 1982), she had cut solo albums and had done backup singing for her sister, Carly Simon, who, along with Judy Collins, contributed demonstration tapes during the composing and arranging of music for *The Secret Garden* (Grabel 13). Norman and Simon soon "moved from a respectful relationship to a real working marriage," says Simon, letting words and music influence each other while composing (Simpson 20). They eventually took a draft to a workshop production at Skidmore College in Saratoga Springs; during those two weeks Norman did a complete rewrite, and together Norman and Simon wrote ten new songs (Grabel 13). A tryout production at Norfolk's Virginia Stage Company in late 1989 convinced them that major reworking was still needed. At this point, Schulman joined the team as the new director.

Like Landesman, Schulman had been a childhood fan of Victorian and Edwardian children's literature, including *Little Women* and "all" of Burnett's books; like Simon, Schulman had had a special fondness for *The Secret Garden*. By age twelve she was also haunting Broadway stage doors, and in junior high school she directed *The King and I* (Wolf 8). As an adult, she had directed many musicals, including a number during her eight years as artistic director of the Pittsburgh Civic Light Opera and a 1989 *Sweeney Todd* on Broadway, for which she received a Tony nomination. Schulman's joining the team apparently created the right chemistry. *The Secret Garden* underwent its final major revision for an October 1990 New York City workshop, and this workshop production elicited the financial backing necessary for an April 1991 opening on Broadway. Development of the musical took three years, "a short time for a musical," according to Norman. "We've done it fast because everyone involved worked so well together" (Mootz).

Asked how *The Secret Garden* was affected by her earlier work on *Big River* and *Into the Woods*, Landesman replied that "one learns negatively," that she wanted *The Secret Garden* to be "less linear, more imagist";[2] in a similar vein, Schulman praised Norman for knowing "how to approach non-literal storytelling" (Wolf 10). The audience of the musical is expected to appreciate the imagist, the nonlinear, the nonliteral from the very start. The set re-creates a Victorian child's toy theater, with proscenium arch inside proscenium arch; overlaying the entire set (including, in New York, the floor) are muted images, reminiscent of Victorian valentines or decoupage—some viewers have been reminded of Joseph Cornell's intricate boxes and collages (see, for example, Rich; Richards). Some images, such as patrons looking down from a balcony, identify the set as a toy theater, but many appear in dreamlike assembly, as in Maurice Sendak's illustrations for *Fly by Night* (1976) and *Outside over There* (1981). Landesman wanted "to portray the world of a child's dreams, including its terrifying images," and so a sinister, horned Victorian mask and a witch on a horse mingle with happier images of birds, animals, flowers, toys, children, and babies.

The suggestion that the stage is at one time exterior—a theater—and interior, within a child's mind, is reinforced by music, words, and action in the prologue to the play. Mary Lennox, in bed, is circled by a dreamlike re-creation of her parents' party, which turns into a nonliteral dramatization of the cholera epidemic. Colonial British partygoers, Indian ayah and fakir, all in white garb, use bloodred handkerchiefs to play a circle game in which participants' elimination indicates that they die. Meanwhile, children's voices sing a minor-key "Mistress Mary, quite contrary" in which the question "How does your garden grow?" receives the reply that the flowers are dying and must be eliminated, like the dancers in their drop-the-handkerchief game: "Dig it up, . . . you're up, you're out, you go" (prologue). The prologue signals the conflation of not only dream and waking worlds but also past and present, living and dead. As the curtain rises, the first voice heard is that of Colin Craven's dead mother, Lily, singing about flowers safe in her garden; in the New York (but not the touring) production, Lily sits in a Victorian picture frame suspended above and behind Mary Lennox, who plays with her dollhouse until her father comes and lifts her into bed.

The first of the two acts is especially nonlinear and nonliteral while Mary, her uncle Archibald Craven, and to a lesser extent Colin are developed as characters haunted by the past and unable to enjoy the present; as Archibald tells Mary later, people who die remain ghosts as long as "someone alive is still holding on to them"

(1.2). When Mary moves to Yorkshire, the ghosts from her past in India go with her, and the portrayal of Mary's first night in Misselthwaite Manor typifies how we are often asked to set aside our usual temporal, spatial, and reality categories. The ghosts, who generally adopt a protective attitude toward the living, sing that this strange house must seem to Mary "like a frightful dream" (prologue). (In the published playscript, the ghosts are labeled "the Dreamers," reversing the more usual notion that it is the living who dream of the dead; I am reminded of Tweedledee's assertion that the sleeping Red King is dreaming about Alice [Carroll 144, 208], which also makes us question our assumptions about who is dreamed and who is dreamer.) Past and present, as well as dream and waking life, are often staged simultaneously. During the presentation of Mary's first night in Misselthwaite, for example, we hear and see Mary's father, Albert, urge his wife, Rose, to take Mary away from the cholera epidemic; meanwhile, Mary is unable to sleep. (Did her parents' conversation occur in her dream or her memory? The ghost scenes often admit more than one interpretation.) Along with the ghosts and Archibald, Mary carries a candle through the corridors of the manor, suggested by three sets of ornate picture frames dropped into a nearly dark stage. What follows is one of many examples of ghosts joining living characters in choral singing; here, as elsewhere, specific lines or slight variations can be credibly sung by several characters. Mary, Archibald, Lily, and the other ghosts sing "I heard someone crying" and posit possible sources of the cry until Mary's parents and Mary herself, Lily, Archibald, and Colin are all, appropriately, nominated by someone (prologue). The living as well as the dead are lost souls crying in the dark, wandering and never meeting.

This emphasis on Mary, Archibald, and Colin as ghost-ridden is a misreading of Burnett's book attributable, no doubt, in large part to Norman. Having loved the Brontës in her youth, she was able to recognize the Gothic elements in Burnett's novel—the parallels between *The Secret Garden* and *Jane Eyre* have been described by more than one reader (Thwaite 220–21; Bixler, *Burnett* 100; Bixler, "Gardens" passim), and the 1987 and 1993 movies heighten the Gothic elements in the book as well. Norman had portrayed the dangers of excessive grief, of inappropriately holding on to the past, in her plays *Third and Oak* (1978), *The Holdup* (1983), and *Traveler in the Dark* (1984) and her novel, *The Fortune Teller* (1987).

In addition, Norman believes that the line between the living and the dead is "very faint"; her reading of Ann Thwaite's biography confirmed her sense that Burnett was a "spiritualist," which Norman defined as someone sharing her own belief that "people are watched over by spirits." Having read Thwaite, Norman must have known that Burnett wrote stories about the living being visited by their beloved dead—*In the Closed Room* (1904) and *The White People* (1917)—although she apparently did not read them. In *Getting Out*, Norman had already written a play simultaneously dramatizing past and present; Arlie's present self, who is trying to make a new start outside prison, shares the stage with her younger, cynical, delinquent self, a past self who comments on the present action. Although Norman had toyed with the idea of having ghosts early in the creative process, they were a relatively late addition to the musical; except for Lily, they appeared after its Norfolk and just before its final workshop production. (However, they were added over a year before the release of the phenomenally popular movie *Ghost*, in which Patrick Swayze, after he dies, manages to communicate with his still-living, beloved Demi Moore.) The team felt that the Norfolk version was too literal, lacking in "magic"; it was "just a nice story with a bunch of nice songs," says Simon. Now their new director, Schulman, confirmed Norman's desire for ghosts and showed how to use them on stage. In addition to providing the nonlinear, nonliteral richness that the team wanted (McGee 70), the ghosts solved a number of musical and theatrical problems. They provided a singing chorus, the lack of which Simon identified as a chief problem in turning Burnett's novel into a musical. (The Misselthwaite house servants provide the chorus in the British musical, adapted by Alfred Shaughnessy of the British Broadcasting Company's "Upstairs, Downstairs" series.) The ghosts also solved some dramatic problems, such as the cholera epidemic, which had earlier been abandoned as unstageable. ("We were very adamant that we didn't want a lot of dead bodies on stage," says Schulman; "the only play that does that successfully is *Hamlet* and then you have blocking problems" [Barbour].) Perhaps above all, the ghosts allowed the musical to be faithful to what Norman has called a crucial "promise" that Burnett's book offers. "That promise is the reason parents read *The Secret Garden* to their children," Norman says, the promise that "no matter where I am, no matter what happens to me, I will always be with you, and you will be all right. You will find a place where you can be happy: There are good people in the world." The birth of her son helped her understand that promise, Norman adds. "I didn't know . . . anything that I would come back from the grave to do until Angus was born" (McGee 70).

Accordingly, as the musical progresses, the ghosts increasingly interact with the living. The ghosts of Mary's ayah and the fakir are often onstage with her, forming a bridge from the Indian to the Yorkshire folk who care for her. The fakir lights the lamp in Mary's room her first night in Misselthwaite Manor (according to my New York notes), for example, and the next morning the ayah's gestures mimic Mary's dismay that Martha expects her to dress herself; the ayah and fakir are also often onstage when Ben Weatherstaff and Dickon Sowerby explain nature's magic to Mary. The ghost of Mary's father also tries to assure continuity in Mary's care. (Schulman notes that the exceptionally "nurturing" Michael De Vries, who played Albert on Broadway, helped enlarge this role.) As if to pass his fatherly role to Archibald, Albert several times stands just behind or next to him, as when Mary asks for "a bit of earth" to make a garden; here, in addition, Archibald's absentminded responses are interrupted by Albert's loving "Happy birthday, darling" (1.4). Also, in the prologue, Albert had gestured an appeal to the ghost of Colin's mother, Lily, asking her to become the protective spirit that Mary's own mother apparently cannot or will not be—the musical is faithful to Burnett's portrayal of Mary's mother as a superficial woman who lacked interest in her child.

Among the ghosts, it is Lily who takes the lead in caring for the living. Making her first appearance suspended from the heavens in a portrait frame, Lily is the dea ex machina who intervenes to bring about the happy conclusion. She does so primarily by bringing first Mary, then Colin, and finally Archibald to her garden. During a stormy night at Misselthwaite, Lily is prominent among the ghosts who help Mary thread her way through the corridors to Colin's room, and act 1 concludes with Lily leading Mary to the garden door. In act 2, after Mary has told Colin about the garden, Lily appears in his room to sing "Come to my garden." Though often onstage, Lily is typically unobserved by the living; exceptions can be interpreted as occurring in a memory or dream, as when Archibald waltzes with Lily in a ball re-created from their courtship (1.2)— from a front seat I noticed that their dance movements were coordinated, but they never touched. Later in Colin's room, however,

Lily sits on his bed and embraces him as they sing a duet (2.5). She likewise embraces Archibald in the penultimate scene (2.9). He is in Paris, having just received a letter from Mary asking him to come home. At the end of their duet, Lily takes Archibald's hand and leads him back to the stage space by now identified as the door to her garden. In this same space, in the final scene, Lily bids farewell to Mary, Colin, and Archibald; having brought them to her garden, where they have become a healthy family, where they have learned to embrace the present, Lily and the other ghosts make a last exit from the garden and from Mary's, Colin's, and Archibald's lives.

As this description suggests, Lily is a centerpiece of the musical's misreading of Burnett's novel. Unlike the other ghosts, she appeared early in the team's creative process, and in the final production she is the only ghost to have a starring role. Simon has said that Lily's was the "easiest voice" "to find," that she "knew her voice exactly," that most of the songs written for Lily remained in the show, the first she wrote for her being "Come to my garden," strains of which accompany the opening and final closing of the curtain.

Lily's prominence provided my own most profound connection with the creators of the musical as misreaders of Burnett's novel when I saw my first production. Some time ago, I noted that *The Secret Garden*, like many of Burnett's stories, contains Cinderella motifs ("Tradition" 203). In the most well-known, Perrault version, Cinderella is assisted by a fairy godmother, but other variants suggest that Cinderella's dead mother is the source of the magic. In the Grimms' version, Cinderella obtains her beautiful gowns from birds who perch on a tree planted on her mother's grave; a similar connection between the secret garden and Colin's dead mother is made in the novel, Mrs. Sowerby at one point telling Colin, "Thy own mother's in this 'ere very garden" (237). Norman used this statement as textual justification for the ghosts in the musical: "Once we had Frances' word for it that there was at least one spirit in this garden, then it was very easy to say, well, there are also more" (Nance). That Colin's dead mother is at work in the house as well as the garden I argued in my last article on *The Secret Garden* ("Gardens" 220–23), citing lines and images also emphasized in the musical. Near the end of the novel, for example, Mary notices that the usually closed curtain over the portrait of his mother is now open; Colin tells her that one night a "patch of moonlight" made him want to pull the curtain cord; he now likes to see her laughing face and observes that she "must have been a sort of Magic person" (228). The obvious image used in the musical is the portrait: Lily's first stage appearance is in a portrait frame, a series of portraits suggest the corridors through which Lily helps Mary find her way to Colin, and a small portrait of Lily is apparently the only possession that Mary is allowed to take from her house in India. The association of the dead mother's power with moonlight is also maintained in the musical when Colin tells Mary about uncovering his mother's portrait (2.6). The image of moonlight was evoked earlier, when Colin, in a song, described for Mary his dreams about nocturnal visits by his father, a "round-shouldered man" who enters Colin's room "on a beam of moonlight" and takes him on a ride "through the moors by moonlight" (1.7). This is one of many times that a word or image— or melodic line or stage blocking—links characters or scenes. Because in one "moonlight" dream the round-shouldered man takes Colin to a secret garden (1.7), we can imagine that Lily is providing magical, moonlight direction in Colin's dreams just as she does in Colin's, Mary's, and Archibald's waking lives.

If the portrayal of Lily in the musical made me think of my own critical writing about Burnett's novel, the portrayal of Mary and Colin made me think of Elizabeth Keyser's article noting that the focus in the book eventually shifts from Mary to "Master Colin" (253), reflecting Burnett's ambivalence about Mary's self-assertiveness. Objections to Mary's being pushed to the background have been repeated in other articles (see, for example, the ones by Marquis and by Paul) and voiced by a considerable number of female readers; and so, not surprisingly, when I asked the creators of the musical to compare their childhood and adult readings of the book, the shift of focus was mentioned most frequently as an adult reaction. Norman, who read the book only as an adult, was particularly resentful, and on this point she consciously made her adaptation a misreading. The first scene that Norman wrote, according to Landesman, was the last in the show. Mary essentially disappears in the concluding pages of the book, but Norman emphasizes her role in the reunion with Archibald; then, Norman wrote up to this final scene to make it emphatically "Mary's story." There were dramatic reasons for this misreading of Burnett's novel—"in a musical you can't shift your central character," observes Schulman (Wolf 10)—but by making Mary central, the creators thought that they were making a statement. When asked how the musical bears their stamp as female creators, how it would have been different if written and produced by men, three of the four answered that women are not afraid to tell a story about a little girl; that men would doubt that a girl could hold an audience for an entire evening, although a boy could, as in *Big River;* that men thus probably would not have undertaken the project. Landesman, however, was undeterred by the many who told her that "only women and children will come to this show." Her response was, "Women buy 70% of the tickets on Broadway. So if that's the audience I get, fine. I will take it" (Simpson 17). (In July 1992, Landesman estimated that the New York audience was 80 percent women and children.)

The decision to make Mary central to the musical means that, compared to the book, Colin's role is considerably diminished and there is more focus on Mary's interaction with adults, especially in that Dickon, like Martha, is played as a young adult. Accordingly, some of the adult characters are developed more than in the book, especially Lily and Archibald. Though apparently incapable, Archibald would like to be a loving father; in the bedtime story that he sings to Colin, he expresses his desire to slay the "dragons" of physical and psychological illness that haunt them both and to someday "race" Colin "to the top of the morning" and tell him directly that he loves him (2.3). For the present, at the direction of Colin's doctor, he tries not to waken and overexcite the boy. The expanded role for Archibald may have been partly inspired by Mandy Patinkin, who opened in the part, but it also came from the creators' reactions to the earlier film adaptations of *The Secret Garden.* Asked for her opinion about these movies, Landesman said that it was essential "to keep Archie on stage" to dramatize the "theme of loss," for if he had been in Paris all the time, he would have been "too removed from the action, so Mary and the audience wouldn't care about him." The emphasis on the parents', as well as the children's, point of view was also no doubt due to the creators' desire to make the musical appealing to ticket-buying adults. "The desire was not to do a children's musical," according to Simon (Barbour); Schulman called *The Secret Garden* "a real family musical," not a "kiddie show" (Wolf 8). Similarly, the creators wanted the musical to appeal to men, not just women. With more developed roles for Mary's father and uncle, the musical "allows men to feel their connection to their children and to the girls in the world and the loved ones they lose," according to Norman (Watts 25). Schulman made a similar point about the emphasis on males as nurturers. After I commented on how often she blocked parallel events, such as Mary's embracing her father and then Archibald on the same stage space, Schulman added, "There are lots of men down on their knees" with children in this musical. Nurturing as a male quality is certainly not absent from Burnett's fiction. Cedric Errol nurtures a haughty earl into a nurturant grandfather in *Little Lord Fauntleroy* (1886); Sara Crewe's father and his male business partner parent Sara in *A Little Princess* (1905); and Dickon and Ben Weatherstaff are among those responsible for Mary's and Colin's alteration in *The Secret Garden*.

Pointedly nonnurturant, however, is one male adult whose role is greatly expanded—and significantly changed—in the musical, Colin's doctor. In the novel Colin accuses Dr. Craven of wanting him to die "because he would get Misselthwaite and be rich instead of poor" (127); although there may be some truth to the charge, the doctor's later appearances show him to be essentially well meaning if provincially incompetent and overly protective. He is primarily just one of the adults whom the children enjoy fooling with their secrets and a foil for Burnett's theories about natural medicine. The creators of the musical, however, individualize him and give more credence to Colin's accusation. Here the doctor is Archibald's younger brother, Neville, who had been in love with Lily himself; having lost her to Archibald before losing her to death, he is doubly embittered.

The expanded role of the doctor as Archibald's brother serves the musical in several ways. Neville provides an adult interlocutor for Archibald, and, because he also loved Lily, he reinforces the theme of loss. In one scene, for example, Neville notices Mary's resemblance to Lily and attributes Archibald's increasingly vivid dreams to Mary's presence in the house; then he and Archibald sing a duet about Mary having Lily's eyes, one of the most haunting songs in the show (1.5). Making Colin's doctor be Archibald's brother also affords one of many examples of effective doubling; the two brothers parallel the two sisters, Lily and Mary's mother, Rose—in Burnett's novel, Colin's mother is the sister of Mary's father. In one scene, a quarrel within each sibling pair results in a musical quartet: Neville argues with Archibald about what to do with Mary at Misselthwaite while, in a re-created conversation from the past, Rose quarrels with Lily about her intention to marry the reclusive

Archibald (2.2). Finally, and not inconsequentially, Neville provides an antagonist for the main character, Mary. After Archibald has gone to Paris, Neville has a decidedly unsympathetic schoolmistress come to get Mary; and, in the most broadly melodramatic and comic scene, Mary, with the assistance of the ayah and the fakir, chants a curse and stages a tantrum, which frightens the schoolmistress away. After she leaves, Neville tells Mary that he will send her away immediately to another school. The appearance of an unsympathetic schoolmistress, like the battle of wills between Neville and Mary, is reminiscent of Sara Crewe's battles with the schoolmistress, Miss Minchin—asked what Burnett fiction she read while preparing to write the musical, Norman recalled only one title, *A Little Princess,* which Landesman, who reread most of Burnett, had given her. Neville is a more sympathetic character than Miss Minchin, for his songs allow us to see his own pain, a personal glimpse largely absent in Burnett's portrayal of Miss Minchin; like Miss Minchin, however, Neville has the aura of a melodramatic villain, eliciting, during performances that I saw, an occasional boo and, at the end, relieved laughter when he is effectively banished from the estate to travel and take up his former medical practice in town.

Some might object that because the musical expands its adult characters and deemphasizes Colin, an important essence of Burnett's novel has been lost, the portrayal of children's delight in having a life secret from adults, and that with this loss a children's novel has been turned into an adult musical. The creative team did in fact struggle, as Norman put it, "to find the balance between the adult characters and the children's story"; the team went "off the track" in the Virginia production, observed Landesman. That production was "much more about Archie and Lily," added Simon (Barbour), who later reflected that this step in the evolution of the piece showed them what the adult part of the story should be. "The big victory came," according to Norman, "when Heidi said, 'We must see this from Mary's point of view'" (Barbour).

Largely because of the focus on Mary, as well as the portrayal of Lily, I myself was not especially upset about the development of several adult characters—a musical or movie can rarely dramatize every aspect of a book. Nor was I much bothered by the charge that a children's novel had been turned into an adult musical, for my observation of four audiences told me that children were enjoying it; indeed, an eight-year-old girl attending with me was much engaged in Mary's plight in the first act, while an adult next to me at another performance declared to his spouse that act 1 was "too psychological" to follow. (In July 1992, Schulman described the audiences as aged five to adult, adding that although many attending were around eleven, the number of younger children had prompted the theater to procure booster seats; moreover, according to Schulman, children from all social backgrounds rooted for initially powerless, "maverick" Mary.)

Finally, I found the changes from novel to musical more provocative than lamentable because, as I suggested in my introduction, I believe, as Roderick McGillis has pointed out, that narratives contain many secrets for a reader to discover—or buried seeds of many other stories, which a reader's imagination can coax into bloom. At a conference I once heard a woman say that as a child, unsatisfied by Burnett's ending, she had invented her own stories about what eventually happened to Mary; similarly, an adult misreader writing a "family musical" may want to fill gaps in the story of Archibald's marriage. Noting that "adults at the turn of the century read eagerly many books which would now be considered for children," Juliet Dusinberre has argued that modernist writers like Virginia Woolf often rewrote children's classics, however unconsciously (30, passim). Taking her cue from Dusinberre, Judith Plotz has argued that "just as a palimpsest reveals an earlier script beneath a later one, so the image" of *The Secret Garden* can be seen beneath D. H. Lawrence's *Lady Chatterley's Lover,* published seventeen years later (1). Like Kathleen Verduin in an earlier article, Plotz points out that each novel features a landless female (Mary Lennox, Connie Chatterley), a disabled aristocratic male (Colin Craven, Clifford Chatterley), and a working-class male (Dickon Sowerby, Oliver Mellors) able to revive others through his special intimacy with nature. Unlike Lawrence, however, Burnett was largely uncritical of the class system, allowing "Master Colin" to take charge of the magical experiments in the garden before marching across the final pages with his father, "the Master of Misselthwaite" (253).

The musical shows the class system in Burnett's story at work in colonial India, as well as in Great Britain. In the game metaphorically portraying the cholera epidemic, it is the fakir who drops the first red handkerchief, dramatizing the foolishness of a British colonial's claim to class insularity: "[The cholera's] exactly what they deserve. Letting their sewage run in the streets" (1.7). As Mary moves to England, it is her proximity to the Yorkshire servant class that pulls her out of her grief; just as in India her ayah had apparently cared more for her than had her mother, so here Martha, Dickon, and Ben tease her out of her pouts and engage her interest in the secret garden, while her self-absorbed guardian ignores her. In giving prominence to the Indian as well as Yorkshire folk, the musical suggests, more than Burnett's novel does, that human wisdom and charity are most likely to be found near the bottom rung of the social ladder. Ben, for example, mixes his garden lore with homespun wisdom, and Dickon, unlike in the novel, helps Mary find the secret garden. After a song in which Dickon helps Mary speak to the bird (represented by piccolo trills) in Yorkshire dialect, Dickon hangs Mary's skipping rope on a plant so that when she later retrieves it, the garden key falls to the ground (1.3).

While Ben and Dickon facilitate Mary's activities outdoors, Martha encourages her battles in the manor and proves subversive of its existing social order. In her first scene, she enters Mary's bedroom singing a bawdy song; learning that in India Mary's ayah dressed her, Martha wonders that "grand folks' children don't turn out fair fools, bein' washed and took out to walk like they was puppies"; as she dresses a sullen Mary, she sings a song listing the household chores that keep her indoors, hinting, perhaps, that Mary should be grateful for her leisure (1.1). Soon, however, Martha becomes Mary's strongest advocate. Near the end, when Mary's self-confidence in her battle with Neville flags, Martha offers some feminist sisterhood and support. Neville, having traded on his authority as a physician, has convinced Mary that Colin's improvement is only apparent. Having taken advantage of the female socialization that encourages her to put others' welfare above her own, Neville has made her feel that she would be responsible should Colin die. Finally, having asserted his authority as her adult guardian in Archibald's absence, Neville has declared that she will go away to school. As Martha helps Mary pack, she also helps her see through Neville's twisted view of the situation; singing "Hold On" (a "power song" inspired by Alison Fraser, who opened the part on Broadway, according to Simon), Martha encourages Mary to circumvent Neville's authority by writing Archibald a letter. It is this letter, coupled with Lily's visitation to his Paris apartment, that brings him home for the final reunion. In the final scene, Martha continues to assert Mary's rights. When, in his excitement about

Colin's recovery, Archibald overlooks Mary, Martha interrupts to ask, "Sir. What is to become of our Mary?" (2.10). In Burnett's portrayal of this scene, Martha and Dickon, like Mary, fade into the background, and Ben appears only to share with Mrs. Medlock a servant's distant, adoring view of Master Colin walking with the Master of Misselthwaite. In the musical Ben, Dickon, Martha, and Mary are all on stage to be thanked by a man who, instead of parading his patriarchal power, accepts a housemaid's correction of his behavior, embraces Mary, and then kneels between his new daughter and his son.

One member of the Yorkshire folk prominent in the novel but absent from the musical (and the 1993 movie) is the archetypal earth mother, Mrs. Sowerby. Asked if she had considered including Mrs. Sowerby, Norman said no, that she had realized early on that she was a "duplication," that she could "get that element in Martha and Dickon." Being more active on Mary's behalf in the musical than in the book, Dickon and Martha do in some ways stand in for their mother, who in the novel acts behind the scenes on the children's behalf before appearing in the garden to bless their efforts. Because in the novel Mrs. Sowerby sometimes speaks and acts on behalf of Colin's dead mother, much of her role is assumed by the ghost of Lily in the musical. And some of her role is, in the musical, taken by Mary; Norman said that she "wanted it to be Mary's story," so she "wanted Mary, not Mother Sowerby [as in the novel], to bring Archie back with a letter."

Norman also wanted the audience to like Mary—Norman and Landesman said that they disliked the children in the movie versions. Once again, Norman was willing to deliberately misread Burnett's novel. "At the beginning," Norman has said, "Burnett depicts Mary as a little brat, but I didn't want to write a 'Taming of the Little Shrew.' So I imply that it's OK for Mary to be a bit nasty since everybody she knows has just died in the cholera epidemic" (Mootz). Burnett's narrator sometimes takes a moralistic attitude toward Mary's behavior, as has been pointed out by the psychiatrist Barbara R. Almond, who cites a passage from the novel implying that "Mary is neglected because she is disagreeable, not the other way around!" (482). Having once worked with emotionally disturbed children at a state hospital, Norman was perhaps especially prone to use a psychological model to understand Mary's behavior; also fitting this model is the far greater emphasis on the past to explain Mary's present behavior—asked why the Indian part of the story was increased in the musical, for example, Landesman said that it "informs us about Mary's behavior; it's an important part of her past." Asked this same question, Norman reiterated that she wanted this to be Mary's story. By helping Mary cast the magic spell in the garden to make Colin well, the Indians help provide a "snapshot of Mary's power," which is needed on stage to replace how, in the novel, Mary "casts a spell over Colin dramatically, through daily interaction"; in the novel, moreover, it is Colin, not Mary, who is in charge of the magic experiments in the garden. The scene in which the Indians help Mary put a curse on the schoolmistress is another instance of the focus on Mary's power. As I saw it acted, Mary's tantrum was playacting and acknowledged to be such by delighted laughter from the audience, particularly its younger part. Rather than having lost control of her emotions, Mary was consciously trying to control her own fate, using a tantrum to control adults, as children may consciously or unconsciously do.

If Norman's work with emotionally disturbed children prepared her to understand Mary, a play that she had recently written and produced with Landesman's help prepared both of them to appreciate the symbolism of the garden in Burnett's classic. Produced in 1984, before Norman had ever read *The Secret Garden, Traveler in the Dark* bears an uncanny resemblance to Burnett's book. Sam, whose mother died when he was twelve, has become a world-famous surgeon; now his nurse has died under his knife, recalling his earlier inability to save his ailing mother. The entire play takes place in the "overgrown garden" beloved by Sam's mother but resented by his father. Here Sam acknowledges how he has kept an emotional distance not only from the nurse—a friend since childhood—but also from his wife and twelve-year-old son. Like Burnett's novel, Norman's play stresses female nurturance—Sam's mother, wife, and nurse have all been self-sacrificingly devoted to him; as in Burnett's novel, renewal of a man and his relationship with his son occur in a "Mother's garden" (act 1).

Deciding how to stage that central healing metaphor, a Mother's garden, proved to be the most difficult challenge in turning Burnett's book into a musical, according to Landesman, Norman, and Schulman. The movie versions had spent too much time showing the children gardening, an activity that is neither "dramatic," according to Landesman, nor, according to Norman, "translatable into movies, the stage, or even magazines, for gardening appeals to all the senses, including smell." Taking the literal approach, using wagons of dirt, did not work, according to Schulman and Landesman; nor could one manage a real bird on stage. "Communing with nature," Landesman concluded, is "best done in song"—as in Dickon's solo conjuring away the winter storms and invoking spring (1.3) or in his duet with Mary explaining how to tell if plants are still "wick" (2.4).

Music is used to create the illusion of not just gardening but the garden itself, especially by evoking the characters' feelings for it. To those who have found too little of the garden in the musical (Rich; Richards), I have wanted to reply, "Did you listen as well as look?" During the first act the music (and much of the dialogue) is saturated with references to and descriptions of gardens. As the curtain rises, the orchestra plays the melody of "Come to my garden" (one of many leitmotifs in the musical, which in this and other ways is operatic), and Lily sings about "clusters of roses"; music takes us from Lily's to "Mistress Mary's" garden, and later, during their nocturnal wanderings, Archibald and Mary sing of a garden in their dreams (prologue). During Archibald's ballroom dream, he and Lily sing of their courtship in her garden (1.2); Ben sings his gardening lore (1.3); and in the library, after Mary has asked for "a bit of earth," Archibald uses garden imagery in a song to contrast Mary's hopeful attitude toward life with his own despairing one (1.4). The melody for "a bit of earth" like that for "Come to my garden" occurs later in musical links between scenes (2.6). Introducing the garden first through words and music, I would argue, invites audiences to imagine their own gardens, much as do the descriptions in Burnett's book. "Every reader sees a different garden," observed Norman; the secret garden is "so much a garden of the mind."

In congruence with this interpretation, the first garden we see is Mary's dream garden, at the opening of act 2. Mary's earlier scenes with Ben and Dickon had been in a greenhouse and a maze (suggested in the New York production by plants shaped like birds and animals). Act 1 ended with Mary at the center back of a darkened stage opening a door into the garden, which is suggested by bright light. When act 2 opens, we are on the other side of that door at a brightly lit garden party. This is the garden as Mary imagines it, the garden of her dreams. Except for Mary's song about the garden, the entire scene is done in pantomime. Mary has her picture taken sitting on the ground between her mother and Lily and also standing in front of her father and a kneeling Archibald; Ben brings her a birthday cake. Everyone is dressed in white, the only color being the red of a handkerchief that Neville drops into Colin's lap, recalling the dramatization of the cholera epidemic. This intrusion of reality ends Mary's dream; and as the characters move offstage, the white sheet on which the party took place is pulled up like an ominous sail or shroud, leaving us in a dark scene in which Archibald and Neville discuss Mary's fate. The second of the three garden scenes in act 2 shows us the secret garden at night. Here Mary works her Indian charm on Colin, and Colin swears the garden community—Dickon, Martha, and Ben are also onstage—to secrecy until he is fully well. Although the stage is dark, scrim and flats suggest foliage with images tucked in it—an Indian child, an Indian on a horse, a snake, an elephant, a rhinoceros. The combination is appropriate for a scene in which Mary's Hindu spell to make Colin well is combined with Martha and Dickon's invocation of spring. (Simon discovered that the modalities of Indian ragas and Yorkshire music are similar, allowing her to juxtapose them in this scene.) Our first full vision of the garden comes in the final scene. According to Landesman, attempts to reveal it before the end did not work, no doubt because subsequent views seemed anticlimactic. Coming after a dream garden and a night garden, this day garden suggests perhaps that we have all just awakened from an unpleasant dream. Like Mary's dream garden, the day garden is well lit; as in the night garden, the foliage on scrim and flats is filled with many images. Here, however, the dominant colors are golds and greens, and the images—many faces of babies and children, birds, butterflies—suggest fecundity. The whole set is flanked left and right by strong female figures, and the several layers of foliage narrowing to the back seemed to me vaginal, perhaps because Burnett's description of Colin bursting from the secret garden into his father's arms (249) has always reminded me of childbirth, underscoring the archetypal theme of rebirth ("Gardens" 222–23).

Norman said that she had not seen this sexual imagery in the final garden set but indicated that the creative team was very much aware of the sexual overtones of Burnett's story. The subliminal sexual appeal of Burnett's book, especially for prepubertal girls—the garden as a metaphor for the female body and place where female

roles can be learned and rehearsed—is discussed by Almond (492–
94). Interestingly, only Almond's article was mentioned when I
asked the four women if they had read any criticism of the novel.
Schulman deliberately read none; the other three read Thwaite's
biography of Burnett; Landesman read some criticism but recalled
only the article by Almond; Norman read only that article and insisted that it was read after the musical was completed, during the
Broadway previews. The creators of the musical were nevertheless
thoroughly conscious of the gender implications of Burnett's story.
Asked what the book meant to them as children, Schulman and
Simon, like so many other women, recalled not the characters or
the plot but the "mystery" and "magic" of the garden setting, of the
garden's being "a secret place to go alone and be safe"; and Schulman gave the recollection a feminist filter. "As a child, I wanted the
garden to be mine but as an adult I was crushed that it is Colin's
garden." Noting that Burnett's book anticipated Virginia Woolf's
Room of One's Own (1929) by almost two decades, Schulman added
that it is "important that Mary control the garden, which is her
body, as we now understand it. It is important that she knows the
door, has the key, and can lock it."

All of these sexual and gender implications are somehow found
in the portrayal of the garden in the second act. The concept of the
garden as a room of one's own is poignantly expressed in Mary's
song in her dream garden—the first song Simon wrote for Mary,
to find her voice. Mary dreams of a garden where she can be herself without feigning for others: "I need a place where I can go,/
Where I can whisper what I know," "a place where I can hide,/
Where no one sees my life inside." Here, in a "place where I can
bid my heart/Be still, and it will mind me," she can control her own
feelings; here, in a "place where I can go when I am lost—/And
there I'll find me," she can nurture herself. The garden has to be
a place that she herself owns, controls, a place "where no one says
to go or stay." She can create her own identity here, perhaps even
by becoming a writer or an artist: "I can make my plans, and write
them down/So I can read them"; "I can take my pen and draw/The
girl I mean to be" (2.1). Schulman has said, "We gave Mary the garden," and the final spoken words and accompanying stage gestures
underscore this major misreading of Burnett's novel. By the end
Mary does in fact own the garden with all that it has come to mean,
including her own healthy female body. Mary offers to return the

garden key, whereupon Archibald lifts her pinafore, places the key in her pocket, and says: "Mary Lennox, for as long as you will have us, . . . we are yours, Colin and I, . . . and this is your home, and this, my lovely child . . . is your garden" (2.10).

Burnett's great-granddaughter said of the musical, according to Norman, that "Frances would love it. Those are exactly the parts that she liked, and that's what she would have done" (Nance). I agree. The Burnett who borrowed from the Brontës and wrote stories about ghosts would have appreciated the use of melodramatic and Gothic elements for psychological analysis of the characters; Burnett the late nineteenth-century feminist would have approved Lily's supernatural mothering, which helps a father to become nurturant; had Burnett been reared during the late twentieth century, she might have focused her entire story on Mary. In addition, Burnett often regarded herself as a "channel" rather than a "creator" (V. Burnett 337) and thus knew that stories are flexible, that they can be told in more than one way. She herself turned a short tale, "Sara Crewe" (1887–88), into a play (1902–3) and eventually into a full-length book (1905), both entitled *A Little Princess;* and she saw some of her stories adapted to film—her last public appearance was at the opening of Mary Pickford in *Little Lord Fauntleroy* (Thwaite 245–46). The Burnett who from childhood enjoyed pleasing audiences (*One* 208–27)—though she did not always please critics—would have liked to know that one of her books would have so many resurrections. She would have liked to know that a line she wrote during her last illness would prove prophetic: "As long as one has a garden one has a future; and as long as one has a future one is alive" (*In the Garden* 10, 30).

Notes

1. In 1992 I saw matinee and evening performances 9 May at the Muny Theatre in St. Louis and 31 July evening and 1 August afternoon performances at the St. James Theatre in New York. These four viewings have been augmented by the original Broadway cast album and the published musical book and lyrics, from which quotations in this article are taken. Additional insights were gained during my 30 July 1992 telephone interviews with Heidi Landesman, Marsha Norman, Susan Schulman, and Lucy Simon.

2. Unless indicated otherwise, statements by and about Landesman, Norman, Schulman, and Simon in this article come from my interviews with them.

122   PHYLLIS BIXLER

Works Cited

Almond, Barbara. *"The Secret Garden:* A Therapeutic Metaphor." *Psychoanalytic Study of the Child* 45 (1990): 477–94.

Barbour, David. "Women of the House." *Bergen County Record* (Hackensack, N.J.), 21 April 1991.

Bixler, Phyllis. *Frances Hodgson Burnett.* Boston: G. K. Hall, 1984.

———. "Gardens, Houses, and Nurturant Power in *The Secret Garden.*" In *Romanticism and Children's Literature in Nineteenth-Century England,* ed. James Holt McGavran, Jr. Athens: University of Georgia Press, 1991.

Bixler Koppes, Phyllis. "Tradition and the Individual Talent of Frances Hodgson Burnett: A Generic Analysis of *Little Lord Fauntleroy, A Little Princess,* and *The Secret Garden.*" *Children's Literature* 7 (1978): 191–207.

Bloom, Harold. *The Anxiety of Influence: A Theory of Poetry.* New York: Oxford University Press, 1973.

Burnett, Frances Hodgson. *In the Garden.* Boston: Medici Society, 1925.

———. *Little Lord Fauntleroy.* New York: Scribner's, 1886.

———. *A Little Princess: Being the Whole Story of Sara Crewe Now Told for the First Time.* New York: Scribner's, 1905.

———. *The Little Princess: A Play for Children and Grown-Up Children in Three Acts.* New York: Samuel French, 1911.

———. *The One I Knew the Best of All: A Memory of the Mind of a Child.* New York: Scribner's, 1893.

———. *The Secret Garden.* 1911. Reprint. New York: Viking Penguin, 1951.

———. *Sara Crewe and Editha's Burglar.* London: Warne, 1888.

Burnett, Vivian. *The Romantick Lady (Frances Hodgson Burnett): The Life Story of an Imagination.* New York: Scribner's, 1927.

Carroll, Lewis. *Through the Looking-Glass and What Alice Found There.* 1871. Reprint, ed. Donald J. Gray. New York: Norton, 1971.

Dusinberre, Juliet. *Alice to the Lighthouse: Children's Books and Radical Experiments in Art.* New York: St. Martin's, 1987.

Grabel, Naomi. "Composer Lucy Simon Shares Her Secrets." *Show Music* (Spring 1992): 12–14.

Jones, Welton. "Heidi Landesman's Callings Are Many." *San Diego Union,* 4 November 1991.

Kermode, Frank. *The Classic.* Cambridge: Harvard University Press, 1983.

Keyser, Elizabeth Lennox. "'Quite Contrary': Frances Hodgson Burnett's *The Secret Garden.*" *Children's Literature* 11 (1983): 191–207.

Landesman, Heidi. Telephone interview. 30 July 1992.

McGee, Celia. "Gambling on a 'Garden': Can a Children's Classic Become a Broadway Hit?" *New York,* 22 April 1991: 65–66, 70–71.

McGillis, Roderick. "'Secrets' and 'Sequence' in Children's Stories." In "Narrative Theory and Children's Literature," ed. Hugh T. Keenan. *Studies in the Literary Imagination* 18:2 (Fall 1985): 35–46.

Marquis, Claudia. "The Power of Speech: Life in *The Secret Garden.*" *AUMLA: Journal of the Australasian Universities Language and Literature Association* 68 (1987): 163–87.

Mootz, William. "Marsha Norman Is Back on Broadway." *Louisville, Ky., Courier-Journal,* 21 April 1991.

Nance, Kevin. "Creating a 'Garden' of Delights." *Lexington Herald-Leader,* 23 June 1991.

Nodelman, Perry. *The Pleasures of Children's Literature.* New York: Longman, 1992.

Norman, Marsha. *The Fortune Teller.* New York: Random House, 1987.

————. *Getting Out.* In Norman, *Four Plays.* New York: Theatre Communications Group, 1988.

————. *The Holdup.* In Norman, *Four Plays.* New York: Theatre Communications Group, 1988.

————. *'night, Mother.* New York: Hill and Wang, 1983.

————. Telephone interview. 30 July 1992.

————. *Third and Oak.* In Norman, *Four Plays.* New York: Theatre Communications Group, 1988.

————. *Traveler in the Dark.* In Norman, *Four Plays.* New York: Theatre Communications Group, 1988.

Norman, Marsha, and Lucy Simon. *The Secret Garden.* New York: Theatre Communications Group, 1992.

Paul, Lissa. "Enigma Variations: What Feminist Theory Knows About Children's Literature." *Signal* (September 1987): 186–201.

Plotz, Judith. "*Secret Garden II; or Lady Chatterley's Lover* as Palimpsest." Paper presented at the Children's Literature Association annual meeting, Hattiesburg, Miss., May 1991. Forthcoming in *Children's Literature Association Quarterly.*

Rich, Frank. " 'Garden': The Secret of Death and Birth." Review of the 1991 musical *The Secret Garden. New York Times,* 26 April 1991.

Richards, David. "Only the Wind Should Sigh in This 'Garden.' " Review of the 1991 musical *The Secret Garden. New York Times,* 5 May 1991.

Schulman, Susan H. Telephone interview. 30 July 1992.

Shaughnessy, Alfred, Sharon Burgett, Sue Beckwith-Smith, and Diana Matterson. The Secret Garden: *A New Musical.* CBS Special Products, P—19920, 1987.

Simon, Lucy. Telephone interview. 30 July 1992.

Simon, Lucy, and Marsha Norman. The Secret Garden: *The Original Broadway Cast Album.* Columbia, CK 48817, 1991.

Simpson, Janice C. "The Women of the *Secret Garden.*" *Theater Week,* 6–12 May 1991, pp. 16–21.

Thwaite, Ann. *Waiting for the Party: The Life of Frances Hodgson Burnett, 1849–1924.* New York: Scribner's, 1974.

Verduin, Kathleen. "*Lady Chatterley* and *The Secret Garden:* Lawrence's Homage to Mrs. Hodgson Burnett." *D. H. Lawrence Review* 17 (Spring 1984): 61–66.

Watts, Patti. "Staged for Success: Four Award-Winning Women Come Together to Turn a Classic Book into a Broadway Musical." *Executive Female* (March–April 1991): 24–25, 40, 70.

Wolf, William. "Tending Her Garden." *Playbill* (May 1991): 6, 8, 10.

Varia

"Tea with Alice of Alice in Wonderland" by Miles Franklin

With an Introduction and Cultural Critique by Sanjay Sircar

A piece on Lewis Carroll's birth centenary exhibition of 1932 organized by the London booksellers J. and E. Bumpus, "Tea with Alice of *Alice in Wonderland*" by Miles Franklin, author of the Australian classic *My Brilliant Career* (1901), lends itself to a critique of once prevalent, perhaps still-existing adult attitudes toward children and their literature. An examination of Franklin's essay, which does not appear in any bibliography of which I am aware, enables us to focus on the production, commercial dissemination, reception, and institutionalization of literature specifically for children. Production and reception take place in a particular cultural or ethnographical context (such as colonialism) and within a capitalist class society (sometimes marked by snobbery, deference, commodity fetishism, and commodification). In this larger context, children's literature can manifest reverence for the good old days and for childhood, it can engender games in which adults take the roles of children and characters from juvenile fiction, and it can foster mythmaking in regard to children's classics generally.

Tea with Alice of Alice in Wonderland
Miles Franklin

How many millions must have wished that they could have tea with Alice and the Mad Hatter!

So it scarcely seemed real when I found myself actually seated at the same table as the one and only Alice herself. But so it was in the wonderland of London, in that particularly seductive establishment, the ancient and honourable book store of Messrs. J. and E. Bumpus, on Oxford street, where Royalty shop. It all happened so simply. Certain people had the pleasure of their company being

Children's Literature 22, ed. Francelia Butler, R. H. W. Dillard, and Elizabeth Lennox Keyser (Yale University Press, © 1994 Hollins College). Franklin's essay is reproduced by permission of the Permanent Trustee Company Limited, Sydney, Australia—Trustee of the Estate of the Late S. M. S. Miles Franklin.

requested at the Old Courthouse for the private opening of the Lewis Carroll Centenary Exhibition. The card of invitation was about eight inches square, and decorated with Alice, the Cheshire Cat, Tweedledum and Tweedledee, the Duchess, and other quaint immortal entities. Mr. J. G. Wilson, the head of Bumpus's, is celebrated for his organisation of unique and delightful occasions, and in this one was conspicuously successful. Those who arrived before the rooms grew too full gained a comprehensive idea of the extensive character and methodical arrangement of the exhibition. Here is all of Carroll, as testified by Mr. Falconer Madan's scholarly catalogue of 116 pages. Here is everything from cheapest reprints, parodies, card games, translations, dramatisations, biscuit tins, up to choicely printed volumes bound in vellum: and those even more costly freak volumes beloved of collectors for a spurious rarity, for which, as a would-be living author, I have lively contempt. They are too often the prizes of the maleficently wealthy in a snobbish sport, the toys of those who, perhaps, lack discernment, generosity or courage to recognise and aid writers in their arduous beginnings. There were endless genuine treasures lent by nearly a hundred owners; journals, letters, photographs, paintings; original drawings by Tenniel, Furness, and others; and, sent by Messrs[.] Macmillan, the 42 original wood blocks for Tenniel's illustrations of "Alice in Wonderland." One bay was full of a large and remarkable collection of Carrolliana sent across the Atlantic by its American owner. Everything imaginable was there, superbly arranged.

But the guests very quickly obscured the exhibits, and the speaking began. The Patroness, H.R.H. Princess Beatrice, was unable to be present, because of an operation on her eye. The chairman, the Very Rev. the Dean of Christ Church (Dr. H. J. White), said that the very same verger who had shown him to his seat when he first entered Christ Church was still alive, and had recently tumbled downstairs without hurting the stairs or himself, though he was 92. He also related how, as an undergraduate in his first term, he had met Mr. Dodgson (Lewis Carroll), as mathematical tutor, and was sorry to say that he did not come up to standard in his Euclid. After a severe interview, Mr. Dodgson said that Mr. White must attend his lectures. He said that the undergraduates dreaded Mr. Dodgson, and in his own case this fear had resulted in concentrated effort. He concluded by saying that to Lewis Carroll had been given the almost unique gift of making more children laugh than anyone else in the world; that hundreds of thousands of children had laughed at his jokes, and not one had ever blushed; and he did not think that any man could have a finer epitaph than the acknowledgment that he was one of the most amusing and purest souls in the world.

Mrs. Hargreaves (the original Alice), in declaring the exhibition open, described herself as a very old person who tired easily, but who remembered the days when she was one of a number of little girls, running about in cotton frocks, who knew Mr. Dodgson before the name of Lewis Carroll had been invented.

Sir Gerald Du Maurier recalled the friendly association between his father, the celebrated "Punch" artist, and Lewis Carroll, and told a new story about Mr. Wills, the great tobacco man, calling at the Du Maurier home at Hampstead, one day, when Lewis Carroll was also there. In those days it was not permissible to mention in a man's presence his business, or the source from which he drew his money, and when Du Maurier was about to take his visitors to see the view from the Heath, he was warned against any mention of tobacco. But no sooner was the famous spot reached from which on clear days portions of eight counties are visible, than Du Maurier remarked: "Here is the most wonderful bird's eye view—oh! I beg your pardon."

Mr. J. C. Squire, a London reviewer and essayist, referred to the long list of notable well-wishers of the exhibition, as the most extraordinary menagerie of people, who could have been collected by no other interest excepting Lewis Carroll, and finished some topical remarks by an entertaining rhyme in honor of "Alice."

The company were then released to tea, and saw such quantities of sandwiches and cakes, including Lewis Carroll's favourite goodies, rock cakes and ginger snaps, that the greediest might have shed a bitter tear if compelled to make any noticeable inroads in such abundance.

The venturesome seized the chairs, the throng milled around, hiding the exhibits, till one lost sight of all but outstanding things placed high, such as the lovely Herkomer portrait of the gentle grey-haired Lewis Carroll (specially lent by the original's old college), the amiable, substantial, respectable, convincing Dodo, or Quentin Matsys' [*sic*] portrait of the pathetically, tragically, inhumanly ugly little Duchess of Carinthia and Tyrol, recently resuscitated as the eponymous heroine of Feuchtwanger's "Ugly Duchess."

The waitresses were desirous of getting some of the people out of the way, but who could be hurried when Alice herself was coming to tea? I sought an inconspicuous corner for the part of invisible and inconsequent Dormouse, while among those present, distinguished in the world of printing presses to-day, to take the larger parts of Mad Hatters and March Hares, Red and White Queens, Duchesses, Knights, or Jabberwock, Carpenter, Walrus, and Gryphon for a frabj[o]us, scrumptious meal, were Lady Dickens, Mr. and Mrs. St. John Ervine, Mr. and Mrs. J. B. Priestly, Capt. Hargreaves, Mr. and Mrs. Kenneth Grahame, Lady Bridgeman, Lady Buxton, the Greek Minister, Miss Horniman, Mr. and Mrs. Leonard Huxley, the Principal of Lady Margaret Hall, Sir Fredk. and Lady Liddell, Mr. E. V. Lucas, Mr. and Mrs. Walter de la Mare, the Master of the Temple, the Provost of Worcester College, Lady Redesdale, Miss Hilda Trevelyan, Miss Irene Vanbrugh, Mr. Henry W. Nevinson, Sir Ernest and Lady Benn, Sir Victor and Lady Gollancz.

But the most consequential were of no consequence compared with Alice herself, attended by the original of Peter Pan (Mr. Peter Davies), carrying red roses (sent her by a lady of 90 who had known her as a little girl in the Deanery), who came, and, as it should have been in a fairly [sic] tale, sat down at the table of the infinitesimal Dormouse. There she was just across the table from me. Alice at eighty, looking not more than 60 or 55, with her fair skin, to which her native climate has been so kind, Alice to-day still so winning that the most matter-of-fact could realise that in this gracious lady, when a child, the greatest of all writers for children had a matchless inspiration and model.

Miles Franklin's "Tea with Alice"

"Tea with Alice" appeared in the 3 December 1932 issue of *All About Books for Australian and New Zealand Readers*, a literary magazine published in Melbourne by D. W. Thorpe. A mishmash of articles, long and short reviews, and unpretentious bits and pieces of literary gossip, this issue includes such articles as "Mr. Galsworthy, Culture and Australia," "Present-Day Poetry," "Some Literary Families," "This Year's Australian Books" (including one by Franklin), "Sir Walter Scott," "New Novels and Christmas Books," along with "The Use of Books for Your Children" by the novelist Storm Jameson, "Children's Books and Libraries," "The Bookless House" by Arthur Mee of the *Children's Encyclopaedia,* and "Books for Children." We note immediately the cultural and commercial significance of so much on children's literature at Christmastime.

The tone of "Tea" does not accord with Franklin's own dismissive attitude toward children's books (even though she wrote an extremely peculiar one herself—*Sydney Royal*, 1947), expressed by her alter-ego heroine in *My Career Goes Bung:* "Gad collected children's books which seemed to me a peculiar hobby for an old bachelor. He read from them. I never had any children's books. Ma thought them trash and I don't believe that Pa ever heard of them" (169). Thus "Tea" is either a genuine acknowledgment of an exceptional work (not "merely" for children) or a journalistic playing along with (and thus a reinforcement of) the mystique of a children's classic. As it stands, "Tea" is competent journalism and follows a simple pattern. Franklin recounts receiving the invitation to the centenary exhibition, lists the exhibits, summarizes the speeches by H. J. White, Alice Liddell Hargreaves, Gerald du Maurier, and J. C. Squire to represent aspects of Carroll (Oxford, children, the stage, humor), and describes the throng, the tea, and the final thrill of sitting across the table from the original Alice.

Although Franklin was a fierce nationalist who consistently repudiated charges of Australian cultural inferiority, the tone of "Tea" is very much that of the country-cousin colonial telling those at home in Australia what she has seen at "home" in England. This is most immediately apparent in the sunburnt-colonial view of Alice Liddell Hargreaves, "with her fair skin, to which her native climate has been so kind." Franklin was one of those who attempted to forge a sense of and pride in an independent Australian identity, but this identity was often defined in terms of inheriting, revering, and treasuring what was presented as the best from the Mother Country. Notions of beauty were among these, and likewise received opinions about the classics.

Franklin was also stridently egalitarian, yet "Tea" is permeated with snobbery about the establishment, both in Franklin's choice of words and metaphors and in what they tell of the proceedings. The snobbery is imperfectly hidden by the facetious inflation of the description of the venue as that "particularly seductive establishment, the ancient and honourable book store of Messrs. J. and E. Bumpus, on Oxford street, where Royalty shop." It comes through clearly in the *News-of-the-World*ish noting of the absence of the "Patroness, H.R.H. Princess Beatrice" because of an eye operation, in Squire's reference to the assembly of "notable well-wishers," and in Franklin's list of people "distinguished in the world of printing presses to-day," four of whom are delineated by educational and diplomatic position rather than by name. The *faux-naïve* simplicity of "It all happened so simply. Certain people had the pleasure of their company being requested at the Lewis Carroll Centenary Exhibition" seems purposefully to convey a snobbish hint that invitations were scarce and that strings had been pulled, for it virtually begs the reader to wonder how Franklin wangled an invitation and what sort of people were selected to attend. Her stated unimportance, as one receiving an unexpected privilege, blurs with her implied importance, as one of those certain people. Clearly it was enjoyable to be at the "private opening," and a whole crowd qualified for invitations.

The emphasis on the grand people present is of a piece with the hyperbolic emphasis on things. These are both "extensive" and "large and remarkable"; they include "all of Carroll," even "everything imaginable." They are "genuine treasures," "specially lent" and "superbly arranged." Interestingly, Franklin stresses that the valuable originals are present: Tenniel's woodblocks, the painting of the Ugly Duchess. And the same imagery extends to people— the "one and only Alice herself," "the original Alice," accompanied by "the original of Peter Pan"; even Dodgson is the Carroll whom Alice knew before he was Carroll, "before the name . . . had been invented." The figure of Carroll himself is the center of commodification and investment with mystique, processes which operate with both people and objects. So we have present in the original "the lovely Herkomer portrait" of Lewis Carroll from "the original's old college," and we have Carroll as the original "amiable, substantial, respectable, convincing Dodo." The power of the word *substantial* spreads from the real man to the fictive Dodo. The portrait is an original object; the man is the original of the author, of the portrait, of the fictive character. The value of man and portrait alike is underpinned in their being originals.

Just as a hierarchy extends from the milling, crushing crowd up to the dignitaries, so does one extend "from cheapest reprints, parodies, card games, translations, dramatisations, biscuit tins, up to choicely printed volumes bound in vellum [an echo of Lear's alphabet?]." The things that can be produced and sold cheaply in quantity rank lower than the expensive, scarce ones. The latter give grace to the former by their juxtaposition on the list and in the exhibition, just as the crowd was presumably edified and elevated by rubbing elbows with and duplicating the actions of the dignitaries in their company. Alice partakes of grace by association with the original man, and Franklin gains grace by contiguity with her. But after mentioning volumes bound in vellum, Franklin, in a different, more personal voice, briefly queries the snobbery relating to valuable things and notable people. She notes "those even more costly freak volumes beloved of collectors, for a spurious rarity, for which, as a would-be living author I have a lively contempt. They are too often the prizes of the maleficently wealthy in a snobbish sport, the toys of those who, perhaps, lack discernment, generosity or courage to recognise and aid writers in their arduous beginnings." Here is a blow for live people against dead things, a touch of what people in the 1930s called socialist red-ragging, a valuing of access to culture (Franklin welcomed the advent of the paperback), and perhaps, too, the envy of one who lacks and wishes for a patron.

Linked by safety and security to the stress on snobbery, hierarchy, commodity, and the original object in "Tea" is the stress on the old, often in conjunction with the very young. We have the ancient and honorable bookstore that sells children's books; "the Old Courthouse"; Alice, "a very old person who tired easily, but who remembered the days when she was one of a number of little girls, running about"; the "old college" of gray-haired Lewis Carroll (who was gray-haired neither at his birth, which the celebrations commemorated, nor at the birth of *Alice*); the "resuscitated" Ugly Duchess; the red roses (emblem of youth) sent by the old lady of ninety who had known Alice as a little girl in the Deanery. Hence, too, the opening of the first address by the Very Reverend the Dean of Christ Church Dr. H. J. White, who recalls his youth when "undergraduates dreaded Mr. Dodgson," when he had a "severe interview," when "fear resulted in concentrated effort," and then cites the many "children [who] had laughed at [Carroll's] jokes." His opening comment about the ninety-two-year-old verger tumbling downstairs unhurt is unconnected to Carroll, except as a reference to Old Father William (whom Franklin does not mention), and reveals the group nostalgia for and worship of old age, both of individuals and eras. Three of the four speakers, White, Hargreaves, and du Maurier, recall the vanished period; indeed, du Maurier's anecdote about an occasion when Carroll was merely present serves solely as a genial evocation of a vanished time and its snobbery (the bird's-eye tobacco).

Hovering about the worship of old people and the Victorian past is a desire for safety and, beyond that, immortality. The old verger is an icon of immortality. "Alice, the Cheshire Cat, Tweedledum and Tweedledee, the Duchess" on the invitation card are not "quaint immortal entities" merely because they are fictions but also because they are quaint (childish, old-fashioned, odd—see the *Oxford English Dictionary*) and because they are images of children, that category of the not-quite-adult human including the dwarf, the animal, and the representational object (cards and chess pieces). Wonderland and Looking-Glass figures, in being neither adult nor human, are child images (by overpowering which the child-protagonist Alice grows closer to adulthood) and images of immortality, being semi-supernatural. So is Quinten Massys's "pathetically, tragically, inhumanly ugly little Duchess," immortalized by him in a painting that is today said to be *after* Massys; identified without evidence as the real Duchess of Carinthia and Tyrol, it is possibly not even a portrait at all but a study in the grotesque. The Duchess was further fictionalized in Lion Feuchtwanger's *Die hässlicher Herzogin Margaretha Maultasch* (1926, translated by Willa and Edwin Muir, 1927; reprinted 1972). Both the painter and the essayist render her as a thing, and she is inscribed as an icon of both adult and child by the sentimentality of Franklin's diction.

The desire for the stable order, the thing, the original, the old, the past, produces an oxymoron in the mixture, odd at first sight, of old age and youth in the nostalgic image of the old safe time of childhood. Actual children are absent (or at any rate unmentioned) in the celebrations, but images of them are present—in the wealthy with their rare toys, in the remembered little girls in the cotton frocks, in the reference to the hundreds of thousands of child readers laughing at Carroll's jokes, in the children of Dickens and the Liddell-Hargreaves families. Indeed, the celebrations and the article remind us that Alice Pleasance Liddell was once both the child inspiration and the child audience for Alice (although the child Peter Davies was not quite the original of Peter Pan but more a member of an original audience). Pretending not to know the difference between a fictive child and a real one who inspired or listened to the first oral version or versions of a text may be silly, but it is salutary. The conceit reminds us that much children's literature does indeed emerge from interactions between real-life children and adults and that the interactions often move from game playing and role-playing to storytelling.

The most interesting thing about "Tea" is that it manifests group regression to a past life-period. We see regression in the pervasive, affectedly childish sweetness, or preciousness, that quality called twee (like but not quite the same as the American *cute*). We see regression in the two similar role-games of the essayist as child and the essayist as Wonderland character (and child) playing the game of "let's pretend we're pretending." Both exemplify the older but still undead tweeness in talk about children's literature. This abrogation of adulthood in what seems affected wonder and playfulness is called the Poohsticks mentality, after those A. A. Milne aficionados who celebrate notable occasions in his life by playing Poohsticks as the climax to pilgrimages to the original places where the Pooh stories were told and which they mention.

I suspect that rather than genuine nostalgia-regression, Franklin's textual mediation as a child or childish persona, with her own equivalent of the wide "dreaming eyes of wonder," involves for her at least half-conscious role-playing. Minxish, gushing *faux-naïveté* is characteristic of the emphatically inconspicuous first-person alterego protagonists of her work all through her career. After the first paragraph, "How many millions must have wished that they could have tea with Alice and the Mad Hatter!" Franklin tells us how the wish was granted in her case in a winner-of-the-Disney-contest, dream-come-true, queen-for-a-day tone. "Tea" begins and ends with how "it scarcely seemed real when I found myself actually seated at the same table as the one and only Alice herself." "It all happened so simply" comes in the voice of wonder at entering a fairy tale and is kept up all through, in, for example, the use of a childish register with "goodies" to express delight in the feast-abundance. It peaks with the meaning, rather than the diction, of the childish, worshiping superlatives of the last paragraph, where Franklin writes of the "matchless inspiration" for the "greatest of all writers," who, "as it should have been in a fairy tale, sat down at the table. . . . There she was just across the table from me." Franklin apparently sat speechless, goggle-eyed at Alice's proximity. The line between children and adults also disappears in White's odd slippage between the two categories of child innocence and adult knowledge. "Hundreds of thousands of children had laughed at

[Carroll's] jokes, and not one had ever blushed" indicates some confusion between the children, who would not blush at what they failed in their innocence to understand, and their book-selecting guardians, who would be the ones to undertake any blushing on their behalf.

The simple wonder of the child entering the fairy tale is allied to the strand of imagery of the second game, dual-sourced, in Franklin's mind and that of the company: playing at Wonderland. It begins with the decorated invitation "about eight inches square," larger than an ordinary one, probably meant to recall the one handed to the Frog Footman. Franklin's own Wonderland–Looking Glass imagery is initiated when she opens "Tea" with the child's wishful fantasy of entering the world of the book, goes on to conflate the person with the fictive character in the metaphor of the "one and only Alice," and extends the conflation to real and fictive space with the phrase "wonderland of London." Then Squire archly calls the assemblage "the most extraordinary menagerie of people, who could have been collected by no other interest excepting Lewis Carroll." The heterogeneous Wonderland–Looking Glass animals are metaphorically children, and so are the adults here assimilated to them.

The adult-regression game is both Franklin's and Squire's; maybe it is shared by all present. Franklin describes the "let's pretend" game with Carrollian or childish diction, or a combination thereof: the "greediest might have shed a bitter tear" at the "frabjous, scrumptious meal," at which are offered the rock cakes and ginger-snaps that were Carroll's favorite goodies (is this actually recorded anywhere?). Franklin then enacts the "let's pretend" game by putting herself in the role of "infinitesimal," "invisible and inconsequent Dormouse": "I sought an inconspicuous corner for the part of . . . Dormouse, while among those present, distinguished . . . to take the part of Mad Hatters and March Hares, Red and White Queens, Duchesses, Knights or Jabberwock, Carpenter, Walrus, and Gryphon" were the list of solid notables. This sentence conjoins the worlds of whimsy to solidity and itself enacts the movement between them. The division in the sentence between plural and singular roles both suggests that fictive roles can be duplicated in the game of enacting them and replicates the stress on the unique original.

The temper of the times and its notion of childhood, the Victorian inheritance, comes through clearly in White's image of Carroll as "one of the most amusing and purest souls in the world." Franklin takes her cue from White in her own image of the "gentle, grey-haired Lewis Carroll . . . the amiable, substantial, respectable, convincing Dodo"—why convincing? It is all very endearing, though it could not always have been so in real life. Franklin's account of Alice Liddell Hargreaves is even more obviously an exercise in myth-making. Franklin evokes the reverent worshipers—"who could be hurried when Alice herself was coming to tea?"—and the converts, "the most matter-of-fact [who] could realise" her power. Alice is not only unique, "the one and only," "herself," but also the age-less immortal, the fairy simultaneously old and young (like George MacDonald's or Charles Kingsley's anima figures): "Alice at eighty, looking not more than 60 or 55," the lady in whom can be seen her lineaments "when a child." She is the muse—"matchless inspiration and model"—and she is the perfect lady, "Alice to-day still so winning . . . this gracious lady." Alice's opening speech is the least interesting of all the addresses, and she does not say anything recordable to her worshiper. Her power is that of perfect femininity, the silent child, the silent woman. She is the daughter figure—the cotton-frocked daughter of the pure man, the memory of whose birth she celebrates. She is the mother figure—mother of children (Captain Hargreaves is present) and figurative mother, who brings to birth and inhabits the literary work. She is the "very old person." And all on one page.

Miles Franklin's "Tea with Alice," which surfaced serendipitously, reminds us that emphemeral accounts of events such as the Carroll centenary celebration can be of value to people interested in children's literature and the institutionalization of the classics. Its naïveté, by rendering a cultural celebration transparent, reminds us, too, that the selective tradition in literature—whereby certain works and authors are hailed and admitted to the canon, allowed to have admiring readers and to bear close scrutiny—operates within children's literature. A cultural celebration like an exhibition is one of the processes of selection and institutionalization. But the exhibition in 1932 did not set out to celebrate a book or books, but their originary point, the author; the order of priority is reversed.

Squire playfully replicates Carroll's role of humorous rhymester when he pays tribute to the *Alice* books in verse (do these verses still exist?), but "Tea" also shows us that the occasion actually focuses on neither the work nor the person but celebrates objects (though it would be claimed that the person was being celebrated through the objects that he inspired). We see, although Franklin does not, that the celebration is an exercise in selling. Mine host Mr. Wilson, "celebrated for his organisation of unique and delightful occasions," of which this is one, is a bookseller, the head of Bumpus, who is organizing the event to publicize his shop and other wares, like Falconer Madan's *Catalogue*. We also see that the celebration is socially biased, exclusive, hymning but not including children. The "guests very quickly obscured the exhibits, and the speaking began," and "the throng milled around, hiding the exhibits, till one lost sight of all but outstanding things." We may, if we wish, read the scene as an allegory. The people hide the things. The things, some of them money-making spinoffs that use *Alice* motifs (the card games and biscuit tins and dramatizations), hide the *Alice* books and their pleasures. The inessential detritus of snobbery and nostalgia hide the possibility that something is being sold and that that something is neither the pleasure nor the appreciation of *Alice in Wonderland* and *Through the Looking-Glass*. But celebrations of culturally significant work and commemorations of culturally significant people do not have to be exhibitions of things nor occasions to gush. To me, a reading of "Tea with Alice" suggests that noncondescending scholarship, criticism, and the cultural study of children's literature are ultimately worth more than huge galas attended by the gliterati of the day.

Works Cited

Franklin, Miles. "Tea with Alice of *Alice in Wonderland*." *All About Books for Australian and New Zealand Readers* 4.12 (3 December 1932): 199.

————. *My Career Goes Bung*. 1946. Reprint. Sydney: Angus and Robertson, 1980.

Madan, Falconer, ed. *Lewis Carroll Centenary Exhibition, Including a Catalogue of the Exhibition, with Notes and Essays on Dodgson's Illustrators by Harold Hartley, and Additional Literary Pieces, Chiefly Unpublished, with Six Illustrations*. London: J. and E. Bumpus, Old Courthouse, 1932.

Timescape at Hemingford Grey: Lucy Boston's Centenary

Peter Hollindale

A centenary suggests historical distance: lives that began a hundred years ago are usually some years ended, and a retrospective salute is a celebration of the past. But Lucy Boston, in this way as in others, breaks the rules. The interaction of past and present, the paramount theme of all but two of her major children's stories, is in her case a matter not only of imagination but of biography.

Lucy Boston was born in 1892, which means that many of the most venerated children's classics were published in her lifetime. The author of *A Stranger at Green Knowe* (1961), in my view the finest modern children's book to explore the tense and tragic relationship between human beings and the rest of the animal world, was two years old when its nineteenth-century ancestor, *The Jungle Book* (1894), was published. The author of *The Children of Green Knowe* (1954), that celebration of what Penelope Lively terms "the presence of the past," was fourteen when Kipling's version of the same theme, *Puck of Pook's Hill* (1906), appeared.

I do not suggest that Kipling directly influenced Lucy Boston. (It is hard to imagine her being directly influenced by anybody.) But important similarities of theme and method between the two writers illuminate both Boston's Victorian origins and the modernity of her response to twentieth-century experience. Comparing *The Jungle Book* with *A Stranger at Green Knowe,* we find the same potentially tragic ambiguity of status in a solitary boy, who is briefly adopted into the animal world but is finally divorced from it by virtue of his humanness. But the biological vision in Boston's novel is notably more somber and pessimistic than Kipling's. Comparing *Puck of Pook's Hill* with *The Children of Green Knowe,* we see that the two writers share an awareness of historical immanence, an acute sense of house or landscape as the store of a living past that can be summoned by the magic of intuitive memory. But in Kipling's book there is a deep security of permanence, which in the Green Knowe

Children's Literature 22, ed. Francelia Butler, R. H. W. Dillard, and Elizabeth Lennox Keyser (Yale University Press, © 1994 Hollins College).

series gradually fades from view beneath the threat and pressure of recent history.

Puck of Pook's Hill is relevant to the study of Boston, because *The Children of Green Knowe* shares with it not only a theme but a narrative method. In Kipling's book two children, Dan and Una (modeled on Kipling's own children, John and Elsie), are acting out scenes from *A Midsummer Night's Dream* on their father's farm when they inadvertently call up the true figure of Puck, an immortal fairy presence in the landscape. Puck introduces them to a series of historical figures, standing for various periods in the past of this one place, and stories are told of their lives and times. The structure is episodic and awkward. Technically it is an uncertain blend of oral storytelling—linked short stories at bedtimes— with the continuity of an extended fiction. But as a loving evocation of a place, peopled over long centuries of habitation, the book is richly imagined. Kipling wrote it when he settled at his house, Bateman's, in Sussex, after years of traveling, and his biographer Charles Carrington notes: "Striking his roots into Sussex, Rudyard now explored the dimension of time as, in his travelling days, he had explored the dimension of space. His old inquiry: 'What should they know of England who only England know?' was taking a new direction. What can they know of present-day England who do not feel its continuity with England's past?" (379).

The similarities with Boston are striking. Both writers produce what might be called timescapes. Both did so having found a much-loved permanent dwelling after years of travel or expatriate living. Both depicted child characters based on their own children. Although Peter Boston grew up long before the Green Knowe series was begun and became its distinguished illustrator, Tolly is Peter as a child. And both authors opted for a "Chinese boxes" technique of inset narratives, which allowed for episodic storytelling. Great-grandmother Oldknow opens up for Tolly, as does Puck for Dan and Una, a vision of the past that is ambiguously placed between story, dream, and truth. The matching technique has disadvantages, and both works are structurally flawed. (A subtler mode of narrative organization to convey the coexistence of past and present in a landscape can be found in Jill Paton Walsh's fine novel *A Chance Child* [1978].) All the same, Boston's work, like Kipling's, powerfully embodies a major theme in which a metaphysical unity of time and place is more important than unity of action and demands something other than linear narrative.

To find that Lucy Boston owes much in imaginative vision and narrative procedure to the best of Victorian and Edwardian children's literature should scarcely surprise us, for she was herself a Victorian child and Edwardian adolescent. It escapes our notice because we think of Boston as a modern writer. And so indeed she is. Her first children's book, *The Children of Green Knowe*, was not published until 1954, when she was over sixty. (Her first book of any description, the adult novel *Yew Hall* [1954], was published earlier the same year.) This was only a year before Philippa Pearce's first novel, *Minnow on the Say* (1955), and only four years before another major celebration of the presence of the past, *Tom's Midnight Garden* (1958). We see Lucy Boston as one of the great inaugurators of the modern period in children's fiction, and we are right to do so. The last of the Green Knowe series and her last children's book, *The Stones of Green Knowe*, appeared as recently as 1976. The time and duration of her writing life are clearly in unusual relation to the formative years of her personal history.

That history closed only in 1990, with her death following a stroke at the age of ninety-seven. Until her final illness she had determinedly lived alone—alert, independent, and formidable—in the Manor House at Hemingford Grey near Cambridge, which is, famously, Green Knowe itself, the chief presence of the past in almost all her children's stories. So her centenary comes on the heels of her death and at a distance of merely thirteen years from her last book, the autobiographical volume *Perverse and Foolish*, which came out in 1979. This work of extreme old age is the one in which she revisits her own childhood, recalling in vivid detail and with singularly pitiless intelligence the experiences of her early years up to her hospital service in France during the Great War.

To mark the centenary year of Lucy Boston's birth, her family arranged for the reissue of *Perverse and Foolish* in a combined volume with her earlier memoir, *Memory in a House* (1973), which begins with her purchase of the Manor at Hemingford Grey just before the Second World War and describes the years that encompassed almost all her writing. The new book, entitled *Memories* (1992), has a brief connecting passage by her son, Peter, which covers the missing period of the interwar years, between the end of *Perverse and Foolish* in 1917 and the beginning of *Memory in a House* in 1939. These were the years of her marriage and its eventual breakup, then several years of music and painting in Italy and Austria until the threat of approaching war brought her home to England, to Cambridge, and finally, bringing permanent enrichment of children's literature, to Hemingford Grey.

Some critics seriously question the pertinence of biographical information to the study of any author, even one like Lucy Boston, whose work is so intimately related to her life. We live in a period that requires us to exercise multiple critical perspectives. We can agree with Roland Barthes that "the birth of the reader is at the cost of the death of the author" and accept that the continuing lives of the Green Knowe books are in the minds of the adults and children who read and take possession of them. Books are like lives: once the umbilical cord is severed, they exist in a series of diverse personal encounters. But the analogy goes further. Encounters with books, like encounters with lives, differ greatly in value. We touch many lives slightly and in passing, others deeply and lastingly. It is possible to read both people and texts in ways that have subjective authenticity for the reader but are nevertheless misreadings, and knowledge of background and context can help us to avoid them. To read the Green Knowe books and help children to read them, it is useful to know about Lucy Boston and about Hemingford Grey.

The main question is why Lucy Boston became a writer for children at all. By her own account it was largely an accident, because she wished *The Children of Green Knowe* to be illustrated by her son, Peter, and because her publisher considered that an illustrated novel was de facto a children's book. In her 1968 talk to the Children's Book Circle she said: "Is there a conscious difference in the way I write for grown-ups and children? No, there is no difference of approach, style, vocabulary or standard. I could pick out passages from any of the books and you would not be able to tell what age it was aimed at." This contention was effectively challenged by Aidan Chambers in his influential essay "The Reader in the Book." Taking representative passages from *Yew Hall* and *The Children of Green Knowe*, he shows the very different expectations of the reader implied by each. But as Chambers rightly affirms, these substantial differences of assumption, tone, and address do not indicate any lowering of standards when Boston moves from an audience of adults to an audience of children. The style and vocabulary differ,

but these skillful modulations are not accompanied by any concessions of intellect. Boston uses her intelligence as forcefully when
speaking to children as to grown-ups, and she assumes reciprocal
intelligence (as opposed to maturity, sophistication, and learning)
in the child.

Boston's intelligence is not at all childlike, except in its ruthless-
ness. In the books, however, she enters into a conspiracy with the
child reader, mediated through Mrs. Oldknow's relationships with
Tolly and Ping, to judge undeserving adults mercilessly, above all
those who are foolish, meddlesome, vulgar, or absurd. The best example of this in the Green Knowe books is Dr. Melanie Powers in *An
Enemy at Green Knowe* (1964), but the practice of subversive equality
of mind between child and adult can often be seen at work—for
instance, when Mrs. Oldknow returns to Tolly from a Christmas
expedition in quest of a partridge for a pear tree. The incident is
"childish," not least in its uncharitable merriment and the practical
expediency of its tailpiece, but the child reader is expected to laugh
at as well as *with* Mrs. Oldknow and Tolly:

> She seemed as pleased to be with him again as he was to be with
> her. They laughed as they ate: they found everything funny.
> They made silly remarks for the sake of laughing at them. She
> told him about an old friend whom she had met for lunch who
> had grown a little queer in the head. "She wore two hats and
> two wrist-watches, neither of which would go: but she knows a
> lot of sporting people. And I *believe* I've got a partridge." [123]

This derisiveness toward ridiculous adults, unrelieved by emolli-
ents of love or duty, is profusely evident in the childhood memories recorded in *Perverse and Foolish*. There is the family's attitude
toward the mother, with Lucy's brother Jas. as principal instigator:
"As time went on Mother's incomprehension of us increased; de-
rision became our normal attitude in private, and in her presence
silence, sometimes broken by an outburst of choking laughter. Jas.
was cruelly witty" (*Memories*, 77). A cousin of the family, who was
also Lucy's future father-in-law, fared no better. "There was nothing so silly this cousin would not say it, and his outbursts were the
joy of his family. . . . In such a house one could count on tumult and
humour all the time" (86–87).

In *Perverse and Foolish*, then, we see the origins and fashioning of
the intelligence that is omnipresent in Boston's children's books—

one that is adult, trained, sophisticated, subtle, but also irreverent, mischievous, and unsparing, especially in its eye for the comic and incongruous, an intelligence, in short, that is remarkably well equipped for talking with children. It is the delicate balance of intelligence and imagination, and the idiosyncrasy of each, that accounts for the originality of Lucy Boston's books for children, and awareness of this informing mind can alert us to features of these books that we might otherwise miss.

The autobiographical works confirm our sense of a necessary distinction that, once recognized, enables better readings of the Green Knowe stories and also of *The Sea Egg* (1967): a distinction between the act of intelligence, which is adult, detached, observant, and judgmental, and the act of imagination, which is childlike, intuitive, sensuous, and empathetic. By her own account the act of intelligence controlled her work as a painter: "I can draw and paint what I am actually looking at, just as I can describe what I experience. I am a reporter but have no pictorial imagination" (*Memories* 288). In the stories, however, both sets of qualities are at work, and sometimes an abrasion between them engenders artistic flaws and yet makes the books unique. Common to intelligence and imagination alike are a peculiar and intimidating directness and a sometimes cruel wit. These are instruments by which children take control of their worlds but which in Lucy Boston have escaped the usual softening and blunting induced by adult life. To read Boston's autobiographical work with the continuity allowed by *Memories* is to recognize the unusual continuum from child to adult life, the seizure of maturity without concessions, which makes her so potent as a children's writer.

Nowhere is the configuration of Boston's imaginative qualities so impressive as in her sense of time and in her celebration of the house that she called Green Knowe. *Memory in a House* records this local habitation in the years 1939–73, a time of accelerated social change in England. As she retraces this period in the autobiography, a gradual change in her attitudes and expectations is revealed, illuminating an aspect of the Green Knowe series that is often overlooked. Writing about her earliest years in the house, she says:

> What I want to evoke is the feeling I had at the time, not fore-
> seeing the future, that the past of the house from the beginning
> still existed—the winds coming off its hay-fields, the clouds

trailing shadows across the familiar woods, all the sounds of song birds, cocks, cattle and sheep, pump and bucket, axe and saw; the overriding tyranny of the seasons, the human fears and isolation, the deep passions and strong earthy loyalties. There was reverence for memory and *et expecto,* the belief in a future. I was lucky enough to have caught it whole. [*Memories,* 258]

Later, when the quiet fields around the house were encroached upon by postwar recreational developments that threatened its tranquillity, she was forced into vigorous defensive measures and a continuing sense of embattlement: "To those for whom what I am preserving is of no value, my embittered defence of it can only seem selfish and anti-social. It was dejecting to find myself . . . forced into the position of public enemy number one in the village, again a position from which there is no escape since as encroachment from every side continues I must always be the *animal méchant qui se défend*" (*Memories,* 285).

It is against this background that we must understand the key statement of *Memory in a House:* "The Manor . . . has an awe-inspiring past and as much of a future as anything can hope for in this blindly destructive present. Over it the sun and the moon have circled day and night for 850 years and the seasons pass in a drama on which the curtain never comes down. . . . If at last I begin to sense the house itself as ephemeral, I feel I am painfully growing up" (*Memories* 274). Here we can see why the Green Knowe books brought Boston's imagination into mingled tension and harmony with her intellect and why the works of art she produced are *necessarily* in the main for children. Imagination in Boston is overwhelmed by a sense of time. Time is perceived as the custodian of enduringness in things. The sense of transience that made her feel she was painfully growing up is expressed in a book that she wrote at the age of eighty about a house in its ninth century. Time in her books is understood as a child understands it. It produces fragile immediacies, as when Tolly in *The Chimneys of Green Knowe* (1958) registers the end of the holidays: "But it was already the last day but one, the last day on which he would not have to say, 'Tomorrow'—" (155). Yet time also stretches dependably into limitless pasts and futures. But time for the adult mind is also an intellectual concept, complex and nonlinear for the physicist but bounded in real life

by historical realities and likelihoods. Time and history are not colleagues and allies, as we commonly suppose. If time is conceived
as a continuum, then history records the erosions that it has suffered. The Green Knowe books can be seen as a sequence in which
time is increasingly belc iguered by history. Boston's implied child
readers are intuitive physicists in their expansionary sense of time,
but history for Boston's adult intellect converts miraculous survival
into ultimate defeat: the house will not always be there.

To consider Boston's mind and her postwar experience in this
way puts a new perspective on the Green Knowe books. It is usual
to recognize that the novels are not equally assured artistic suc-
cesses. Not only the awkward narrative of *The Children of Green
Knowe* but the anarchic fantasy of *The River at Green Knowe* (1959),
the supposed disproportions between menace and countermeasure
in *An Enemy at Green Knowe*, and lapses of characterization in several of the books have all attracted criticism. Although the series
as a whole is a work of accepted distinction, only *The Chimneys of
Green Knowe* and *A Stranger at Green Knowe* are generally seen as
individual masterpieces, free of notable technical limitations.

That the homogeneity of the cycle goes largely unquestioned is a
tribute to the power of the house itself as a unifying symbol. Few
commentators observe the gradual darkening of the series as it progresses. The first three novels in the sequence, *Children*, *Chimneys*
and *River*, are largely happy books—*River*, whatever its failings as
undisciplined fantasy, almost exuberantly so. They are marked by
an underlying confidence in the sturdy enduringness of the house.
The second half of the sequence no longer has that same tone of
civilized playfulness.

In *Perverse and Foolish*, the young Lucy learns that the critic I. A.
Richards has said that she is "uncivilised": "I recognised this as
true and was much discouraged" (*Memories* 128). In her last years
the civilized intellect of Lucy Boston the adult, the connoisseur of
music and buildings and gardens, made a profound alliance with
her uncivilized self—which delighted in the animal world, in the
expression of unprudish sensuous human joy, and in ancient pieties
both pagan and Christian—to confront the barbarism of civilization in its more destructive postwar guises. Hence the tragic figure
of Hanno the gorilla in *A Stranger at Green Knowe*, a wild, caged,
displaced creature exciting protective indignation in his own right
but also standing as symbolic victim for mindless human rapacities

of other kinds. Hence the battle against the destructive invasiveness of Dr. Melanie Powers in *An Enemy at Green Knowe*. And hence the overpowering sense of loss and consequent elegiac tone of *The Stones of Green Knowe* (1976). When Roger d'Aulneaux, the young Norman boy in this last book, murmurs his invocation of time's blessing, " 'O my house,' he thought. 'Live for ever!' " (110), his creator has already sadly accepted that the wish will not be granted. The Green Knowe sequence shows a gradual erosion of confidence in time's ability to protect and a gradual complication of ideas about the meaning of civilization. *The Stones of Green Knowe,* published twelve years after the other five books, is a pessimistic coda to the series, far darker and bleaker than anything that preceded it. The mutilation of landscape that occurs when the Stones of Green Knowe are uprooted and transferred to a museum is the sign of a decadence in which vandalism has become endemic in civilization itself. This harsh conclusion bears out a growing sense in the later books that time is being damaged by history, a verdict confirmed by the personal experiences recounted in the autobiographical texts.

A short poem, written in old age and printed in her collection *Time Is Undone* (1977), is a distillation of Lucy Boston's attitudes toward time, the house, and the generations of its occupants. Like the autobiographical books, it helps us not to misread the Green Knowe sequence. From the studied archaism of "my liking," which means "beloved," as in the medieval carol "Lullay, My Liking," to the imagined future when grandparent and grandchild will themselves be perceived as household ghosts by their descendants, the poem embodies the sense of continuity that Boston's imagination celebrates so unforgettably. But in the reference to "this ruined place," her candid intelligence accepts the fate that must eventually befall the house. The poem is called "A Grandson Touring."

> I said, my liking, that these walls shall keep
> Our thought, our voices and our love.
> But those astonished hours would sleep
> With unheard ghosts who joy or weep
> If neither you nor I were there
> To sense them in the conspiring air.
> They would be dreaming deep.
> Perhaps some stripling, born like you
> Out of long lineage, bearing still your face,

May say "Was I then here before?
This silence holds my heart. And who
So loved this ruined place
And haunts it evermore?"

Works Cited

Boston, Lucy M. *Yew Hall*. London: Faber and Faber, 1954.
————. *The Children of Green Knowe*. London: Faber and Faber, 1954.
————. *The Chimneys of Green Knowe* (in the United States: *Treasure of Green Knowe*).
London: Faber and Faber, 1958.
————. *The River at Green Knowe*. London: Faber and Faber, 1959.
————. *A Stranger at Green Knowe*. London: Faber and Faber, 1961.
————. *An Enemy at Green Knowe*. London: Faber and Faber, 1964.
————. *The Stones of Green Knowe*. London: Bodley Head, 1976.
————. *The Sea Egg*. London: Faber and Faber, 1967.
————. *Memories*. Introduction by Jill Paton Walsh and linking passages by Peter
Boston. Cambridge: Colt Books with Diana Boston, 1992.
————. *Memory in a House*. London: Bodley Head, 1973. Reprinted in Boston, *Memories*.
————. *Perverse and Foolish*. London: Bodley Head, 1979. Reprinted in Boston, *Memories*.
————. *Time Is Undone: Twenty-Five Poems*. Privately printed, 1977.
Carrington, Charles. *Rudyard Kipling: His Life and Work*. London: Macmillan, 1955.
Chambers, Aidan. "The Reader in the Book." *Signal* 23 (May 1977): 64–87.
Kipling, Rudyard. *The Jungle Book*. London: Macmillan, 1894.
————. *Puck of Pook's Hill*. London: Macmillan, 1906.
Pearce, Philippa. *Minnow on the Say*. London: Oxford University Press, 1955.
————. *Tom's Midnight Garden*. London: Oxford University Press, 1958.

Cat-Quest: A Symbolic Animal in Margaret Wise Brown

Suzanne Rahn

For the 1986 annual conference of the Children's Literature Association, Trina Schart Hyman planned "a vicious diatribe," subtitled "How to Survive Twenty-Five Years of Illustrating Children's Books Without Putting Clothes on Animals" (Hyman 5). Although the lecture she delivered was on another subject altogether, the question session afterward gave her the opportunity to explain why anthropomorphic animals were her "pet peeve." "Every other picture book for small children," she complained,

> doesn't even mention that these characters are animals. It says, Henrietta's First Trip to the Dentist. Well, Henrietta's a raccoon, you know, with Nikes and a little pink dress on. And the dentist is a rhinoceros. . . . Why couldn't Henrietta be a kid and why couldn't the dentist be a real dentist? Is that because we're taking the easy way out and we're afraid to show real people in questionable situations? Not only that, don't you think that this is giving kids the idea that animals are supposed to behave and think and have the same values as us? And that's really wrong. [13]

For the lay public, "children's literature" is indeed all but synonymous with cute talking animals. Would-be writers for children have driven some editors to the point of advertising in *Writer's Market* that "no talking animal stories will be accepted." Even in highly regarded picture books, species are assigned to characters with little or no concern for the nature of the animal. A child will learn nothing about badgers from Russell Hoban's Frances books, or about grizzlies from Else Minarik's Little Bear. Such animal characters are not really animals but, as Margaret Blount calls them, "Ourselves in Fur."

We could trace the clothed animal syndrome back to the turn of the century and Beatrix Potter, yet her characters are still in a sense

Children's Literature 22, ed. Francelia Butler, R. H. W. Dillard, and Elizabeth Lennox Keyser (Yale University Press, © 1994 Hollins College).

true animals, their small lives dominated by the need to find food and shelter, raise families, and survive the lethal attacks of predators. A stronger case could be made against Margaret Wise Brown. The popularity of her books for small children, steadily growing since the 1940s, may well have influenced the picture-book makers of today. And many of her numerous animal protagonists seem only nominally animal. The Runaway Bunny, though sharing Peter Rabbit's impulse to leave home, has neither an overpowering desire to gorge himself on vegetables nor a Mr. McGregor to watch out for. In *Goodnight Moon,* the animal-human question was not decided until the final editorial meetings; a little boy might be sleeping in the "great green room" today had Clement Hurd not been better at drawing rabbits than children (Marcus 197). For other books, the animal species seems to have been chosen almost at random. The animal family in *Wait till the Moon Is Full* consisted originally of rabbits, but were changed to raccoons (Marcus 229). The animals in *Little Fur Family* and *Three Little Animals* do not even possess a species—only a generic furriness.

Yet it does seem to matter, at some level, whether these characters are animals or not. We feel instinctively that to replace the rabbit with a little boy would change the great green room. To me, the animality of her animals is essential in Margaret Wise Brown, if not to her imitators. I will even argue that she chose which species of animal to use in a given context—not scientifically, nor always consistently, but in harmony with a poetic logic of her own.

Leonard Marcus's sensitive portrait of Brown in *Awakened by the Moon* suggests that the boundaries between children, animals, and self were more fluid for her than for most adults. At the Bank Street School, for example, "Brownie" amazed her peers by her ability to achieve "as if by second nature" the "unselfconscious identification with the young child's experience" for which the other students strained and strove (Marcus 61). In later years, Brown's periodic vacations alone on her Maine island seem to have kept her in touch with her animal self as well. "Everything is so astonishingly wild and beautiful here," she wrote, "and I have developed the ears of a rabbit and the eyes of an eagle. . . . Michael used to say that only a great saint or a beast could live alone and I seem to have described the beast" (Marcus 259).

Brown's unforced kinship with both children and animals was fundamental to her creative work. Her comments on writing for children often couple the two together. "Children are keen as wild animals and also as timorous," she states in "Creative Writing for Very Young Children" (Marcus 249). She speaks of "the small animal dignity that children and puppies and shy little horses struggle so hard to maintain" as an inspiration for her work. She compares writing for young children—"the sudden starts and stops, the sounds and silences in the words"—to writing for puppies and kittens and even suggests that dogs would enjoy listening to her Noisy Books (Bader 258).

Although adults often sentimentalize small animals and children, the animals and children are not sentimental about themselves, and Brown was not sentimental about them either. To write for children, she said, "one has to love not children but what children love" (Marcus 251). Adults might be dismayed to learn that Brown's favorite sport was beagling—hunting rabbits cross-country on foot with a pack of beagles—but in fact Brown's animal self included an unmistakable predatory streak. Her love of hunting expressed itself not only in beagling but, as Marcus has observed, in her choice of metaphors. He notes how she refers to "the child I will chase" in a Bank Street research project, and to "catching" the stories and poems that children improvise (65); he points out that *The Runaway Bunny* is a magical hunting tale (149). As a child, Brown skinned a dead pet rabbit for its fur, and boasted that she would be a "lady butcher" when she grew up (16). As an adult, she carpeted her living-room floor with polar bear skins and had *Little Fur Family* bound in rabbit fur. Yet the goddess Diana, the huntress, was also the protector of all wild animals, and Brown clearly identifies with small, harmless creatures, too; she and her lover, Michael Strange, corresponded as "Bun" and "Rab."

Rabbits were clearly a special animal for her. She had kept pet rabbits as a child, and was "captivated," says Marcus, by the "comforting softness and sensuality" of their fur and their "quickness and vulnerability" (16). From these early experiences, furry feelings of comfort, coziness, and emotional security—but also of flight and elusiveness—came to cluster around the animal. *The Runaway Bunny*, fluctuating between escape and security, freedom and love, expresses perfectly what rabbits meant to Margaret Wise Brown. And it is evident in this picture book that the animals are not interchangeable with human beings. No child can run away as well as a bunny can. At one point, Brown even foregrounds the distinction by having the bunny threaten to "become a little boy and run into a house"—as if this were the wildest idea he could come up with. *The Golden Egg Book,* with its lonely rabbit who finds an unexpected friend, also deals with the need for a loving relationship. The child character in *Goodnight, Moon,* with its deep sense of comfort and security, did need to be a rabbit rather than some other animal. The essence of rabbitness permeates all these stories.

The personal symbolism of other animals is less obvious in Brown's work. Sometimes, as in *Little Fur Family,* it seems that mere furriness was enough to connect her creatively with the keen senses and deep emotions of her child-animal self. Yet a close look at Brown's cats—with rabbits and dogs, her most numerous animal protagonists—suggests that they, too, had a special significance for her.[1]

In a previous article, "Cat-Child," I defined the characteristic roles of cat protagonists in children's literature. Unlike the straightforward dog, who is inevitably "man's best friend," the cat, with its ambiguous status as a not quite domesticated domestic animal, can move in a number of directions. It can serve as a magical guide or intermediary to another world (as in Lloyd Alexander's *Time Cat* or Dr. Seuss's *Cat in the Hat*). It can belong to a sophisticated society parallel to our own (as in the Cat Club books of Esther Averill), or simply enter our world on equal, adult terms (as T. S. Eliot's cats do). It may represent the nonconformist in society, like Kipling's "Cat Who Walked by Himself." Or, especially as a stray, it can become the child in search of love and security, as in Wanda Gág's *Millions of Cats* or Beverly Cleary's *Socks* or Paul Gallico's *The Abandoned.*

Brown's cats, however, belong in a "category" of their own. On a questionnaire Brown once listed her hobby as "Cat Life—which means doing nothing and just watching" (Marcus 146). Cat Life was what she pursued in solitude on her Maine island, where she recharged her acute sensory awareness of the natural world. Her fictional cats express what Cat Life is and what it can do. It is curious without being predatory, receptive without being passive, alone without being lonely. The "wonder and surprise at the world" of a kitten on its own for the first time inspired her as a writer, she says (Bader 258). Her cat stories reflect this same surprise and wonder.

We can see instantly how different her cats and her rabbits are by comparing *The Runaway Bunny* to the short-short story "One

Eye Open," the first of a series called a Page for Children that Brown did for *Good Housekeeping* in the late 1940s. The bunny's need for security outweighs his need for independence; in the end, he gladly surrenders to his mother's protecting love. The kitten, on the other hand, is determined to take off: "Once there was a little cat who wanted to see the world. So he stuck out his whiskers and went pussyfooting over to tell his mother good-bye. His mother was asleep. But she had one eye open. 'Why do you want to see the world, you funny little kitten?' she said. 'Why not just curl up by me and eat and sleep?' 'Because I want to see the world,' said the kitten, 'and off I go.' 'Good-bye,' said his mother. 'Look where you're going. Look before you leap, and always keep One Eye Open'" (94). "To see the world" is repeated three times in this very short story; the mother cat tells her kitten to "look where you're going" and "look before you leap," and she, too, keeps "one eye open." As just watching, the basic principle of Cat Life, led Brown into creation, her cat characters' desire to see leads them to explore, to investigate, to experiment, and sometimes to create as well.

Other *Good Housekeeping* Pages for Children reinforce this image of the cat. "Where Have You Been?" contrasts the stolid conservatism of the dog with the enterprise and curiosity of the cat.

> Little White Dog,
> Little White Dog,
> Where have you been?
> Sitting on a log,
> Said the Little White Dog.
>
> Little Gray Cat,
> Little Gray Cat,
> Where have you been?
> To see this and that,
> Said the Little Gray Cat. [93]

And "Pusscatkin and the Pumpkin," from the same series, takes Cat Life a step further.

> Pusscatkin found a pumpkin.
> He looked inside it.
> Suddenly the pumpkin's eyes turned green
>   and the pumpkin began to purr.
> But where was Pusscatkin? [86]

The cat's wondering curiosity leads it first to look inside the pumpkin and then to transform the pumpkin into something new and surprising—even magical (fig. 1).

Pussy Willow, a Little Golden Book published in 1951, is also based on a kitten's wonder and surprise at the world. This "little pussycat not much bigger than a pussywillow" and "just as soft and gray and furry as those little flowers clinging to the branches all about him" is born into "a wide green world" of spring flowers and small creatures. When the pussy willows disappear, replaced by seed tassels and green leaves, Pussy Willow goes in search of them, climbing trees, exploring a garden, hunting along the seashore, asking every creature he meets where the pussy willows are. The seasons pass as he searches, and when spring returns, he finds his pussy willows once more—just where he left them. The story celebrates the ever-changing beauty of the natural world, experienced through the senses of a kitten fearlessly on its own. The quest, being unnecessary, becomes an end in itself.

The nonpredatory nature of Cat Life is especially noticeable in *Pussy Willow.* Pussy Willow encounters a bug, a frog, a deer mouse, and a butterfly—without pouncing on any of them. He even shares a nest with a family of baby birds. Only by making her kitten "not much bigger than a pussywillow" (and avoiding all mention of what he eats) could Brown cast even a thin veil of plausibility over such unnatural behavior.

Like the symbolic rabbit, the symbolic cat represents not one trait or tendency but a cluster of them, stressed differently in different characters and with differing degrees of humanization. In *The Little Island* (1946), as in *Pussy Willow,* Brown places a self-aware, solitary kitten in a setting of great natural beauty—the very island that Brown could see from the window of her house in Maine (Marcus 190–91). The kitten's situation is a miniaturized version of her own. *A Pussycat's Christmas* (1949) focuses on the sensory awareness of the cat, and falls at the least humanized end of her scale. Evoking what a real cat might experience on Christmas Eve, Brown describes everything in terms of sensory input.

The little cat Pussycat knew that Christmas was coming.
The ice tinkled when it broke on the frozen mud puddles.
The cold air made her hair stand straight up in the air.
And the air smelled just as it did last year.

Pusscatkin and the Pumpkin

Pusscatkin
found a pumpkin.

He looked
inside it.

Suddenly the
pumpkin's eyes
turned green
and the
pumpkin
began
to purr.
But where
was
Pusscatkin?

A PAGE FOR CHILDREN, BY MARGARET WISE BROWN
DRAWINGS BY GARTH WILLIAMS

Fig. 1. "Pusscatkin and the Pumpkin." Text by Brown, by permission of the Estate of Margaret Wise Brown; illustration by Garth Williams, by permission.

What did it smell like?
Could she smell Christmas trees?

Of course she could.
And Tangerines? And Christmas Greens? And Holly?
And could she hear the crackle and slip of white tissue paper?
And red tissue paper?

She certainly could.

For children, too, Christmas is at least half anticipation, triggered by such sensory cues as these.

Just twice in *Pussycat's Christmas,* Brown suggests realms beyond the comprehension of a cat. As evening falls, Pussycat is still outside when she hears the sound of bells "coming from far away off up the snowy road. . . . What was it?" (You turn the page.) "She saw it! She saw the sleigh go jingling by." And you, too, see a sleigh drawn by reindeer spread across both pages through the falling snow, and Santa himself waving a hand at you.

Only the cat—and you—is allowed that glimpse of Santa Claus. The moment evokes the cat's traditional alliance with supernatural powers but is also a kind of object lesson in the value of Cat Life. Only because Pussycat is there, just watching, does she witness something magical.

On the last pages, Brown ventures deeper still into what Christmas is. Pussycat's anonymous "people" have gone to church, and she hears the carol singers outside in the darkness singing "Silent Night." "Pussycat listened for a long time. Of course she didn't understand the words, but she liked the mystery of it all. Then she pushed open the living room door with her paw and there in the silent house was the Christmas tree." There is no pretense that a cat can understand what Christmas really means—no sentimental miracle. By keeping her eye firmly on the cat, Brown captures the excitement and wonder of Christmas Eve, hints at the mystery behind it, and quietly backs away, leaving the cat to contemplate the glory of the tree. Nothing could be more effective than the restraint she shows here.

At the opposite end of the humanization scale is *The Color Kittens: A Child's First Book About Colors* (1949): "Once there were two color kittens with green eyes, Brush and Hush. They liked to mix and make colors by splashing one color into another. They had buckets and buckets and buckets and buckets of color to splash around with." Brush and Hush can talk to each other, they dream fantastic color dreams, and in the pictures by Alice and Martin Provenson they wear cute little caps and overalls and walk on their hind legs.

Yet Brush and Hush share the qualities of Brown's symbolic cat, though here the emphasis is not on receptive watching, but on the experimental curiosity that makes Pussycat bat at Christmas tree balls, the kitten in "One Eye Open" set off to see the world, and Pusscatkin climb into the pumpkin. As in "Pusscatkin," what begins with sensory awareness (in this case, of colors) proceeds to exploration (mixing colors), and ends in the creation of something new and wonderful. Not content with discovering how to make their favorite color, green, Brush and Hush dream of lands where the colors obey entirely different rules:

> Of a purple land
> In a pale pink sea
> Where apples fell
> From a golden tree.

And the next morning, "wild with purring and pouncing, . . . they knocked over the buckets and all the colors ran out together. There were all the colors in the world and the color kittens had made them."[2]

It is tempting to see Brown's symbolic cat as a paradigm for her own creativity, just as the rabbit seems to represent emotional needs, vulnerabilities, and satisfactions. The cat's contemplative ability, coupled with acute sensory awareness, produces the state Brown called Cat Life—the inner condition from which active creativity arises. The curiosity of the kitten exploring its new world may remind us of Brown's eagerness to experiment with the form and content of the picture book. The cat is also proverbially a loner, rather than a social animal. Brown recognized in herself a lifelong tendency to aloofness and detachment from close relationships, which caused her a good deal of unhappiness (see Marcus 158, 233), but may have been necessary for her creative work. The Runaway Bunny stays home with his loving mother, but the kitten in "One Eye Open" detaches himself from her so that he can see the world.

If the cat analogy holds true, what is Brown telling us about her art in *The House of a Hundred Windows* (1945)? This experimental picture book combined simple two-color lithographs by Robert de Veyrac with photographs of paintings by artists ranging from Samuel Ryder and John James Audubon to Henri Rousseau, Max Ernst, and Yves Tanguey. The text tells how a small black cat lives in a house with a hundred windows; each window looks out into the landscape of a different painting. Brown does not inform the young reader that these are paintings, or what famous artists painted them; each "window" speaks for itself, with its own vision of the world (fig. 2). Many of the paintings are masterpieces of surrealism, and their effect in this context is hauntingly magical. Through each window we see a strange new world.

Brown's own houses reveal her fascination with the magical possibilities of doors and windows. A door in her Maine house, called the Witch's Wink, opened onto a fifty-foot drop to the rocky shore below; on the opposite wall, a group of small mirrors, each framed differently, reflected multiple images of the sea (Marcus 165). In the cottage she built for Michael Strange, an ornate antique frame was hung to outline not a painting but a window looking out onto a dark forest of spruces (Marcus 237). This Picture Window, as Brown called it, an exact reversal of the Hundred Windows, raises the same speculations about the power of the frame, and the relation of art to reality. In *The House of a Hundred Windows,* Brown transforms a personal aspect of her creative life into a way of sharing the creativity of all artists with her young audience. As art appreciation for children, the book is still unique of its kind, and Brown herself must have felt stimulated by it, for she left notes for two sequels and a television version among her papers (Marcus 286–87).

The House of a Hundred Windows is a fair example of a book whose main character might seem interchangeable with another animal— a dog, say, or a mouse. Or, as Trina Schart Hyman might ask, "Why an animal at all? Animals don't look at paintings. Why not a child instead?"

But in the context of Brown's feline symbolism, the small black cat of the *House* seems inevitable. As it moves silently from room to room, gazing with wonder through the different windows, the cat once more personifies the total sensory awareness and receptive contemplation of its species. Here Cat Life moves beyond the natural world to embrace the artist's world of the imagination.

Yet the story takes a startling turn. Suddenly, for the first time, the cat finds a door that leads not into some artist's private vision but out into the real world. Will the cat go back into the house or

Fig. 2. Cat looking at *Melancholy and Mystery of a Street* by Giorgio de Chirico, from Brown, *The House of a Hundred Windows*. Text copyright 1945 by Margaret Wise Brown, illustration copyright 1945 by Robert de Veyrac, reprinted by permission of HarperCollins Publishers.

THE DOOR WAS OPEN.

IT WAS UP TO THE CAT.

Fig. 3. Last page of *The House of a Hundred Windows*. Text copyright 1945 by Margaret Wise Brown, illustration copyright 1945 by Robert de Veyrac, reprinted by permission of HarperCollins Publishers.

outside, into a world it has never seen before? The book ends there (fig. 3). The cat stands hesitating on the threshold, as cats do, but the decision must be made by the young reader. Most children, I think, will decide that the cat must venture out into the real world, now that it knows the world is there. But did Margaret Wise Brown go out? Or back in? Or did she feel that she was poised, forever, on that threshold between two worlds?

Notes

1. According to Marcus, as a child Brown had a black cat named Ole King Cole, about whom she used to tell stories to her younger sister (13). Although we hear more in his account of her Kerry blue terrier Crispian, cats remained a part of her life. Her black cat with white paws stars in the posthumously published *Seven Stories About a Cat Named Sneakers* (1955), and her cat Bobby in *The Little Island* (1946 [Marcus 298, 191]).

Brown's dogs deserve an analysis of their own. Her own Crispian had "an unusually wild and contrary temperament, even for a Kerry. . . . Crispian was a terror—and this, doubtless, was what Margaret liked about him. He was the wildness of small children, hers at times to rein in, at other times hers only to keep pace with" (Marcus 182). The strong, almost undoglike individualism of Crispian became the focus of Brown's *Mister Dog: The Dog Who Belonged to Himself* (1952). Even Muffin, the protagonist of Brown's Noisy Books, seems less doggily dependent on his "people" than dogs generally are in fiction and almost catlike in his investigations of the sensory world.

2. Brown planned a sequel to *The Color Kittens* called "The Number Bears," a counting book, but it was left unfinished at her death (Marcus 286).

Works Cited

Bader, Barbara. *American Picturebooks from* Noah's Ark *to* The Beast Within. New York: Macmillan, 1976.

Blount, Margaret. *Animal Land: The Creatures of Children's Fiction.* New York: Morrow, 1975.

Brown, Margaret Wise. *The Color Kittens: A Child's First Book About Colors.* New York: Golden Press, 1949.

———. *The House of a Hundred Windows.* New York: Harper, 1945.

———. "One Eye Open." *Good Housekeeping* 126 (April 1948): 94.

———. "Pusscatkin and the Pumpkin." *Good Housekeeping* 127 (October 1948): 86.

———. *A Pussycat's Christmas.* New York: Crowell, 1949.

———. *The Runaway Bunny.* New York: Harper, 1942.

———. "Where Have You Been?" *Good Housekeeping* 126 (May 1948): 93.

Hyman, Trina Schart. "Illustrating *The Water of Life.*" In *Proceedings of the Thirteenth Annual Conference of the Children's Literature Association,* ed. Susan R. Gannon and Ruth Anne Thompson. West Lafayette: Education Department, Purdue University, 1988.

Marcus, Leonard S. *Margaret Wise Brown: Awakened by the Moon.* Boston: Beacon, 1992.

Rahn, Suzanne. "Cat-Child: Rediscovering *Socks* and *Island Mackenzie.*" *Lion and the Unicorn* 12.1 (1988): 111–20.

Margaret Wise Brown: Awakened by You Know Who

Angela M. Estes

One purpose of literary biography is to send the reader with quickened interest in pursuit of the life and works of its subject. Leonard S. Marcus's biography of the complex and endlessly engaging author Margaret Wise Brown, *Margaret Wise Brown: Awakened by the Moon,* not only meets this mark but also heralds a literary event in children's literature and literature by women. As in running to hounds—a sport of which Margaret Wise Brown was very fond—such a work can afford the reader a good hunt even if the rabbit escapes.

Physicists and literary theorists alike have been telling us for some time now that we tend to find in the objects of our study what we bring to them, what we need and want to see, conditioned by what and how we have been taught to see. This dictum holds true for the biographer, who creates the life of a chosen subject, as well as for the reviewer of that biography, who reads, comments on, and thus re-creates the narrative of the life in question. Of the various approaches or lenses that we may bring to bear upon a text, each of us has one which enables us to focus clearly, and for Leonard Marcus the lens through which he most effectively views the life of Margaret Wise Brown is that of children's literature.

The product of more than nine years of research and writing, which included examining unpublished letters and family papers and conducting dozens of interviews with Brown's friends, colleagues, and relatives, Marcus's portrait of Margaret Wise Brown is compelling. Marcus excels in his accounts of Brown's years at Hollins College, Virginia, and her emergence as a writer of children's books in the mid-1930s. He carefully delineates her pivotal role in the creation of the modern picture book from the late 1930s through the 1940s and 1950s, the period now considered the golden age of the American picture book.

Brown began writing books for children during her association with Lucy Sprague Mitchell at the Bureau of Educational Experiments, known as Bank Street (its Greenwich Village address).

Children's Literature 22, ed. Francelia Butler, R. H. W. Dillard, and Elizabeth Lennox Keyser (Yale University Press, © 1994 Hollins College).

Under Mitchell's tutelage, Brown became immersed in what Mitchell termed the "Here and Now" world of the very young. A progressive educator, Mitchell believed that the immediate and urgent sense impressions of children and their own daily experiences should form the basis of their education and reading; she proposed the creation of a new kind of juvenile literature: "a developmentally sound here-and-now literature based on [Mitchell's] own observations of children aged two to seven" (Marcus 52). To enhance her literary experiment, Mitchell enlisted the trainees in Bank Street's Cooperative School for Student Teachers (one of whom was Brown herself) to write stories, try them out on young listeners at the school, and then revise the stories based on the children's responses.

Marcus provides a thorough and lively account of the half-century-long "Fairy Tale War" that ensued. Under Mitchell's guidance, Bank Street writers advocated a literature grounded in a young child's sensory impressions and everyday experiences (disparagingly referred to by one writer as the "Beep beep crunch crunch" school of children's literature), while traditional arbiters of the standards for children's books—notably the children's librarian Anne Carroll Moore of the New York Public Library—continued to regard childhood as a state of innocence, which should be nurtured with "once upon a time" folk and fantasy literature (161). According to Marcus, a purchase order from the New York Public Library was regarded as not only a "major critical endorsement" but also an assurance of respectable sales for a children's book. Thus, the omission of Bank Street–inspired children's books from both the library's purchase orders and its "annual fall lists of new books recommended for holiday gift giving" (55)—an omission prompted by the Fairy Tale War—posed long-term publishing difficulties for writers of the Bank Street persuasion.

From her first creative efforts at Bank Street, Brown went on to become the first editor and best-selling author of the fledgling and experimental publishing house of William R. Scott. Eventually she wrote books for several publishers, including Harper and Brothers and Simon and Schuster, becoming the most sought-after author in her field. At the time of her death from a blood clot at the age of forty-two, Brown had written more than a hundred books for children; according to Marcus, from the immense number of unpublished manuscripts found after her death, more than twenty additional books were published posthumously.

In addition to her own inexhaustible creative efforts, Brown discovered, befriended, advised, and generously helped to further the careers of numerous book illustrators with whom she collaborated: Leonard Weisgard, Clement Hurd, Edith Thacher Hurd, Garth Williams, Esphyr Slobodkina, and Jean Charlot, to name a few. Although Brown by all accounts could be exacting in her work— often insisting on controlling the details of her books, including size, paper, binding, colors, and the placement of text—Clement Hurd's remark, quoted by Marcus, echoes the consensus regarding her genius: "[A]ll Margaret's main illustrators did their best work in her books" (290).

Concerning the genius of Margaret Wise Brown as the author of books for children, Marcus's biography leaves no doubt, and he is at his best where he reconstructs her energetic, imaginative, and dazzling career. But perhaps the most fascinating moments occur when we catch glimpses of the woman and the artist. In the words of those who knew Brown, she was "an original"; she was "mer-curial," "quixotic," "an experimenter," "the 'most creative' person they had ever known" (3). There is Margaret Wise Brown the child, freely revising and adding details to traditional fairy tales as she reads them to her younger sister. This same child raises pet rab-bits and, when one dies, skins the rabbit for its fur. There is the college woman whose favorite place for a rendezvous is the last pew of St. Patrick's Cathedral and who playfully annotates her best friend's calendar with reminders of herself—suggestions to send her a present, write to her, or underline a favorite book and send it to her. Then there is Margaret Wise Brown, member of the Long Island socialite group the Buckram Beagles, who loves to hunt rab-bits on weekends, running strenuously for miles with the hounds. We see this woman, paradoxically, alongside the woman who cre-ates the warm and intimate world of *The Runaway Bunny* (1942). Finally, there is the woman who continually reshapes and redesigns her homes: one in fur, one with live trees and uncaged birds, one with a door that opens onto a "sheer fifty-foot drop . . . to the rocky shore below." Perhaps most telling of Brown's interior designs is the one on the wall directly opposite this door; Marcus describes it as "a collection of small mirrors, each differently framed and made flush with its neighbors, so that when the door was open each mirror reflected a different image of the sea to produce endlessly shifting effects of multiple perspective and light. To step before the wall was to glimpse oneself as fragmentary, ever-changing, harlequin-esque—'plural,' in Margaret's own word" (165).

If Brown had a genius for reshaping her surroundings, she had no less genius for reshaping her self. Her spontaneous ability to generate for herself new nicknames (Tim, Brownie, Goldie), pseudonyms (Golden MacDonald, Timothy Hay, Memory Ambrose, Juniper Sage), and epithets (Old Horror, the Bun, Your Favorite Jailbird) seemed endless. In fact, at the end of one letter to Lucy Sprague Mitchell she signed her name, "Brownies—they get more and more plural" (160). Perhaps this proliferation of selves helps to account for the reader's sense at the close of the biography that Margaret Wise Brown remains as elusive as the quarry that perpetually escapes its pursuers.

Brown's multiplicity of selves clearly presents a problem for the biographer, and for the most part Marcus admirably illuminates Brown's myriad facets. Not surprisingly, the book is most convincing with respect to those aspects of Brown's life and work involving Marcus's field of expertise, children's literature. Even when examining less familiar terrain, however, he delivers in most cases an evenhanded account. For example, while Marcus does not pursue an analysis of Brown's life and works in terms of race, class, and gender, neither does he conspire to suppress Brown's anti-Semitism or classism. He includes in his portrayal of Brown both her acknowledgment of and her questioning of her anti-Semitism with respect to her friend Esphyr Slobodkina. Likewise, Brown's own sense of privilege is prominent in remarks such as "Comforts aren't for me . . . luxuries are" (164) and in an incident related by Marcus in which Brown, on her way to a luncheon appointment, drives her Chrysler Town & Country convertible through a crowd at Union Square, shouting "Make way for the rich!" (212).

Marcus's bias is evident, however, when he attempts to interpret and explain the relationship—which lasted more than ten years—between Margaret Wise Brown and the glamorous socialite, writer, actress, and poetry performer Michael Strange and again when he imposes an overall shape on Brown's life. Marcus's rendering of the bond between Brown and Strange is strongest when he allows the relationship to stand alone, revealed through letters between the two women and interviews with mutual friends. In fact, the letters of Brown are some of the most intriguing material in the book; even from a distance of almost fifty years, passages from these letters often leap into the reader's imagination, turning another facet of Brown's personality into view and making the reader yearn for more.

Marcus is less successful, however, in his attempts to explain—and, it often seems, to explain away—the relationship with Michael Strange. At points, he seeks motivation for the union between the two women in Brown's need for an older woman–mentor–mother figure. He also terms the deep and lasting connection a "worthy experiment" that Brown was willing to engage in (although she "had shown no such interest before") because of "her loneliness and her frustrated attempts at love in recent months and years" (168). And at other times, he deems the connection "self-destructive" (as the jacket cover puts it) and "damaging" (175), a relationship that Brown finally outgrows.

The reader first begins to question Marcus's account of the relationship when Marcus interprets as autobiography two short stories written by Brown during the early stages of her involvement with Strange. One can, of course, read fiction in the light of autobiography, and vice versa. When, however, one constructs an interpretation of a life by reading fiction as autobiography, one courts the danger of viewing the life as necessarily congruent with fiction. Where Brown ends her story "The Scent" with a woman resting alone in her bed, refusing to answer messages or meet visitors, Marcus finds evidence of Brown's "troubled conscience," suggesting "the depth and disturbing nature of the passionate feelings that Michael Strange had unexpectedly aroused in her" (127–28). This reading of fiction as autobiography would seem to be especially inappropriate in the case of a writer such as Margaret Wise Brown, who, as Marcus notes, recalled that "Story teller" was "a polite word in our family for . . . liar" (250).

Moreover, Marcus's interpretation seems partial with respect to Brown's redesigning of one of her homes. When Brown and Strange began living together, in apartments across the hall from each other on East End Avenue, Brown moved her huge Victorian four-poster bed into her small front room. According to Marcus, upon entering this parlor, "[f]irst-time visitors were taken aback; one felt as though one had entered the apartment by the wrong door and somehow landed in a more private quarter of the premises than one had planned" (170). Marcus attributes two motives to Brown's rearrangement of her bed: her desire to be able to watch the river traffic from bed and her pleasure at "the hint of a scandalous life" (170) suggested by the arrangement. While Brown may indeed have acted on the basis of both these motivations, Marcus does not note what might seem a more plausible impetus for her action. By placing the bed in her front room, Brown symbolically placed her sexuality—and her sexual relationship with another woman— at the center of both her own life and the awareness of others. Her actions thus seem entirely in keeping with those of a woman newly in love who desires recognition of that love.

Brown's symbolic movement of her bed to the front of her home is consistent, too, with her statements about the significance of her love for Michael Strange. In letters to Strange written long after the initial delight of the relationship had waned and their involvement had become exceedingly painful, Brown wrote, "There was a time I felt well loved by you and it was the warmest time in my life. . . . It is the center I come back to and revolve about" (211). Brown's own words and actions are thus curiously at odds with the feelings attributed to her by Marcus, as his references to her "troubled con- science" reveal. It is unlikely that any woman living in the United States during the 1940s could have entered a relationship with another woman without conflicting feelings, but Marcus's interpre- tations often appear to minimize and oversimplify possibilities that Brown herself envisioned.

The important point is not whether or to what extent Brown may have been a lesbian. Rather, by not exploring the possibilities that Brown herself may have found in her relationship with Michael Strange, we may be losing a whole other perspective—or lens—by means of which we can view her life and art. Perhaps when seen through this lens, the apparent quirks and eccentricities of Brown would not seem so odd, and perhaps the fragments of her life that remain in view would appear less like the pieces of a puzzle that never quite fit together no matter which way they are arranged. Through a different lens, we might, for example, see Brown's re- lationship with Strange as a pas de deux similar to that performed by the bunny and its mother in *The Runaway Bunny*. In this way, we might gain insight into the ways in which Michael Strange—all the while believing that she would lead in the dance and that Brown would follow—in fact may have provided, as does the mother in the story, the opportunity for Brown to express and live out other possibilities for her life, possibilities for which American culture of the 1940s and heterosexual institutions did not allow.

What emerges from Marcus's book is Margaret Wise Brown's urgent and incessant need to create a self, to create significance for herself, since she found suitable none of the roles available to her. She was perpetually fascinated by what Alice James in her *Diary* terms "that most interesting being, *myself*" (25). Above all, in her focus on herself, Brown was very much an outsider. One of her professors at Hollins College remembered her as a "law unto herself" (Marcus 26), and the staff psychologist at Bank Street later noted that Brown "operated in a highly individual mode" (61). Perhaps most telling of all, in a book that Brown considered one of her most important, *The Dark Wood of the Golden Birds* (1950), she wrote of the struggle of the artist, whose heart is finally pierced by a golden feather, "the symbol of his difference" (245).

In spite of the privilege of her class and race, then, Brown was an outsider, and as Marcus convincingly relates, she confronted daily both the pain and the delights of her difference—the latter undoubtedly made possible by her privilege. The narrative that Marcus imposes on Brown's life oversimplifies the richness and complexity of the life so vividly detailed elsewhere in the book. In the narrative Marcus constructs, Brown first moves from isolation, loneliness, and frustrated attempts at love to the destructive "experiment" with Michael Strange. When Brown emerges "from the shadow of Michael Strange's influence," according to Marcus, she develops a "new steadiness and certitude" (249), along with a "new-found self-possession" (264), that culminate in the heterosexual love relationship with her fiancé, James Stillman Rockefeller, Jr. Such a reading of Brown's life privileges the traits of self-possession and certitude and the institution of heterosexuality. And Marcus makes clear that Brown was frequently at odds not only with heterosexuality but also with the "adult" emphasis placed upon certainty and maturity. More important, Marcus's narrative order neglects to take into account recent work in developmental psychology by researchers who point out that females tend to form relationships not on the basis of differentiation, hierarchy, and separation, but on the basis of connection and community.

Another possible narrative that we might employ to shape the life of Margaret Wise Brown is the story that Brown seemed to tell about herself—the story of an outsider. Brown continually re-imagined and re-created her life, pushing it beyond the bounds of ordinary expectations and conventional narratives; in both her life and her art she sought new forms of expression, what she termed "a more fearless baldness of the heart to say the things we never say and the other never knows." In a late letter to Michael Strange, Brown revealed that she had "always longed for another language before it is too late" and called herself the "Rabbit poet." As she put it, "I believe in the excess" (215). Ezra Pound, had he known her, perhaps would not have understood Brown's reference to herself as "Rabbit poet," but he undoubtedly would have described her as one of "the antennae of the race"—one of those artists whose life and work form a template for the stories that we eventually use to shape our own experiences.

That there might be a special appeal for children—outsiders to the constructed world that adults are privileged to name and shape—in the perspective offered by the outsider is an area in the study of children's literature that deserves more attention. Likewise, as Marcus's biography makes vividly clear, the study of the works of Margaret Wise Brown—as poet and woman writer—has just begun. If women writers have been excluded from the traditionally male realm of what has been deemed significant literature, Brown has also been left out of virtually every study of American women writers, including those inspired by the feminist reconsideration of women's writing that has taken place in the last twenty-five years.

Marcus is to be commended for introducing to us Margaret Wise Brown as a modernist woman writer, for in doing so he begins the task of rewriting the traditional literary histories that have excluded so much. His biography makes clear the influence on Brown of Virginia Woolf and Gertrude Stein—Brown's favorite authors. Stein especially appears to have been influential for Brown, and it was at Brown's suggestion that Stein wrote her own children's book, *The World Is Round* (1939).

Stein, Woolf, and Brown were modernist writers for whom the multiplicity of selves—rather than the fostering of a single, balanced, possessed self—was of utmost importance and delight. As Marcus writes, "The power to change oneself, to be a part of the ceaseless changefulness of life, was always for Margaret a transcendent ideal" (156). All of these writers were women working within and at times against the dominant traditions and cultural expectations with which they were confronted. They were all women who pursued, at varying lengths, intense relationships with other women. They were all women, in short, who were outsiders. In addition, however, they were women who by virtue of class and race were privileged outsiders, and as such, an understanding of their lives and works will require an examination of the unique intersection of race, class, gender, and sexual orientation at which they wrote.

The title of Marcus's book, with its allusion to Brown's *Goodnight Moon* (1947), encourages us to read the biography as a mystery: Who or what is the moon that awakened Brown? Intriguingly, this question is never answered, nor, in fact, is it even overtly addressed. The moon can be read as a female symbol, or perhaps for Margaret Wise Brown it was a personal symbol, since it appears in so many of her works. One book, *The First Story* (1947), is even "dedicated to the Moon" (217). In any case, if the moon of Marcus's title is a metaphor, it is a metaphor in search of a tenor so that understanding the title of the book itself becomes a circuitous, Gertrude Stein kind of game with the reader. Ultimately, then, it is a tribute to Marcus that in this first biography of Margaret Wise Brown the question posed by the title remains unanswered, leaving the identity of both the moon and Brown playfully enigmatic. Although the narrative structure of biography has dictated that Marcus shape Brown's life to meet the needs of the genre, Brown has eluded this shaping; her life remains for readers—and even for her biographer—as complex as she felt and lived it. After all, as this always provocative and endlessly imaginative author wrote on a cryptic note slipped under her best friend's bedroom door at Hollins College, "Life is damn queer" (32).

Works Cited

James, Alice. *The Diary of Alice James.* Ed. Leon Edel. New York: Penguin, 1987.
Marcus, Leonard S. *Margaret Wise Brown: Awakened by the Moon.* Boston: Beacon, 1992.
Pound, Ezra. *ABC of Reading.* New York: New Directions, 1960.

Reviews

Humane Ideology

Perry Nodelman

Language and Ideology in Children's Fiction, by John Stephens. London and New York: Longman, 1992.

Ideology is what those who disagree with us believe; what we believe ourselves is the way things are. So it is claimed by those who object to what they derisively call politically correct approaches to literature—the wide variety of feminist, Marxist, and New Historicist analyses of the ideological content of literary texts. These objectors are convinced that reality as they view it themselves—in almost every case, as it has been traditionally understood and described by white upper-class and middle-class males of European extraction and their female companions—is all the reality there is. Worthwhile literary texts, particularly those in the canon of great literature, do nothing more than reflect the essence of that one true and truly universal reality. These texts are, therefore, above the transience and silliness of ideology—they are not political at all. And any texts that do have ideology in them are just ephemeral trash—propaganda for bad ideas.

But as John Stephens points out in this important and persuasive book: "Ideologies . . . are not necessarily undesirable, and in the sense of a system of beliefs by which we make sense of the world, social life would be impossible without them" (8). No living human being is or ever was separate from the ideology of a specific time and place and culture, and that includes Shakespeare and Milton—and Beatrix Potter and Lloyd Alexander: "a narrative without an ideology is unthinkable" (8).

Indeed, Stephens insists that "if you read a book and discover that it is utterly free of ideological presuppositions, what that really means is that you have just read a book which precisely reflects those societal presuppositions which you yourself have learned to subscribe to, and which are therefore invisible" (50). Stephens's major purpose in *Language and Ideology in Children's Fiction* is to render that invisibility visible, to reveal the extent to which the chil-

Children's Literature 22, ed. Francelia Butler, R. H. W. Dillard, and Elizabeth Lennox Keyser (Yale University Press, © 1994 Hollins College).

dren's books of our time confirm and sustain specific societal and cultural presuppositions.

His enterprise is timely; despite the impressive progress that critics of adult literature have made in recent years in uncovering and understanding the ideological implications of literary texts, far too many commentators on children's literature prefer to remain blind to its societal and cultural presuppositions. Most reviews in such popular organs as the *Horn Book* and even a surprising proportion of the articles in professional journals devoted to children's literature (including this one) work from the unstated assumption that children's literature—or, at any rate, worthwhile children's literature—exists outside ideology. Stephens offers a powerful corrective to the unconsidered, somewhat egocentric, and far too common habit of believing that the children's books that most accurately reflect an adult commentator's own unacknowledged vision of reality are the good ones.

I expected a book with the word *ideology* in its title to concentrate on issues of gender, race, and class. But Stephens has surprisingly little to say about any of them; instead, he focuses on the assumptions that underlie those matters—on the essential vision of reality that so many children's books and so many commentators on children's literature (including, I have to admit, myself) take for granted.

As scholars, educators, and librarians, as believers in the power of ideas to change lives, we tend to assume the liberal humanist view that reality is a place in which individuals have the power to define and control their lives. We love children's books in which characters must make choices that define their existence and its meaning. We particularly admire those in which the choices have to do with the rejection of socially conformist values or pressures and the assertion of individual self-governance, especially in the face of political repression or bleak economic conditions. When poor black or oppressed Jewish characters find the courage within themselves to believe in their individual integrity despite massive attempts to undermine and destroy it, we cheer like crazy and throw handfuls of Newberys and Carnegies and Governor-General Awards at the books describing them.

But liberal humanists remain blithely unconscious of the contradiction at the heart of these assumptions, and even previous discussions of ideology in relation to children's fiction have failed to address it. These commentators all assume that individuals are, on the one hand, deeply implicated in and affected by their social circumstances (and thus by ideology) but, on the other hand, somehow essentially separate from and therefore in some important way untouched by that which has formed them. For instance, most objections to the racism or sexism of certain children's books operate on the self-contradicting assumption that child readers have not yet absorbed the values of their families, their class, and their culture and are therefore absolutely free to choose to accept these pernicious ideas from books. Although the books are ideological and dangerous, the children are, thus far at least, separate enough from ideology to be at risk from it, or so we suppose. Peter Hunt's *Criticism, Theory, and Children's Literature* (1991) offers a more sophisticated analysis of ideology and espouses a more optimistic view of children, but it expresses exactly the same contradiction: even though children's books have ideological content, children are inherently independent, free spirits whose imaginative spontaneity allows them to triumphantly escape the intended ideological indoctrination.

Stephens himself is more toughminded; he understands that child readers are already implicated in ideology, not separate from it at all. And because he understands that, he is able to perceive and to analyze the repressive impulse of exactly those texts which we most admire and which seem most to encourage children's sense of their own individuality. He does so by focusing on a paradox: texts that strongly encourage child readers to value individual will and choice over social conformity are in fact demanding not only agreement with their adult writers' values but also conformity to the mainstream values of our culture, particularly mainstream definitions of what it means to be an individual. Most important, he shows that the ways texts by authors as diverse as Judy Blume and Ursula Le Guin encourage agreement are themselves manipulative and therefore strangely repressive of readers' individual freedom. Texts like *Are You There, God? It's Me, Margaret* and *The Tombs of Atuan* appear to affirm individuality but actually work to deprive readers of their freedom to think differently or to be truly individual, because they offer readers only a narrow range of ways to be individual—ways that discourage readers from any action or thought that might threaten the peaceful maintenance of the social whole as currently constituted.

Stephens believes that such texts forcefully manipulate readers into espousing socially acceptable ideas about who and what they individually are by offering specific positions or points of view from which fictional events are perceived and understood and then encouraging readers to occupy those positions themselves; as he says, "readers . . . , in taking up a position from which the text is most readily intelligible, are apt to be situated within the frame of the text's ideology; that is, they are subjected to and by that ideology" (67). The key word here is "subjected"; in developing subjectivity (what less ideologically conscious writers call selfhood or individuality and see as separate from ideology), we become subjected to ideological pressure; to become subjective is to be subjected.

Stephens is thus highly suspicious of a strategy for making sense of literary texts that commentators almost universally encourage: young readers' identification with fictional characters. Coupled with reader-focused approaches to texts that purport to value the individuality inherent in a young reader's supposedly individual response, this "is a dangerous ideological tool and pedagogically irresponsible. It fosters an illusion that readers are in control of the text whereas they are highly susceptible to the ideologies of the text, especially the unarticulated or implicit ideologies" (68). Stephens himself encourages, first, the development of reading strategies that allow a wider spectrum of possibilities—not just identification but also various means of gaining critical distance from characters—and, second, the reading of texts that offer readers a choice of subject positions.

Finally, however, he announces his agreement with one specific form of subjectivity, "an ideological perspective deeply embedded in Western social practice: the self is an amalgam of all its experiences and of every other with which it has had significant contact, but essential selfhood is a negotiated separateness" (286). Although this definition sounds much like the contradiction that I outlined earlier—the idea of a self affected by exterior pressures but somehow still essentially separate from them—there is a key difference: the word *negotiated*. According to Stephens, we develop knowledge of the individuality of our own subjectivity by knowing enough about the subjectivities of others to be able to consider how they are unlike our own; we do not so much identify with what we resemble as *not* identify with what we do not resemble. We become conscious of who we are by constantly negotiating between what we have become through earlier negotiations with texts and the social world and what texts and the world around us are constantly encouraging us to believe we are.

Speaking of this sort of negotiated separateness, Stephens says, "I think myself it is the best and most humane subject position available to us as human beings" (287). But even here Stephens is refreshingly conscious of the pressures of ideology: "I also recognize that in reaching it readers are thoroughly subjected to the text's processes" (287). True, but what impresses me about Stephens's approach is the degree of trust that it implies in the ability of children to move through uncertainties, arrive at their own conclusions, and take a key part in the construction of their selves. Faith in the good sense of children is rare and commendable, especially when it never denies the extent to which cultural pressures control our perceptions of others and ourselves.

So far I have discussed ideology and said nothing directly about the other key word in Stephens's title: *language.* But I have been talking about language all along, for, as Stephens points out, all language is ideological, "since language does not merely reflect the world but is crucial to the very constitution of the world" (12). An earlier attempt to place children's fiction in the context of ideologically oriented theory, Jacqueline Rose's *Case of Peter Pan; or, The Impossibility of Children's Fiction,* took that thesis for granted. Rose's argument seemed like gassy theorizing because she discussed no text other than the one she acknowledged to be freakishly unique, Barrie's *Peter Pan.* One of the great strengths of Stephens's book is that he not only asserts that language is ideological but shows how. He provides detailed, ingenious, and persuasive analyses of the ideological implications in texts as diverse as Maurice Sendak's *Where the Wild Things Are,* Babette Coles's *Prince Cinders,* and Le Guin's *Tombs of Atuan.* Informed by a rich understanding both of the general characteristics of language as described by linguists and of the specific narrative uses of language as described by narratological theorists, these analyses offer intellectual pleasure as well as understanding.

Not only is *Language and Ideology in Children's Fiction* a strong and persuasive critique of common and dangerous assumptions about childhood subjectivity and children's literature, but Stephens manages the critique without even suggesting what doctrinaire theorists like Rose insist on: that children's literature as a whole is a mistaken enterprise, nothing more than a nastily repressive effort to manipulate children by totalitarian adults. Instead, Stephens expresses his own deep pleasure in some of the typical forms of children's fiction and defends it as good for children, even though he never forgets important ideological concerns. Even more important, his acceptance of the inevitability of our adult responsibility to help children construct their subjectivities leads him to suggest ways of exercising that responsibility that never deny its inherent repressiveness and therefore always express a humane respect for young, malleable human beings.

Widening Circles: Readers, Classrooms, Cultures

J. D. Stahl

Kinderbuchanalysen II: Wirkung—kultureller Kontext—Unterricht, by Reinbert Tabbert. Frankfurt am Main: dipa, 1991.

Reading *Kinderbuchanalysen II* is like wandering through the workshop of a master craftsman whose work of different phases lies open for inspection all about. Reinbert Tabbert, professor of English at the Pädagogische Hochschule Schwäbisch Gmünd, is a supple, prolific, and far-ranging critic and educator. This volume, number 22 in the series Jugend und Medien edited by Winfred Kaminski and successor to Tabbert's earlier *Kinderbuchanalysen* (1989), is a collection of articles and papers spanning the period 1975–91. As the subtitle suggests, it is organized into three thematic sections. The first is concerned with the effects of children's literature on its readers and is heavily influenced by reader-response theory, particularly the work of Hans Robert Jauß and Wolfgang Iser, who in turn is indebted to the Polish philosopher Roman Ingarden. The second section is an examination of national cultures, stereotypes, and myths. Instructional models and methods are the subject of the third section.

In section 1, "Aspects of Reader Relativity," Tabbert investigates issues that can be broadly classified as *Kommunikationsästhetik,* which it is probably a mistake to translate as "aesthetics of communications," because the German term casts a far wider net than most English speakers will associate with the word *aesthetics.* As Tabbert says in his first essay: "In Germany we have a tried and true method of approaching the unknown: we construct theories about it" (9; this and the following translations are mine). Indeed, *Kinderbuchanalysen II* is theoretically sophisticated, but despite the gentle self-mockery, theory is not applied narrowly here. Tabbert considers many different dimensions of the communicative process involving children and literature with flexibility and acuity. Whether he is interviewing Astrid Lindgren or constructing a theory of *"Rezeptionsästhetik"* in children's literature, his writing displays an admi-

Children's Literature 22, ed. Francelia Butler, R. H. W. Dillard, and Elizabeth Lennox Keyser (Yale University Press, © 1994 Hollins College).

rable awareness of the multiple contexts in which children's literature can and should be read. His analyses of writers as diverse as Ivan Southall and Edward Lear, Hilke Raddatz and Maurice Sendak, display a combination of psychological perceptiveness, historical consciousness, and alertness to cultural differences.

The last is central to the second section, where Tabbert reflects on different cultural values and concepts in children's books. Especially fascinating is the lead essay, "National Myths in Three Classical Picture Books," which was originally presented in 1989 at the Ninth Symposium of the International Research Society for Children's Literature in Salamanca, Spain. Here Tabbert examines three picture books about animals—Beatrix Potter's *Peter Rabbit* (1901), Jean de Brunhoff's *Story of Babar* (1931), and Fritz Koch-Gotha's *Die Häschenschule* (School for little rabbits, 1924)—as embodiments of national myths in animal form, with resonances across the cultural landscapes of English, French, and German history. Peter Rabbit reflects the English love of gardens. Babar, very much an urban creature, is a symbol of the importance of Paris as the luminous center of French culture, and the forest in *Die Häschenschule* (no English word quite captures the romance of the German word *Wald*) represents a mythic region of enduring influence in Germanic *Lebensgefühl*. With absorbing insight Tabbert discusses the animal and human traits and clothing, together with the implications of the characters, who reveal so much about the collective experience and consciousness of each nation.

Wisely and accurately, if sadly, Tabbert notes in "Picture Books Between Two Cultures" (1990) that "the initiation of understanding of foreign cultures, as desirable as it may be, appears to have little chance under present market conditions" (131). He concludes that translators, editors, and publishers should, as far as possible, retain explicit cultural self-representations in the translation of picture books from one language or cultural group to another, a practice often avoided for fear of loss of sales. When the attempt is made to adjust a text to the expectations of a targeted audience in a different culture from that of the original author and illustrator, there is a danger of creating jarring discrepancies between the messages of the words and the pictures, making it easy to miss the opportunity to encounter an unfamiliar world of experience. Tabbert urges the retention of cultural uniqueness—the strangeness of a foreign culture—as far as is possible, and demonstrates his point persuasively with close analyses of picture books that succeed or fail to different degrees and in the ways they convey a sense of cultural diversity. He examines, among others, the German translations of Munro Leaf's *Story of Ferdinand*, Philippe Dumas's *Laura sur la route*, Christophe Gallaz and Roberto Innocenti's *Rose Blanche*, and Leo Lionni's *Swimmy*. The most detailed investigation, in an essay entitled "Ein Bunyip ist vieles, aber kein Umir" (A bunyip is many things, but not an umir), is devoted to the German version of an Australian picture book, Jenny Wagner's *Bunyip of Berkeley's Creek* (1975), translated into German by Renate Nagel in 1978.

The essay "Children in West German Children's Books" (1988), first presented in Osaka, Japan, at the German-Japanese conference Childhood in Contemporary Children's Books, is an informative survey, necessarily simplifying but usefully summarizing the stages of development that West German children's literature has passed through since World War II. From the idealistic and idealizing phase, often referred to as *heile Welt*, that emerged directly after the war, West German children's literature moved through a period of political engagement, often incorporating a radical critique of society; this second phase started in the late 1960s, a time when conflict and disharmony entered children's literature to shape a new realism. In the third phase, which began in the late 1970s, authors and readers generally turned inward, reflecting imaginatively on the emotional experience of the child.

To round out the second section of his book, Kaminski includes Tabbert's interview with the Gaelic author Finlay Macleod. Fionnlagh Macleoid, as his name is written in Gaelic, is concerned with encouraging the production of children's literature in so-called Lesser Used Languages in Europe. Last comes an excellent crosscultural study of the possibilities for young readers in Germany and Australia to identify with the figure of the Australian bushranger as found in Randolph Stow's *Midnite* (1967), translated into German by Sybil Gräfin Schönfeldt as *Käpt'n Mitternacht* (1972).

The third section shifts the emphasis to pedagogy as Tabbert turns to foreign language and German literature instruction as sites for the examination of cultural values. Exemplary in several respects is his investigation of "Australian myths in the teaching of English," which shows with clarity and skill how the Australian national myths of the "jolly swagman" as embodied in "Waltzing Matilda" and myths of the heroism of Anzac forces at Gallipoli can be deconstructed. He juxtaposes a selection from an uncritical patriotic school text (*The Story of Australia*) with "The Band Played Waltzing Matilda," a protest song that effectively merges the legend of the freedom of the bushranger with the painful emotional reality of a soldier's experience at Gallipoli and after.

Literary theory, psychological insight, pedagogical adeptness, and respect for cultural specificity combine in the essays of this section. Included are a discussion of foreign children in German children's literature; a case study of a popular novel from the German Democratic Republic, with an eye to its significance as a means of preserving a critical but sympathetic memory of life in the GDR; and an account of a university seminar, conducted with the Australian children's literature scholar Rhonda Bunbury, about *The Bunyip of Berkeley's Creek* and its watered-down German version, *Die Reise des einsamen Umirs*. Throughout he argues for the value of children's and young adult literature in foreign language instruction, and offers excellent suggestions for playful and engaging uses of language forms and games in teaching.

Tabbert moves gracefully from vivid metaphor to the language of theory to illustrative examples, and the scholarly substance of his discussions is leavened by touches of humor and by a humane awareness of the value of spontaneous responses from child and adult readers alike. All in all, *Kinderbuchanalysen II* is the mature work of a talented scholar, critic, and teacher. It demonstrates admirable cultural sensitivity and breadth, valuable historical awareness in its accounts of children's literature and criticism, and sound pedagogical insights with many practical suggestions for teachers. Finally, it represents a feature of German children's literature criticism that the American children's literature establishment would do well to learn from, namely, the close relation between pedagogy on the one hand and literary theory and criticism on the other—a relation that has traditionally been and continues to be more productive and comfortable in Germany than in the United States.

Hawthorne's "New Literature for the Young"

Elizabeth Goodenough

Hawthorne's Literature for Children, by Laura Laffrado. Athens: University of Georgia Press, 1991.

Published between 1835 and 1853, Nathaniel Hawthorne's writings for children are representative of every kind of literature for the young that burgeoned in antebellum America. In forms as diverse as history and fairy tale, biographical sketch and Sunday school tract, geography and myth, these writings span the two decades of Hawthorne's emergence as a major literary artist. Nevertheless, because they were considered hackwork, students of Hawthorne have neglected them until recently. Calvin Schorer's unpublished dissertation (University of Chicago, 1948) remained the only extended examination of this material until Nina Baym included it in *The Shape of Hawthorne's Career* (1982) and Frederick Newberry devoted a chapter of *Hawthorne's Divided Loyalties* (1987) to *The Whole History of Grandfather's Chair* (1851). Of this now forgotten New England history, Baym startled Hawthorne scholars by claiming that the author "had never been in firmer control of matter and manner than in this series," then praised *A Wonder-Book for Girls and Boys* (1852) as "his most complex and successful framed narrative." Because Hawthorne adapted the first classical myths for children into English and is often credited with inaugurating the American literary focus on the child in "The Gentle Boy" (1832), a book-length study of all his writings for and about children is long overdue.

Laura Laffrado's *Hawthorne's Literature for Children* fills a significant gap simply by calling attention to what a rich field of inquiry Hawthorne's six books for children represent. Surveying *The Whole History of Grandfather's Chair* (originally published in 1841 as three brief volumes: *Grandfather's Chair, Liberty Tree,* and *Famous Old People*), *Biographical Stories for Children* (1842), *A Wonder-Book* (1851), and *Tanglewood Tales* (1853) in four chapters, Laffrado points out that all of his juvenile works are collections. She examines his use of the framed narrative as a way of lending adhesion to these

Children's Literature 22, ed. Francelia Butler, R. H. W. Dillard, and Elizabeth Lennox Keyser (Yale University Press, © 1994 Hollins College).

texts, emphasizing that through fictive narrators like Grandfather, Mr. Temple, and Eustace Bright the author systematically distances himself from the stories that he tells. Arguing that in writing for children Hawthorne "is attempting to establish a certain mode of discourse, a way in which he can write confidently" (3), she sees him escaping financial insecurity and his struggles as a writer, "his own daily reality and personal history" (8), through three auctorial personas who differ from him in age, status, and experience. In the fireside storytelling of *Grandfather's Chair* Laffrado presents him experimenting with what he called "neutral territory," described a decade later in the preface to *The Scarlet Letter* as "somewhere between the real world and fairyland, where the Actual and the Imaginary may meet, and each imbue itself with the nature of the other" (7). Adducing this unusual domain, which Hawthorne later attested was congenial to the romance writer's work, Laffrado finds a plausible formula for explaining the success of both the *Whole History* and *A Wonder-Book*.

Laffrado's biographical framework thus relates the production of children's books to the familiar contours of Hawthorne's career—a protracted and solitary apprenticeship, a burst of creative power, then a sudden, painful decline. The sunny pastoralism of *A Wonder-Book for Girls and Boys* is inevitably associated with the golden age of Hawthorne's personal and professional life, and the discussion of *Tanglewood Tales*, the final product of the author's two most prolific years, offers some biographical facts to suggest why Hawthorne's vision had soured so dramatically in a sequel written only eighteen months after the first book of myths. It is less clear, however, in chapter 2 why *Biographical Stories for Children*, written within a year of the *Whole History*, remained unfinished and is so inferior a work. Why, for example, does Laffrado liken Hawthorne in 1841, returning from Brook Farm eager to marry Sophia Peabody, to Edward Temple, suddenly "confined in misery-inducing circumstances," blindfolded in a darkened room (42)? Although her secondary sources are meticulously documented, primary research materials—family journals and letters, *The American Notebooks*—might have added fresh perspectives to a study so biographically grounded.

Unfortunately Laffrado does not examine much of the cultural ferment that produced these works, although attitudes toward children, childrearing, schooling, and children's literature changed radically during Hawthorne's lifetime (1804–64). Ralph Waldo Emerson, reflecting on this shift in sentiment, quoted a "witty physician" who lamented that "it was a misfortune to have been born when children were nothing and to live until men were nothing" (Cable 101). Although Hawthorne never completely relinquished the stern Calvinist view of childhood by which he was raised, his ambition to "revolutionize the whole system of children's literature" (2) should be seen within the context of the romantic spirit of reform. In the vanguard was his energetic future sister-in-law, Elizabeth Peabody, who not only published Hawthorne's first three children's books but drew the writer out of his isolation in Salem to a wider readership and into the intellectual atmosphere of Transcendentalism. Recommending him as "a man of first rate genius" to Horace Mann, the new secretary of the Massachusetts Board of Education who would soon marry her sister Mary, Elizabeth even tried to arrange for Hawthorne's "new literature for the young" to become part of the district school libraries, which Mann planned to endow in the early 1840s (Peabody 199).

The tension between Puritan and romantic conceptions of the child in Hawthorne's fiction also influenced his fascinated, sometimes frightened observation of his own children. Of Una he wrote in *The American Notebooks:* "I now and then catch a glimpse of her, in which I cannot believe her to be my own human child, but a spirit strangely mingled with good and evil" (8:430–31). The complexity of his view runs counter to Laffrado's assertion that "children throughout his fiction correspond closely to nineteenth-century ideals of cherubic, flower-children." The restlessly physical and pragmatic Charley, who seems to learn nothing from Grandfather's history and rams the antique chair with his wheelbarrow, hardly conforms to her notion that "child auditors featured in the frame tales . . . fit this mold without exception" (141). Even the wild and prescient Pearl of *The Scarlet Letter* is portrayed unproblematically, as a psychologically comprehensible character with "natural empathy" (5).

At times the book's strength, its exclusive focus on Hawthorne's writings for children, seems related to a failure to reckon with the dark and ironic side of Hawthorne's genius. There is also some carelessness in details: Hawthorne located the "familiar room" of his neutral territory not on "the upper floor of the Salem Custom House" (7) but in the deserted parlor of his own home; *A Wonder-*

Book for Girls and Boys is consistently mistitled *A Wonder Book for Boys and Girls.* Nevertheless, *Hawthorne's Literature for Children* breaks new ground by offering an overview of the diverse characters, themes, and techniques that Hawthorne developed for a child audience. The appendix provides publication data and some interesting facts about the moderate remuneration and other compensations that he earned for all his efforts. It is satisfying and thought provoking finally to ponder the six children's books in uninterrupted sequence and in relation to each other. Finding *A Wonder-Book* and *Tanglewood Tales* still available today in paperback legitimizes Hawthorne's pride in not writing "downward" to children and ratifies his delight in young auditors, who "possess an unestimated sensibility to whatever is deep and high, in imagination or feeling" (*Wonder-Book,* preface).

Works Cited

Cable, Mary. *The Little Darlings.* New York, 1972.
Hawthorne, Nathaniel. *The American Notebooks.* In *The Centenary Edition of the Works of Nathaniel Hawthorne,* vol. 8, ed. William Charvat, Roy Harvey Pearce, and Claude M. Simpson (Columbus: Ohio State University Press, 1972).
———. A Wonder-Book *and* Tanglewood Tales. In *The Centenary Edition of the Works of Nathaniel Hawthorne,* vol. 7, ed. William Charvat, Roy Harvey Pearce, and Claude M. Simpson (Columbus: Ohio State University Press, 1972).
Peabody, Elizabeth Palmer. *Letters of Elizabeth Palmer Peabody.* Ed. Bruce A. Ronda. Middletown, Conn.: Wesleyan University Press, 1984.

Audaciously, Archetypally American

John Cech

Audacious Kids: Coming of Age in America's Classic Children's Books, by Jerry Griswold. New York and Oxford: Oxford University Press, 1992.

Jerry Griswold's study of a dozen well-known nineteenth- and early twentieth-century American children's books is, true to its title, an audacious work of criticism. In a time of unprecedented and often impenetrable critical discourse, this book is deliberately jargon free and accessible—without mysterious hermeneutics and neological obscurities—to both scholarly and general audiences. It is written with clarity and humor, with inventive energy and an agile, synthesizing intelligence. Most important, rather than engaging in the nearly requisite diatribes or revisionings, it presumes to practice an ideologically neutral cultural criticism that provides a context in which Griswold can make some basic sense of an archetypal story, a theme and its variations, that has worn its way deep into the grain of American children's literature.

The thesis of *Audacious Kids* is that a similar narrative pattern repeats itself with uncanny frequency in American juvenile literature, especially in a group of well-known works from the golden age of children's books, which Griswold dates from 1865 to 1914. The books that he considers are strikingly different, ranging from the feminist concerns of *Little Women* (1868) to the macho social Darwinism of *Tarzan of the Apes* (1914). With other examples of how this archetypal pattern is represented, Griswold explores *Hans Brinker* (1865), *Little Women* (1868), *The Adventures of Tom Sawyer* (1876), *Toby Tyler* (1881), *The Prince and the Pauper* (1881), *The Adventures of Huckleberry Finn* (1885), *Little Lord Fauntleroy* (1885), *The Wizard of Oz* (1900), *Rebecca of Sunnybrook Farm* (1903), *Pollyanna* (1913), and *Tarzan of the Apes* (1914). These disparate works, Griswold finds, are bound together by their fundamental similarities into an "Urstory" that he entitles, borrowing ideas and approaches from Otto Rank and Joseph Campbell, "The Three Lives of the Child-Hero"

Children's Literature 22, ed. Francelia Butler, R. H. W. Dillard, and Elizabeth Lennox Keyser (Yale University Press, © 1994 Hollins College).

(5). With due recognition of other possible patterns that can be created from these same elements, Griswold outlines the primal, mythic story that he sees emerging from these "classics."

A child is born to parents who married despite the objections of others. For a time, the family is well-to-do, members of the nobility or otherwise happy and prosperous. Then the child's parents die, or the child is separated from its parents and effectively orphaned. Without their protection the child suffers from poverty and neglect and (if nobly born) is dispossessed. The hero then makes a journey to another place and is adopted into a second family. In these new circumstances the child is treated harshly by an adult guardian of the same sex but sometimes has help from an adult of the opposite sex. Eventually, however, the child triumphs over its antagonist and is acknowledged. Finally, some accommodation is reached between the two discordant phases of the child's past: life in the original or biological family and life in the second or adoptive family. [4]

The connecting links between these elements are psychological, Griswold argues, and the child-hero (who has at least a dozen faces) lives these three lives in order to resolve a number of commonly shared developmental tasks, beginning with the problem of dealing with "separation from parents to achieve autonomy," an upsetting but necessary passage that leads to "familiar fantasies of being orphaned, hungry, impoverished, mistreated, exposed" (10–11). In the "Second Life," the child-hero contends with normal Oedipal emotions, which are transformed through "the child's triumph over the antagonist (signaled by the death or humbling of that same-sex parent figure) . . . a salutary symbol of the child's resolution of these Oedipal problems and the achievement of independence" (12). With this settling of animosities, in the "Third Life" a return is possible to those "vanished happy times" before the child was cast out into the world (12). Often, however, because the child-hero is on the brink of maturity at the end of the story, he or she is asked to strike an informed balance between past struggles and the realizations that accompany present empowerment. Dorothy, for example, discovers that she "cannot escape her troubles by going elsewhere. The last words of the movie, 'There's no place like home,' really amount to 'There's no place *but* home'" (40).

Griswold is quick to anticipate challenges to his representation of this universal pattern of psychological experience as uniquely American. Other writers from other traditions have been instinctively drawn to similar plot devices; the adventures of the orphaned child, for example, are a recurrent motif in fairy tales and in Dickens, and the child's Oedipal struggle with same-sex antagonists is, well, as old as the Greeks. But what other national literatures do not have, Griswold compellingly and credibly asserts, is the psychohistorical perception, from the colonial period on, of the country as a metaphoric child. Since the Revolution this conception of "America-as-Child" has been a "pervasive pattern" in our collective cultural thought; we cast ourselves as "an orphan, estranged and engaged in Oedipal rebellion against its parents, making its Declaration of Independence and achieving autonomy" (16). To amplify this reading of America as child, Griswold adds a number of other particularly American characteristics that figure frequently in the works he discusses: the national obsession with health; "an advocacy of positive thinking" and the reciprocal control, as in *Hans Brinker*, of "those oceanic feelings that threaten to break through the dykes of self-control" (18); and the belief that the only antidote to the foolishness and faults of the world is the innocence of the child-hero, like Pollyanna, "whose comprehensive optimism is often mistaken for empty-headedness but whose naiveté turns out to have a contagious and redemptive effect in her community" (19).

In a series of quick paragraphs at the end of his introduction, Griswold also sketches, with remarkable insight, a number of cultural concerns that affected both writers and the general reading public during the latter half of the nineteenth century, further sensitizing them to the figurative child. During this period a dramatic change occurred in American culture, and this paradigmatic shift had to do with the vision of the child. "The child became a public figure, seized on as a vehicle for nostalgia or as a symbol of the future's promise, brought from the shadows as original sinner and put on center stage as original innocent, ministered to by educators, health professionals, humanitarians, and politicians. Given this milieu and these obsessions it may not be so surprising after all that many of the best sellers of the period were children's books" (24).

In the twelve chapters that follow, Griswold works through the archetypal pattern that he has identified with its attendant variations in each of the selected books. He freely admits that his Urstory is one of many patterns of meaning to be found in these books or in the many other works that he does not consider but that could be included in other studies of this period. Often he focuses his critical attention primarily on certain distinct features of a work or group of works: the Oedipal dynamics of *Huckleberry Finn* and *Rebecca of Sunnybrook Farm;* the nationalistic subtexts of *Little Lord Fauntleroy, Tarzan of the Apes,* and *The Prince and the Pauper;* the "gospel of optimism" in *Hans Brinker, The Secret Garden,* and *Pollyanna* (185). But in each case, Griswold takes pains to show how a work may be said to conform to or, as with *Huck Finn,* significantly modify the seemingly neat story template.

Inevitable as some repetition may be in this study, Griswold admirably avoids sounding as though he is mechanically repeating the outlines of his pattern, and he lets each consideration of a variation of the Ur-story offer us a unique opportunity to contemplate the myth. His discussion of *Huckleberry Finn,* for instance, begins with an analysis of Twain's stream-of-consciousness approach in creating the sequence of episodes and the appropriateness of a psychological reading of the story to such a method of composition. His interpretation of Pollyanna's "radical innocence" starts with a summary of the amazing popularity of the book—the enormous sales and the "testimonials to the book's transformative power [that poured] in from stockbrokers, clergy, missionaries, millionaires, dowagers, file clerks, and a sobbing Philadelphia newspaperman" (216). The Glad Game that Pollyanna plays in the book led some of Eleanor Porter's fans to found Glad Clubs of their own—complete with smiling-child buttons—"which included the Glad Kids, a group of prisoners in a penitentiary whose ages ranged from thirty-two to seventy-six" (217).

To his credit, Griswold acknowledges the complexity of individual works and their resistance to unqualified archetypal categorization. But one sometimes wishes for deeper, fuller analyses of a given novel, the kind of exploration that is not possible given Griswold's critical intentions in this study. In the chapter on *The Wizard of Oz,* for example, Griswold could have more carefully delineated between the book and the film, rather than conflating the two. The film appeared at a time of greater psychological consciousness, and it is one of the rare movies that are much better than the books on which they are based. Griswold could have taken advantage of this discrepancy, especially in his discussion of Dorothy's Oedipal passage. The closeness of Judy Garland's Dorothy to womanhood, and Auntie Em's dismissal of Dorothy's dream, makes the ending of the movie ambiguous and unsettling and, arguably, a more complicated variation of the pattern, one that is perhaps fitting in a decade that registered a more complex vision of the child.

But such reservations are slight and infrequent, and when they occur they mark Griswold's capacity for readily engaging the reader in one of his implicit objectives: to generate a lively, ongoing discussion of American children's literature in relation to both our personal journeys as readers and the patterns of concerns that can be traced in the cultural past. *Audacious Kids* begins a long-awaited, collective consideration of these key works of the national literature, and it is to be hoped that its energy will stimulate other studies of these and other works and periods in our national myth-making. This fascinating book leads us back to a pivotal moment in the history of American childhood and children's literature, touching chords that are both universal and peculiarly American. For the mythic orphan children are with us still in the works of Maurice Sendak and Jerry Spinelli and Francesca Block, and Griswold has shown us in his compelling study where to look for their appearance, how to understand their journeys, and how to welcome them home.

The Anne-Girl and Her Critics

Anne K. Phillips

Such a Simple Little Tale: Critical Responses to L. M. Montgomery's Anne of Green Gables, edited by Mavis Reimer. Metuchen, N.J.: Scarecrow Press and the Children's Literature Association, 1992.

As Mavis Reimer notes in her introduction to *Such a Simple Little Tale,* the concept of collecting a series of essays on L. M. Montgomery's *Anne of Green Gables* arose when the publications committee of the Children's Literature Association realized that over a period of years the editors of prominent children's literature publications had published more articles about *Anne* than about any other single book. Of the thirteen essays included in this collection, eight originally appeared in Children's Literature Association publications—five in the *Quarterly,* two in the published proceedings of conferences, and one in the first volume of the Touchstones series edited by Perry Nodelman. The remaining five essays, drawn from *Canadian Children's Literature, Studies in Canadian Literature, English Studies in Canada,* and the *Journal of American Culture,* place Montgomery's first novel in her Anne series in diverse and provocative contexts. In all, the collection is a welcome development in Montgomery studies. In conjunction with Mary Rubio and Elizabeth Waterston's publication of the third volume of Montgomery's journals, *The Selected Journals of L. M. Montgomery* (Oxford University Press, 1992), the essays that appear in *Such a Simple Little Tale* call attention to Montgomery's artistic merit and affirm her important position within the children's literature canon.

Reimer has organized the collection chronologically, beginning with Muriel A. Whitaker's "'Queer Children': L. M. Montgomery's Heroines" (1975) and leading to the final essay, Temma F. Berg's "*Anne of Green Gables:* A Girl's Reading" (1988). Many of the essays appeared in or after 1985, products of the critical and popular attention generated by the publication of the first volume of Montgomery's journals and Kevin Sullivan's Canadian Broadcasting Company production of *Anne of Green Gables* (televised in

Children's Literature 22, ed. Francelia Butler, R. H. W. Dillard, and Elizabeth Lennox Keyser (Yale University Press, © 1994 Hollins College).

America on Wonderworks for the Public Broadcasting System) the same year.

The chronological organization indicates the trends in critical approaches. In the essays provided here, individual authors move from the formalist strategies of Nodelman or Marilyn Solt to the feminist-informed approaches of Nancy Huse or Eva Kornfeld and Susan Jackson—demonstrating the broader impact of feminist criticism on children's literature. Berg draws on Lacan, but, as Reimer notes, "much more work could be done in reading *Anne* by the light of recent theories of culture, language, and subjectivity" (188). Although Reimer identifies many scholars' seeming unfamiliarity with and infrequent references to other Montgomery criticism, several of the authors included in this volume do incorporate and build on the work of earlier commentators. Berg's essay in particular neatly rounds out the collection with its references to the work of several of the preceding authors, among them Janet Weiss-Townsend, Susan Drain, and Carol Gay, whose essays originally appeared in the special Montgomery issue of the *Children's Literature Association Quarterly* in 1986.

The chronological approach also has disadvantages. It entails movement between essays in which Montgomery's work is considered in strikingly different contexts and between essays in which Montgomery is the primary focus and those in which her work is only marginally discussed. Particularly rough transitions occur between Nodelman's "Progressive Utopias," in which he constructs an archetypal girls' story, and Catherine Ross's "Ghost of the Old-Time Heroine," in which she analyzes the modes of romance and realism as they are utilized by several Canadian writers, including Margaret Atwood, Alice Munro, Sara Jeanette Duncan, and Margaret Laurence, as well as Montgomery. Nodelman treats *Anne of Green Gables* as children's literature; Ross places Montgomery's novel squarely within a distinctly adult tradition in Canadian literature. A different kind of disjunction occurs between Huse's excellent "Journeys of the Mother in the World of Green Gables" and Kornfeld and Jackson's "Female Bildungsroman in Nineteenth-Century America." Although neither essay focuses exclusively on *Anne,* Montgomery's work is central to Huse's comparison of the mother experiences of three important female characters in the series—Marilla, Anne, and Rilla. Montgomery's fiction is only the final (and somewhat marginal) example in Kornfeld and Jackson's essay, which draws more heavily on *Little Women, Five Little Peppers and How They Grew,* and *Rebecca of Sunnybrook Farm.* Each of the essays in *Such a Simple Little Tale* deserves inclusion, but under a different organizing principle (perhaps a thematic one?) they might have been displayed to greater advantage.

A more significant problem with the chronological approach is that it applies only to the essays. In the introduction Reimer refers to early reviews and reactions to *Anne,* yet the reader must proceed to the final section of the book, "Suggestions for Further Reading," to find sample excerpts from these reviews. Why not adhere to the chronological design and situate the reviews before the essays? In addition, the suggested readings on scholarship and criticism more than once include summaries of essays included in the volume—essays which readers would presumably already have read and which are even more fully summarized in the introduction. Reimer is undoubtedly attempting to provide the larger critical context for the essays included in this volume, but the effect is redundant. A more effective organizing strategy might have overcome these limitations to the design of the volume.

The suggested readings on Montgomery and *Anne* are divided into bibliographies, notes on the series, life and letters, early reviews, and contexts and history of reception, in addition to the section on scholarship and criticism. In two of these components Reimer identifies Elizabeth Waterston's 1966 essay on Montgomery as worthy of special attention; according to Reimer, it is "the beginning of the detailed critical study of *Anne*" (179). Why, then, hasn't the essay been included here? Reimer details its publication history—including its reprinting in the 1975 Montgomery issue of *Canadian Children's Literature*—and may have felt that it was already familiar to Montgomery scholars. Yet several of the essays included in *Such a Simple Little Tale* also have prominent publication histories —including Mary Rubio's "Anne of Green Gables: The Architect of Adolescence," drawn from the first volume of the Touchstones series. Waterston's essay would have contributed to the breadth of Reimer's volume both as the earliest serious discussion of Montgomery's novel and as an application of theories of adolescent development.

In the introduction and "Suggestions for Further Reading," Reimer raises significant issues. Concerned that critics lose sight of Montgomery's intended audience, she notes more than once that

Anne was aimed at girls, not adults. Reimer argues against strictly biographical readings of Anne, Emily, and other Montgomery characters: "While it seems certain that readers will persist in questioning the correlation between Anne and her creator, the availability of Montgomery's journals makes it possible to set that question in broader contexts" (169). In addition, Reimer suggests in her introduction that one of her objectives is to demonstrate distinctions between American approaches to *Anne of Green Gables* and Canadian approaches and "to alert readers of Montgomery in both countries that claim *Anne* as part of their literary heritage to the conversations under way in the other country" (4–5). American critics, according to Reimer, place Montgomery's novel within familiar literary traditions—as local color, domestic fiction, sentimental fiction—whereas in Canada "*Anne* is seen as a singular, if not anomalous, achievement" (4). Reimer admits that such a distinction is often a tendency rather than a divergence and cites essays within the volume that include Montgomery's work within established Canadian traditions in literature. Readers may wish that Reimer had more clearly explained her proposed distinction: certainly, the material in this volume fails to provide the necessary support for the argument.

The Children's Literature Association and Scarecrow Press are to be applauded for making distinguished, scholarly analysis of children's literature accessible through the publication of *Such a Simple Little Tale*. Readers may wish for more historical contexts, more journal excerpts, more personal letters, indeed, more volumes in the future, but the present work is certainly a handsome beginning for what may become a preeminent series.

Fiber, Bone, and Sinew Aplenty

Mary V. Jackson

Moral Instruction and Fiction for Children, 1749–1820, by Samuel F. Pickering, Jr. Athens: University of Georgia Press, 1993.

In the preface to *Moral Instruction and Fiction for Children, 1749–1820,* Samuel Pickering indicates that his distinguished scholarly work *John Locke and Children's Books in Eighteenth-Century England* (1981) lies behind this newest study. Yet the recent book—he would evidently have us believe—is less tough fibered than its predecessor, not merely different in approach. Noting the difficulty of writing about simple matters without sounding simpleminded, he tells us that he has eschewed luring us to marvel "at a Jamesian figure hidden in the carpet of children's literature." He would rather have us know well and truly "the carpet itself, its texture and colors, perhaps even a sense of its place in the House of Fiction" (viii). We are also warned not to expect his study to grapple with the thorny problem of the readings' influence on children. Instead, he will focus on the books themselves to demonstrate his findings on "narrative practice and authorial intention" (viii). Finally, he says, the book is "a covert celebration of imaginative instruction" undertaken because it was fun; his choices for discussion were dictated by his "penchant for sweets." He urges those who do not have his critical sweet-tooth to go forth into the libraries, where thousands of little books with more "fiber and bone, gristle and sinew" await their attention (ix–x).

This caveat is misleading. There are sinew, bone, and fiber aplenty in the particular fancy-filled sweets that he has chosen to discuss, and no lack whatsoever of mature critical judgment, backed by scholarly knowledge of the social and literary history of the age.

The many strengths of the book stem directly from Pickering's decision to quote liberally and to retell in some detail portions of many books. He has a knack for deftly seizing upon the most salient features of a narrative and re-creating a sense of the whole and of the means, the imaginative devices, that render these intensely

Children's Literature 22, ed. Francelia Butler, R. H. W. Dillard, and Elizabeth Lennox Keyser (Yale University Press, © 1994 Hollins College).

moral stories prepossessing and on occasion even enchanting. Not only does this tactic convey a lively sense of the drama and humor in these teaching tales but it is probably the most convincing way to demonstrate one very important point that he makes. We often think of early children's books as being divided into two hostile, if not mutually exclusive, camps (fancy versus morality), but "this division is too simple. Although much early fiction warned children against the dangers of the imagination, it did so in imaginative stories . . . [that] led children across marvelously drawn landscapes, woods and meadows which may have delighted readers as much or more than fairyland" (viii–ix).

Moral Instruction, which is divided into seven chapters, organizes a huge number of works, some never before examined, around (1) genres, (2) imitations of central literary works, and (3) motifs significant to early children's literature generally. In the first chapter, "Allegory and the Eastern Tale," Pickering examines symbolic fictions that blend the "ordinary with the unusual," explaining how the adaptability of allegory made it equally if differently fruitful for both religious and secular writers and revealing numerous fresh and several surprising parallels between juvenile allegories and *Pilgrim's Progress.* Pickering delineates the eastern tale's appeal but shows that there was ambivalence toward it, chiefly among conservatives like Sarah Kirby Trimmer, who judged such tales insufficiently "favourable to the Christian Cause": "It is a great affront to the *divine majesty* . . . to ascribe to a Genii . . . that mediation which belongs to the son of god alone" (23).

In the next chapters, "School Stories," *"Robinson Crusoe,"* "The Foundling," and *"Pamela,"* Pickering explores scores of tales, explaining the artistry of each type, the moral issues inherent in them, and how and to what end writers of differing persuasions chose to utilize them. Differences in the codes of life that such books offered boys as opposed to girls, and the prosperous as opposed to the poor, are touched on briefly and sporadically in the early chapters, then focused on in the final chapters, "Servants and Inferiors" and "Liars and Tell-Tales." Without sounding a doctrinaire note, Pickering explores complicated issues of gender and class, shedding light on the standards evolving in the literature and on unresolved contradictions in the society. He shows more clearly than anyone else to date how the middle class strove with surprising success to remake in its own image not only the lowly orders but the aristocracy as well.

Because the works discussed in each chapter and the appendix were written over a period of more than seventy years, *Moral Instruction* yields an additional bonus. Each literary genre and model is shown to be both a key to elucidating "bundles of messages" packed into a single book and a guideline to clarifying permutations of religious and cultural values in children's moral fiction.

It may seem ungrateful to find fault with a work so well conceived and executed and filled with valuable insights and no little wit, but I do have one suggestion and one query.

First, it is inconvenient not to have a bibliography of both primary and secondary works in a text that scrutinizes so large a field and introduces titles likely to be unfamiliar to many. Bibliography is a tricky matter in early juvenile books. We do not always know the dates of first editions, and too often we think we know, only to find an earlier volume extant. Such problems with publishing history notwithstanding, it is a handicap to have no guide, as is the case here. Pickering's endnotes cite the editions he used, including American reprints of early English books—a sensible decision. But I would like to be able to consult a concise list of these and not be forced to scour the notes to remind myself who wrote what approximately when. Furthermore, it would be helpful, especially for students and scholars new to the field, to supply the earliest publishing data even when citing a later edition. In most cases, the dates of the English and American editions are close enough to cause no problem in the discussions.

Although Pickering does not anatomize like and unlike aspects of American and English society, I find myself wondering if his assumption of great similarities in British and American values and expectations for childhood (in many senses true) does not inadvertently raise questions about dissimilarities. *Moral Instruction* ends officially at 1820, but there are comments on later works: Twain's *Huckleberry Finn* (1884), Kipling's *Kim* (1901), even Dickens's *Hard Times* (1854). In Britain juvenile moral fiction altered significantly between 1780 and 1820, let alone 1854. And the disparity between British and American cultural and moral givens in children's fiction—particularly concerning class and wealth and religious faith—increased during the nineteenth century. But these are matters for another book, and it is to Pickering's credit that he leads us to think about and to rethink critical issues.

Indeed, Pickering's book can be seen as a model for effective studies of didactic fiction for children. Like his earlier *John Locke and Children's Books,* it is a fine blend of scholarly rigor and critical incisiveness, lightened by wit and conveyed in lucid prose devoid of cant terms and pedantic posturings. No serious student or scholar in the field, and certainly no research library, should be without it.

Folktales and Traditional Morality

Christa Kamenetsky

Off with Their Heads! Fairy Tales and the Culture of Childhood, by Maria
Tatar. Princeton, N.J.: Princeton University Press, 1992.

Maria Tatar has searched out parallel didactic trends in early children's literature and European folktales. With great ease she crosses
centuries and national boundaries in tracing recurring patterns of
virtues and vices in educational tracts, folktales, fantasies, classical
mythology, and the Bible, as well as in the works of Shakespeare,
Petrarch, and Boccaccio. Working on the premise that the history
of children's literature has suffered from an unusually cruel streak,
one that especially affects women and children, she singles out
"moral correctives" in selected works of James Janeway, John Bun-
yan, Jane and Anne Taylor, Mrs. Sherwood, Carlo Collodi, Heinrich Hoffmann, Hans Christian Andersen, and Lewis Carroll and
then looks for corresponding trends in contemporaneous folktales.

Didactic patterns in folktales have become more prominent in
recent centuries, Tatar claims, because the oral tradition has been
supplanted by printed texts intended for children. Individual folktale collectors supposedly also rewrote folktales in accordance with
prevailing social and educational concepts, as well as their personal
likes or dislikes, thereby not only eliminating coarse, bawdy, erotic,
and incestuous scenes to protect children, according to Tatar, but
also emphasizing acts of cruelty, violence, brutal intimidation, big-
otry, and coercion, mainly to utilize the tales as "lessons" (64–65).
An increasing concern with productive socialization led collectors to
intensify an already existing gender bias. Male protagonists usually
reaped rewards for such virtues as humility, compassion, and faithfulness, yet they often escaped punishment for crimes committed in
the course of adventurous actions. Female protagonists, in contrast,
were not rewarded for the same virtues, though these were often
taken for granted as preconditions for marriage, which was usually
their only chance to move to a higher class. Self-willed or adventure-
some actions by women were condemned. If women failed in obedi-

Children's Literature 22, ed. Francelia Butler, R. H. W. Dillard, and Elizabeth Lennox
Keyser (Yale University Press, © 1994 Hollins College).

ence, humility, diligence, or endurance, they were chastised, often having to sacrifice their self-esteem by assuming a servile attitude, like Catskin or Allerleirauh. In contemplating the "seven sins" of female protagonists and their gruesome consequences, Tatar traces this gender bias in such works as a tale of Boccaccio, Shakespeare's *Taming of the Shrew,* and an eighteenth-century manual on how to subdue unruly wives. In European folktale variants she examines similar patterns of punishment associated with female disobedience, pride, selfishness, greed, gluttony, and unfaithfulness. After establishing some common sociocultural attitudes toward stubborn and self-willed women through the ages, she concludes that women were treated cruelly and coercively because men considered them to be "children" and inferiors (105–7, 135).

In a chapter entitled "Beauties and Beasts," Tatar pays special attention to the themes of female obedience and self-denial. She uses the Greek myth of Cupid and Psyche in Apuleius's version and a number of folktale variants on this theme as a testing ground, observing that de Beaumont's "Beauty and the Beast," the Grimms' "Singing, Spring Lark," and the Norwegian "East of the Sun and West of the Moon" show a shift in emphasis toward didacticism. Whereas the myth dwells on the theme of female jealousy, the folktale variants emphasize the sin of female curiosity and state more explicitly a demand for modesty, obedience, endurance, compassion, and complete subordination. Here Tatar employs feminist and sociocultural interpretations of the theme by Carol Gilligan, Torberg Lundell, Jack Zipes, and others (260).

According to Tatar, adulterous women are punished with special cruelty in folktales. To illustrate her point, she refers to two passages describing the death penalty for adulterous females, one from "The Three Snake Leaves" in the collection of the Brothers Grimm and one from "The Lion's Grass" in Italo Calvino's anthology of Italian folktales. In the first tale, the unfaithful woman is "sent out to sea with her accomplice in a boat filled with holes," and in the second the woman is condemned in the following terms: "Hang her first, then burn her, and then throw her ashes to the wind" (118). Even the most skeptical reader might lean toward accepting Tatar's thesis that folktales are biased against women, for hardly a folktale in the world depicts an equally cruel punishment for an adulterous male. What she does not mention, however, is that in both cases the women committed not only adultery but murder. The first woman killed her husband on the high seas and threw his body overboard, and the second issued a court order to have her husband killed by hanging, even though she owed him her own life and happiness. Even if we reject the cruelty and the death penalty itself, it becomes difficult to consider these women victims, for in both cases the death sentence arises from the traditional concept of retribution. Had Tatar related the full extent of their crimes, she might have done better justice to the sociocultural contexts of the tales.

Children, too, are punished violently in folktales. To prove her point, Tatar refers to the Grimms' tale "Frau Trude," in which a girl's stubbornness and curiosity result in death: she is turned into a block of wood and casually tossed into the fire. In "The Stubborn Child," the Grimms convey an equally disagreeable lesson when the mother enforces obedience beyond the grave by smacking the arm of her buried child that is sticking out of the soil. Tatar takes both stories at their face value without consulting the Grimms' own notes, which dwell not on behavioral lessons for children but rather on superstitions. In one variant they knew, the Devil takes the place of Frau Trude, and in another one the arm sticking out of the grave points to the common folk belief that the dead communicate with the living. Moral teachings, it seems, sometimes lie in the eye of the beholder rather than in the folktale itself.

"Festive violence" is the theme that strikes Tatar as most abhorrent and pointless in children's books and folktales. Among others, she cites Lewis Carroll's Queen ("Off with his head!"), relating to this gruesome command some equally horrifying scenes from the Russian folktale "Vasilissa the Fair," as well as some bloody rejuvenation tales by Giambattiste Basile and the Brothers Grimm, the Ogre's massacre of his seven daughters in "Tom Thumb," and absurd violence inflicted by needles and flying objects in "Herr Korbes" and "Riff-Raff." Taking these stories literally, she finds no excuse for scenes of violence or torture anywhere, not even if they appear in the form of slapstick humor or grotesque exaggeration (171).

Tatar's sociocultural approach is more convincing when she ties the recurrent theme of childhood death in early children's books to some revealing statistics on the high infant mortality rate in the nineteenth century. The discussion illuminates basic survival problems related to poor health and poverty, conditions often reflected in early children's books. She explains how some Puritan or didactic books, such as James Janeway's *Token for Children* or Heinrich Hoffmann's *Der Struwwelpeter,* used the theme of childhood death to keep children in line with adult expectations. Yet here, too, her approach shows certain limitations. Perhaps she might have emphasized some differences in the orientation of these two works and others, for Janeway's Puritan vision has little in common with Hoffmann's emphasis on proper behavior. Stylistic differences also set these books apart from each other, for there is certainly no room for laughter in *A Token for Children.* The same question of emphasis applies to Tatar's discussions of some other historical children's books, in which a consideration of style, intent, and literary quality is overshadowed by her analysis of sociocultural aspects and gender-related topics. The need for a more careful approach to types of writing for children is especially evident in her comparison of Janeway's *Token for Children* with Wilhelm Grimm's *Dear Mili* (79–93). Inspired by Grimm's loving concern for a child and influenced by a religious legend, this tale is neither a religious tract nor a fantasy, nor does it qualify as a folktale. As Tatar herself acknowledges, it is merely a personal letter to a little girl named Mili. Because it was never meant for publication, it is not well suited to a comparative discussion of a prevailing publication trend. Tatar is also sidetracked by the question of why Maurice Sendak chose to illustrate what has since become known as a picture book; such an inquiry belongs to a different study, one that would take up the artistic dimensions of his choice.

Cannibalism and incest are the focus of attention in several chapters. By citing a great number of detailed examples, mostly from older folktale collections, Tatar relates these themes to Freud's *Totem and Taboo,* as well as to studies by Melanie Klein and Robert Darnton (201–5). She cannot find any merit in these recurrent themes, however, except that they empower children to use their wits in working through anxieties about abandonment and aggression (209). At the same time, Tatar rejects Bettelheim's theories on the therapeutic value of cruelty in folktales because they do not sufficiently take into account such unacceptable excesses as cannibalism or the coercive actions of "god-like" husbands against their wives (199).

Tatar admits that the themes of coercion and incest are more evident in older folktale collections intended for an adult audience, yet she claims that, disguised, they persist in modern folktale collections intended for children. She contends that folktale editors have

attempted to suppress the socially unacceptable themes by shifting the blame to the mother or stepmother. In "A Girl Without
Hands," Tatar argues, the Grimms replaced the godlike father with
the Devil, thus "masking" the father's sexual desire for his daughter. She considers such masking a "brilliant move on the part of the
Grimms" (125), implying that they consciously reshaped the story
in accordance with their own social and moral codes. Following
the theory of female disempowerment and John M. Ellis's theory
of substitution, she believes that the father has been absolved of a
serious crime and turned into a kind yet cowardly figure, "one not
unlike the fathers in 'Hansel and Gretel,' 'Snow White,' and 'Beauty
and the Beast'" (121).

Occasionally Tatar supports her findings by comparing the
Grimms' published folktales with some older printed folktale variants listed in their notes, assuming that such listings constitute
proof that the Grimms used their notes as sources for the published
tales (57). The basis for such an assumption may be questioned,
for the Grimms often cited older printed variants for comparative
purposes only, without necessarily acknowledging them as sources.
She further claims that they purposely selected from among the
available variants those that corresponded to their own values. For
example, the particular variant of "Mother Holle" that they chose
for their collection (54–57) emphasizes female diligence and hard
work, rather than the theme of good luck that was predominant in
some older printed sources.

The claim that the Grimms rewrote the tales by selecting their
favorite variants may be disputed by comparing their corresponding notes for the tales in the third volume of the *Kinder- und Hausmärchen* (1822). In most cases, their preferences point to the available oral variants, whereas the older printed variants are merely
listed for comparative purposes. This procedure also pertains to
"Rotkäppchen" (Red Cap), for which they relied on a German oral
variant, not on Perrault's "Le petit chaperon rouge," as Tatar claims
(36). They give credit to Perrault for publishing the first and only
printed variant known to them, yet they do not acknowledge the
tale as a source, influence, or model. It is possible that the French
Huguenots introduced the tale to the region of Hesse.

Tatar also charges the Grimms with anti-Semitism in "The Jew in
the Thornbush," for they supposedly selected from among numerous versions available to them the one tale that features a Jew being

forced to dance to the music of the magic fiddle until his clothes are torn to tatters by thorns. Because two other versions mention a clergyman in the role of the Jew, Tatar charges the Grimms with having used and amplified a racial stereotype (180). Such observations are justified in the light of the current concern to be fair, just, sensitive, and democratic in a diverse society, especially in regard to gender, race, and religion. Publishers have long recognized the merits of replacing the title "The Jew in the Thornbush" with the nonreligious "The Miser in the Thornbush."

But did the Grimms indeed lack sensitivity? Their notes to the tale reveal no interest beyond choosing available oral variants over older and apparently less authentic printed variants, among them two folk comedies from Vienna. They related observations on the folkloristic motif of the magic fiddle (or magic flute) that forced listeners to dance. No other tales in the Grimms' collection feature the Jew as a character, and a single quotation from Jacob Grimm (cited by Tatar out of context) can hardly be used as proof of anti-Semitism. The male victims appearing in other tales in their collection represent a broad spectrum of German society and the world beyond, including innkeepers, peasants, beggars, priests, kings, giants, monsters, the Devil, and Saint Peter himself. In the folktale world no one is immune from victimization, it seems, as no one is immune from ridicule. Had the Grimms been xenophobic or racially prejudiced, would they have bothered to collect and review hundreds of folktales from other countries, including Palestine (Grimm and Grimm, vol. 3, pt. 2)? For them the acid test was authenticity, not pedagogical concerns or personal prejudices.

Did the Grimms take sadistic pleasure in intensifying the suffering and humiliation, especially of female characters? In tales like "Ashputtel," in which Tatar identifies an enhancement of the themes of humiliation, suffering, and cruelty in comparison with the French "Cinderella," of which it is a variant, did the Grimms purposely insert motifs like ashes to evoke children's sympathy for pedagogical purposes (5–7)? The Grimms' notes do not bear out such assumptions, for again they show that the Grimms chose the available oral tale variant rather than the printed versions, most of which already contained the ash motif. Among these were Danish, Norwegian, and Slavic variants and one German variant in which the main protagonist was a boy who did the dirty work, slept in the ashes, and was abused by his brothers. This note should serve as a reminder that the victims in the Grimms' collection are not pre-dominantly female. Next to Dummling who with his naïveté, kind-ness, and empathy righted wrongs and set the world in order was Däumling (Tom Thumb), who, even though disadvantaged by na-ture, possessed the wit and resourcefulness to come out on top.

Tatar is puzzled by an apparent contradiction in the Grimms' approaches to folktales: How could they try to capture in their collection "the authentic voice of the people in all its purity" yet simultaneously impose on the tales their own value system by cre-ating an "educational manual" (16, 243)? The Grimms never used the expression "educational manual." Wilhelm Grimm perceived in the tales the potential for an education in poetry, a concept that is diametrically opposed to their use as a handbook on manners and morals. In his introduction to the 1819 edition of the *Kinder- und Hausmärchen* he wrote:

> We wish to offer with our collection not only a service to the history of poetry but simultaneously the intention to make effective the poetry itself that is alive within it: to delight those who are capable of enjoying it. It is for this reason that it should become a true book of education. [Kamenetsky 96n]

> Wir wollten indes durch unsere Sammlung nicht bloss der Geschichte der Poesie einen Dienst erweisen, es war zugleich Absicht dass die Poesie selbst, die darin lebendig ist, wirke: erfreue, wen sie erfreuen kann, und darum auch, dass es ein eigentliches Erziehungsbuch daraus werde. [Grimm and Grimm xii]

To make effective the poetry within folktales meant to make young and old receptive to the poetic imagery and naive worldview. The concept of a book of education was more precisely based on the romantic term *Naturpoesie* (nature or folk poetry), which em-braced folktales, myths, legends, epics, children's games, and folk beliefs. According to the Grimms, Naturpoesie was reflected in the symbolic language of folktales and myths, as well as in archaic ex-pressions and colloquial speech patterns.

In pursuing an eclectic approach to folktales, Tatar limits her comparisons by focusing almost exclusively on depressing examples of suffering and violence at the expense of such balancing themes as love, kindness, empathy, courage, faith, and justice. There is more to the Grimms' tale "Star Coins" than the "virtue of misery and suffering" that is rewarded with "cold hard cash" (43).

Wilhelm Grimm emphasizes the complementary nature of the mythical forces in folktales, which include darkness as well as light, evil as well as goodness and its reconciling powers. Bruno Bettelheim, too, points to the consolation in folktales that permit the triumph of good over evil (9); Max Lüthi praises their sublimating qualities that transform reality (15, 93); and Italo Calvino considers the "realistic" aspects of folktales merely "a sort of springboard into wonderland, a foil for the regal and the supernatural" (xxxii). He suggests that the themes of love and kindness have a tendency to be associated with the "wondrous," even when closely allied with morality (xxx). Granted, there are many ways of interpreting folktales, but a little more attention to their mythical, symbolic, aesthetic, and poetic qualities may leave the reader less puzzled at what Tatar presents as their cruel and paradoxical nature.

"No fairy tale is sacred" (229), Tatar concludes, urging creative writers and storytellers to create their own new versions of the tales. This call for creativity emerges logically from her reference to Carolyn G. Heilbrun's concept of the challenge "to produce fictions" (230) and Stanley Fish's concept of reading as an active process that engages the reader in constructing the text (xvi, 239n). Such an invitation appeals to a sense of freedom while taking into account the possible needs of individual children, as well as showing a sensitivity to issues of race and gender.

Tatar argues that the very existence of variants justifies an "inventive" approach to the subject, for storytelling consists of "unceasing negotiations between the creative consciousness of individuals and the collective sociocultural constructs available to them" (230). Yet are "cultural stories" in that sense identical with traditional folktales? Folklorists might question such an assumption, even though the dividing line between folktale and fantasy has often been the subject of debate. The Grimms might agree with Tatar that a fixed *"Urmärchen"* does not exist, for they thought that storytellers were inspired by a "pendulum movement" between the "substance" of tradition (also called the "core" or "spirit") and their own sense of improvisation. Yet unlike Tatar, the Grimms emphasized the need for responsibility to the spirit of tradition and consistently rejected stories that appeared made up or invented.

At what point do folktales cease to be folktales and assume the form of fantasies or satires? How far can we go without investing them with a new form of didacticism—even if only in the interest of promoting a bias-free society? Tatar does not answer such questions, yet they will remain with us for some time to come.

Tatar's analysis would be helped by a differentiation between children's books that explicitly spell out moralities and others that merely imply them, such as Gillian Avery's historical studies of "fairy tales with a purpose" and "fairy tales for pleasure." Especially welcome would be a clearer distinction among various types of folktale collections, for, in spite of some flaws, the Grimms' collection was conceived as a more serious, scholarly endeavor than those of Benjamin Tabart or George Cruikshank, for example, who both willfully used (and abused) folktales for the sake of promoting moral messages or social propaganda. The assumption that all collectors impose their own biases on the tales is no justification for ignoring existing scholarship on great variations in quality, style, and intent in the tales by Ludwig Bechstein, Achim von Arnim, or Albert Ludwig Grimm (who, as Tatar notes, was not a relative of the Brothers Grimm).

Like the Brothers Grimm themselves, Tatar advises scholars to consult folktale variants from different collections and cultures before analyzing a single folktale theme all by itself. The Grimms spent a lifetime exploring the interconnections among folktale variants from many lands, searching, like Johann Gottfried Herder before them, for common themes reflecting the Naturpoesie of humankind. Yet Tatar does not use the Grimms' comparative notes systematically and sometimes only selectively to drive home sociocultural and feminist theories. On the whole, however, Tatar's broadly conceived study will undoubtedly challenge readers to reexamine some historical children's books and European folktale variants across time and space. The detailed chapter notes, inclusive bibliography, and thorough index are valuable aids to the researcher.

Works Cited

Avery, Gillian. *Nineteenth Century Children: Heroes and Heroines in English Children's Stories 1780–1900*. London: Hodder and Stoughton, 1965.
Bettelheim, Bruno. *The Uses of Enchantment: The Meaning and Importance of Fairy Tales*. New York: Random House, 1977.

Calvino, Italo, comp. *Italian Folktales.* Trans. George Martin. New York: Harcourt Brace Jovanovich, 1980.

Grimm, Jacob, and Wilhelm Grimm. *Kinder- und Hausmärchen.* 2nd ed. 3 vols. Berlin: Reimer, 1919–22.

Grimm, Wilhelm. *Dear Mili.* Trans. Ralph Manheim; illus. Maurice Sendak. New York: Farrar, Straus and Giroux, 1988.

Hoffmann, Heinrich. *Der Struwwelpeter.* Frankfurt: Volksausgabe, [ca. 1845].

Janeway, James. *A Token for Children: Being an Exact Account of the Conversion, Holy and Exemplary Lives, and Joyful Deaths of Several Young Children.* London: Frances Westley, 1825.

Kamenetsky, Christa. *The Brothers Grimm and Their Critics: Folktales and the Quest for Meaning.* Athens: Ohio University Press, 1992.

Lüthi, Max. *Once upon a Time: On the Nature of Fairy Tales.* Trans. Lee Chadeayne and Paul Gottwald. Bloomington: Indiana University Press, 1976.

Interrupting the Critical Line from Rationalism to Romanticism

Lissa Paul

Romanticism and Children's Literature in Nineteenth-Century England,
edited by James Holt McGavran, Jr. Athens: University of Georgia Press, 1991.

The best essay in *Romanticism and Children's Literature in Nineteenth-Century England,* a collection edited by James Holt McGavran, Jr., is "Romancing the Moral Tale: Maria Edgeworth and the Problematics of Pedagogy" by Mitzi Myers. With a brilliant mix of scholarly breadth and compassionate, critical insight Myers illuminates a world that is usually opaque, even to children's literature specialists. Although the essay appears in the middle of the book, I am situating it at the beginning of the review, not just because the essay is an exemplary work of criticism, but because it offers a glimpse of what the collection might have been.

With the provocative collision of romancing, moral tale, and pedagogy in the title, Myers interrupts the traditional straight and narrow line from rationalism to romance. She questions beliefs received from Harvey Darton (and often parroted by children's literature scholars) that didactic tales are undifferentiated, boring aggregates and not up to the original art of the romantic writers. Through her analysis of Maria Edgeworth's *Simple Susan* as a "nurturing fantasy masquerading as rational moral tale" (111), Myers demonstrates how to read moral tales against the grain and so release forgotten "maternal pedagogies" and a "plurality of meanings." She shows how to open up relations "between nurturance and autonomy, connectedness and individuation, child and parent, dependence and dominance, feeling and reason, and, finally, between experience and the discursive practices that configure or constitute it" (98).

When Myers explains how late twentieth-century poststructuralist criticism destabilizes the privileging of nineteenth-century romanticism over eighteenth-century rationalism, she is explaining

Children's Literature 22, ed. Francelia Butler, R. H. W. Dillard, and Elizabeth Lennox Keyser (Yale University Press, © 1994 Hollins College).

how we can revise our assumptions about the period—and so discover readings unlike the ones we knew. Myers is joined in this endeavor by other contributors to the book, particularly Jeanie Watson, Alan Richardson, Patricia Demers, Michael Hancher, Phyllis Bixler, and Anita Moss. All write about un(dis)covering received ideological assumptions—and that, it seems to me, is a good reason for assembling a collection of critical essays about romanticism and children's literature in nineteenth-century England. To demonstrate what I think is best about the collection, I will focus first on the critical lines in essays by Richardson, Bixler, and Hancher. With those examples up front, my difficulties with the collection as a whole will be easier to explain.

In "Wordsworth, Fairy Tales, and the Politics of Children's Reading," Alan Richardson uses a New Historicist approach to explore how the didactic writers of the early nineteenth century did not so much censor the fairy tale as appropriate it. He reveals the blurring of genre distinctions. Like Myers, Richardson shows that the boundaries between the fairy tale and the didactic story are not as clear as they have been assumed to be. And that contention opens up a radical new project for children's literature criticism. He suggests a possible direction: "Rather than maintain a simplistic opposition between didacticism and fantasy, indoctrination and a negative 'natural' education—a model inherited from the Romantics themselves—critical studies might profitably develop more complex approaches attuned to the intricate politics of literacy and education in the Romantic period" (49).

In the same spirit of redefining relations between rationalism and romanticism, Phyllis Bixler uses the insights of feminist theory to focus on the community of mothers in *The Secret Garden*. She reads beyond the subjugation of Mary within the story and extrapolates why Mary continues to be celebrated by female readers despite the way she apparently recedes into the background of the narrative. Bixler reads the feminist "webs of symbolic imagery"—especially the house and garden—as "a celebration of nature's power, . . . a primarily female power" (209). To use the terms of "ecriture feminine," Bixler "thinks through the body" in order to reveal a feminist reading of "the maternal body" in *The Secret Garden*.

Another essay that awakens alternative interpretive strategies for reading nineteenth-century children's literature is "Alice's Audiences." Michael Hancher takes the old problem of trying to figure out whether or not the Alice stories are for children and puts a new spin on it. He changes the question by pointing out that the audiences for the Alice stories were unstable from the beginning. The stories, after all, were oral tales told by Charles Lutwidge Dodgson that moved through a network of private friends, through the privileged mediation of John Tenniel, then through other languages, nursery versions, and a range of dramatic versions. The revelation of the instability of child-adult oppositions—like instability in didactic-imaginative oppositions—is part of current critical practice and part, I think, of a larger postmodern project, one that shifts away from the authoritative desires of formalist critical enterprises. When Hancher says that *Alice* "is a happily overdetermined and polymorphous text" thriving "in an indefinite number of forms" (202), he is aligning himself with a sensibility that celebrates multiplicity, diversity, and instability. That postmodern sensibility permeates the best essays in the collection—and brings me to my problem with the others.

The essays in the collection that had me riveted to the texts are about rereading nineteenth-century children's literature against the grain of conventional binary oppositions between rationalism and romanticism. Alan Richardson, Mitzi Myers, Patricia Demers, Judith Plotz, Michael Hancher, Phyllis Bixler, and Anita Moss all write in the poststructuralist idiom that celebrates uncertainty and instability and questions the gaps between what is said and what is meant. Some essays in the collection, however, are written in an authoritative idiom that jars in tone and content against the others. All are well researched and documented. All are scholarly. But in the context of the poststructuralist essays their authority looks suspect. Here is an example. In "The Idiot Boy as Healer," Ross Woodman says that he is going "to explore the poem ["The Idiot Boy"] as Wordsworth's most joyous account of . . . a healing nature bathed in maternal love under the rule of an eternal child that constitutes Wordsworth's naturalized world of faery, the proper domain of children's literature" (73). In the light of surrounding essays—Richardson's "Politics of Reading"—"eternal" children and the "naturalized world of faery" are suspect terms. Like Richardson, I am more curious about "our own investment in the Romantic idealization of childhood and its fairy tales" (49).

Although collected essays are bound (literally and figuratively) to set up conversations with each other, what I miss here is an editorial rationale for the collection. The title, *Romanticism and Children's Literature in Nineteenth-Century England,* does not offer enough clues about the content. And all that McGavran offers in the introduction to "orient the reader to the perspectives of the writers of this collection" is this: "The first five essays (by Jeanie Watson, Alan Richardson, James McGavran, Ross Woodman, and Mitzi Myers) focus on writings of the Romantic Period; and the remaining six (by Patricia Demers, Roderick McGillis, Judith Plotz, Michael Hancher, Phyllis Bixler, and Anita Moss) explore Victorian literature and document further development and complication of the Romantic conflict over childhood" (5). That is not enough of a rationale for the book—even though McGavran does go on a bit about the essays in slightly more depth later. Besides, judging from the essays by Myers and Richardson especially, it is not simply the romantic conflict over childhood that is at issue but our understanding of it as it pertains to our views on romanticism, rationalism, children, education, the moral tale, and the fairy tale—to name just a few.

While musing on the problems of assembling collections of essays, I thought about the perils of peritextual clues. The dust jacket of *Romanticism and Children's Literature in Nineteenth-Century England* is dark pink and put me in mind of two pink-covered collections of essays I like very much: *Writing and Sexual Difference,* edited by Elizabeth Abel (University of Chicago Press, 1982), and *The Poetics of Gender,* edited by Nancy K. Miller (Columbia University Press, 1986). And it put me in mind of a very funny essay, "Annie Leclerc Writing a Letter, with Vermeer," by Jane Gallop (included in *The Poetics of Gender*), in which Gallop plays on the pink cover of *Writing and Sexual Difference:* "Pink then becomes THE color of sexual difference, carrying alone within it the diacritical distinction pink/ blue" (138–39). In Gallop's comment about relations between color coding and gender coding—even when applied to the color of academic books—I begin to understand my unease with McGavran's collection. To maintain good relations with the authoritative (blue) readings of people like Woodman, McGavran politely holds back from embracing the radical (pink) readings in the essays by Myers and Richardson. So his collection lacks the radical sense of purpose that I find so attractive in both *Writing and Sexual Difference* and *The Poetics of Gender.* The editors of both books are explicit about their intention to disrupt the status quo and rethink interpretive strategies. McGavran is not.

As I wrote this review, the book sat next to my computer available for reference. I kept glancing at the cover illustration by Arthur Hughes (from *At the Back of the North Wind*) of North Wind, floating, prone, her hair flowing invitingly around her. I wished the cover designer had juxtaposed it with one of Sendak's illustrations of Ida from *Outside over There,* the one where she is floating in her yellow raincoat. Then the two similarly posed nineteenth-century and twentieth-century mothering figures could have communed with each other on the cover. They might even have communed with McGavran himself, who hints at the very end of his introduction that there are evocative relations between nineteenth-century and twentieth-century children's literature. McGavran alludes to Sendak (as well as Philippa Pearce and Virginia Hamilton) as authors "who continue to be haunted by, and thus to redefine, the Romantic figure of the child" (11). I would have liked the collection better had it contained more haunting and redefining. But there is enough, especially in the essays by Myers and Richardson, to make the collection worth having anyway.

Victorian Fantasy Fiction Is No Longer Just for the Childlike

Glenn Edward Sadler

Victorian Fantasy Literature: Literary Battles with Church and Empire, by Karen Michalson. Vol. 10 of *Studies in British Literature.* Queenston, Ont., and Lewiston, N.Y.: Edwin Mellen Press, 1990.

For the Childlike: George MacDonald's Fantasies for Children, edited by Roderick McGillis. Metuchen, N.J.: Children's Literature Association and Scarecrow Press, 1992.

The fantasy fiction of Victorian authors has yet to receive the critical attention that it deserves. Even though it continues to be popular with the general reader, it is either neglected by critics or relegated to the Tolkienian nursery. Both Karen Michalson's historical study *Victorian Fantasy Literature* and Roderick McGillis's collection of essays *For the Childlike: George MacDonald's Fantasies for Children* are attempts to rectify this situation.

Michalson's study is in some ways informative and offers a perceptive treatment of the literary rejection of nineteenth-century fantasy fiction, but the book is tedious to read because of its thesis-like style and weak organization. It is an odd mixture of historical literary criticism, fictionalized biographical sketches, which are sometimes irritating, and scattered comments on individual authors and their works. The book consists of nine chapters. Three (not grouped together) trace the reasons for the historical rejection of fantasy fiction, and five treat representative authors and works: John Ruskin and *The King of the Golden River;* George MacDonald and *Phantastes;* Charles Kingsley and *The Water Babies;* Henry Rider Haggard and *She;* and Kipling and *The Jungle Books* and *Puck of Pook's Hill.*

As Michalson points out, why "fantasy fiction" has received less critical acceptance than the "realistic novel" is an interesting question: "The bias in favor of realism in the formation of the traditional canon of nineteenth-century British fiction" can be traced to "non-literary and non-aesthetic reasons" (i). Apparently, "both Church

Children's Literature 22, ed. Francelia Butler, R. H. W. Dillard, and Elizabeth Lennox Keyser (Yale University Press, © 1994 Hollins College).

and Empire needed a canon of realism to promote their own brand of conservative ideology" (ii). Educational institutions and reviewers of the period (including Samuel Taylor Coleridge) helped in the literary battles against the acceptance of fantasy fiction, which Church and Empire considered a threat to the status quo. Fantasy was equated with irrationality and opposition to dogma. "To say that a work or idea was 'fantastic' was to dismiss it as unrealistic and therefore as unworthy of the time or consideration of a truly rational, scientific, progressive inheritor of the Enlightenment" (2). The subjects of fantasy fiction—fairies, magical beings, and occurrences of the impossible—further argued against its acceptance and made such works an easy target for ridicule. Michalson suggests that Coleridge's theoretical separation of Imagination and Fancy, making Fancy a secondary faculty, contributed to the destruction of fantasy as an art form. According to Owen Barfield, however, the author of *What Coleridge Thought,* Coleridge did not consider Fancy to be intellectually inferior and gave it "an honorable status, in 'the world of intelligences with the whole system of their representations'" (Barfield 85). In his own works Coleridge elevated the fantastic and the supernatural, but other reviewers of the period, like "the hanging judge," Lord Jeffrey, disapproved strongly of the irrational or "the fantastic" and condemned Wordsworth's poetry. As Michalson notes of Wordsworth's poem "Strange Fits of Passion Have I Known," the speaker is quite ordinary and the situation representational of real life (5).

The historical rejection of fantasy is linked by Michalson to "the realism bias of evangelicism" and "was picked up and sustained by educational institutions in the later part of the century" (36). I cannot help but wonder how much influence Evangelical Christianity had in shaping public opinion and the canon. Possibly the audience—such works of fantasy were ostensibly meant to be read by women and children—had as much, if not more, to do with the rejection of fantasy as an art form.[1]

Certainly the classic triad of Victorian fantasy fiction—John Ruskin, George MacDonald, and Charles Kingsley—shared a common interest, as Michalson notes, not only in creating new myths or subverting established ones but in offering in their fiction an imaginative alternative to Evangelical Christian dogmas. Ruskin's *King of the Golden River* is, according to Michalson, "the only example of an evangelical fairy tale in Victorian English literature" (43). It has

been neglected by critics because "the tale subverts two antithetical genres, the fantasy oriented fairy tale and the evangelical moral
tale, by combining them" (44). The tale "is a myth that offers redemption . . . not through faith, the central doctrine of Evangelism,
but through human acts of goodness" (59). But Ruskin is not unique
in his subversive use of the fairy tale: MacDonald also created his
own anti-Victorian myth in *Phantastes* and *Lilith,* in which there are
the recurring themes of self-denial and opposition to established
religious dogmas. Both MacDonald and Kingsley shared a dislike
for "dogmatic forms of Christianity" (116), and in *The Water Babies*
Tom is a threat (like Anodos in *Phantastes*) "to any kind of Christian
hierarchical organization because he knows what he wants without
reference to doctrine" (117).

Michalson draws heavily in her study of these authors on her
own imaginative re-creation of biographical facts, making critical
assumptions that at times seem farfetched, for example, that the
"personal life of George MacDonald in many ways resembled that
of Jesus Christ" (61). Her conclusions, however, are valid and suggest convincingly that "the history of nineteenth-century fantasy
literature is one of literary challenges to culturally and socially entrenched belief systems" (259).

Like Michalson, Roderick McGillis explores the unique aesthetic
power of fantasy fiction to delight and instruct readers of all ages.
There recurs throughout the fifteen essays in this collection the
well-established central idea that MacDonald's fantasies have a two-
dimensional appeal. As Stephen Prickett says in his essay, "The
Two Worlds of George MacDonald," "His work is both didactic and
symbolic, clear and puzzling, realistic and fantastic. . . . Such oppositions suggest MacDonald's Dialectic method" (2). Prickett defines
this dualism as consisting of "two worlds, co-existing in time and
space, superimposed upon one another," and it is "one of the most
persistent themes of George MacDonald's fantasy writing" (17).
Michael Mendelson claims that "no one employs as fully or as effectively as MacDonald the fundamental elements of this very ancient
genre" of the fairy tale (45). In defense of the so-called structure-
less narrative in MacDonald's *Phantastes,* McGillis traces in it the
theme of "the community of the center" (63), or an "inward and
outward" movement "at the same time," and reminds "us that at the
center we find the cosmos."

As interesting as these approaches to MacDonald may be, there

is not much originality here. Earlier critics of MacDonald, starting
with his own contemporaries, have made some of the same observations. Throughout the essays several well-known ideas are repeated,
such as C. S. Lewis's famous description of MacDonald as a maker
of myth (Frank Riga 112) and Louis MacNeice's often quoted comment that he is a master of the parable form (Cynthia Marshall
104; Roderick McGillis 149; Melba N. Battin 208–9, 217). In "The
Golden Key," a fantasy-parable not often read by children, Cynthia
Marshall detects in the "Narrative Strategies" of the fantasy "difficulties" with the tale in terms of a "feminist response." Marshall's
"chief concern is whether Mossy's having the key and Tangle's not
having it can be called thematically meaningful" (100)—a point
about the story that seems inconsequential. She suggests that the
"tale's theology" has its source in the gospel of Matthew (20:1–
16) and attempts to explain "how MacDonald's symbolic structure
mystifies, and occasionally alienates, readers" (101). What Marshall
seems to overlook is that MacDonald intentionally used ambiguous
symbolism in order to prevent the reader from taking an allegorical
approach to the meaning of the tale.

Although this volume of essays offers occasional insights into
MacDonald's imaginative process as a writer of fantasy, the contributors rely too heavily on ideas expressed by earlier critics of
MacDonald's work—C. S. Lewis, Robert Lee Wolff, Richard Reis—
and are reluctant to formulate new approaches to his work. (William
Raeper's essay, "MacDonald, Hogg, and the Scottish Folk Tradition," is an exception and offers the kind of fresh approach to
MacDonald that is needed.) But for all the repetition of ideas, *For
the Childlike* is an interesting and occasionally informative summary
of critical approaches to MacDonald's fantasy fiction by those who
admire it.

Note

1. See *Forbidden Journeys: Fairy Tales and Fantasies by Victorian Women Writers*, ed.
Nina Auerbach and U. C. Knoepflmacher (Chicago: University of Chicago Press,
1992). This revealing collection of fantasy writings by women writers demonstrates
the significant role of women in the creation of fantasy works during the period and
that such works were in public opinion often identified with women and children.

Work Cited

Barfield, Owen. *What Coleridge Thought*. Middletown, Conn.: Wesleyan University
    Press, 1971.

Dissertations of Note

Compiled and Annotated by Rachel Fordyce

Alderman, Belle Yarbrough. "Setting in Australian Children's Novels." D.L.S. diss. Columbia University, 1984. 365 pp. DAI 45:3128A.

Alderman examines settings in children's novels by major and minor Australian authors to determine the extent to which locale reflects an Australian ethos and the biography of the author who writes about it. She focuses specifically on five patterns in the novels: "setting as a way of life," where "life in a particular locale or . . . cultural or historical milieu" is described; setting as a control over life; setting "as a catalyst of character change . . . usually through an environmental catastrophe"; setting as a metaphoric expression of the relation between people and place; and setting as mythology and tradition, where "traditions and myths concerning the environment" are explored. She finds that the novels reinforce traditional images of Australians and the bush country and stress courage, moral strength, endurance, and love for the land. Moreover, "rural life is viewed as offering a physical and spiritual salvation" not associated with "civilization."

Almerico, Gina Marjorie. "The Portrayal of Older Characters in Children's Magazines." Ph.D. diss. University of Florida, 1987. 149 pp. DAI 48:2030A.

In a content analysis of eleven children's magazines published in 1985 Almerico appraises the image of the elderly and concludes that they are barely represented in terms of numbers, gender, "ethnic/racial composition, financial status, living arrangement, marital status, and occupational status." Nor are they represented in their multiplicity of interests or abilities. Those older people who do appear are generally portrayed in positive roles, but they are also depicted as bland, neutral, uninvolved, or uninteresting. Though not "victims of blatant discrimination," they are condemned to banality and insipidity.

Aspatore, Jilleen Valentine. "The Military-Patriotic Theme in Soviet Textbooks and Children's Literature." 2 vols. Ph.D. diss. Georgetown University, 1986. 523 pp. DAI 48:1466A.

Aspatore emphasizes the "seriousness with which Soviet authorities approach the military-patriotic program" in the Soviet educational system, in children's literature, and among children's presses. She examines the methods used to inculcate a hatred of class and a "willingness to defend the homeland" and finds them generally effective as of 1986. Primary themes are "love of homeland, the Party and youth organizations, Lenin, the Revolution and Civil War, The Great Patriotic War, internationalism (the Soviet View of the world order), and the Soviet Army today," although Aspatore does note numerous articles by Soviet authorities acknowledging some unrest among young people.

Bagnall, Norma Hayes. "Children's Literature in Texas: A History and Evaluation." Ph.D. diss. Texas A & M University, 1984. 162 pp. DAI 45:2873A.

Bagnall traces literature for children set in Texas from its inception in 1855 through 1980 and evaluates its "literary, historical, and cultural importance" as regional and national literature. The dissertation is in two parts and contains an analysis and an annotated bibliography of the more than two hundred books that she discovered. Bagnall notes that the majority of the works analyzed have a rural setting, are historical in nature, have "Anglo protagonists," and, perhaps

Children's Literature 22, ed. Francelia Butler, R. H. W. Dillard, and Elizabeth Lennox Keyser (Yale University Press, © 1994 Hollins College).

most important, are "overwhelmingly ordinary," although some books of real merit exist.

Bevan, Ellen Sternberg. "Family Matters: The Fiction of Hawthorne, Alcott, and James." Ph.D. diss. University of Rochester, 1991. 409 pp. DAI 52:1326A.

The second chapter of Bevan's dissertation treats Alcott's "idealized domestic relations—families learning to conform to a set of internalized cultural relations—undercut by a subversive strand in the adult novels and the thrillers which suggests a feminist view of family relations." Bevan also compares Alcott favorably with James and Hawthorne in her ability to analyze the tautness and unease of nineteenth-century family relationships and struggles. She concludes that "the family ideal is implicit in each writer; the attainment of family harmony and security remains, however, an ideal, rather than an attained actuality." This ideal merits analysis in relation to Alcott's novels for children.

Burgess, Virginia Aleine. "Portrayal of Alaskan Native Americans in Children's Literature." Ph.D. diss. University of South Carolina, 1990. 219 pp. DAI 51:2742–43A.

In an appraisal of the treatment of Aleuts, Eskimos, and Athabascan Indians in seventy contemporary books for children Burgess finds both negative stereotyping and positive portrayal. The former occurs most often in the form of "unrealistic illustrations or cultural generalizations," the latter when characters are portrayed as leaders who perform noteworthy acts. She concludes that Native American Alaskans are more realistically portrayed now than they were before 1970.

Butterworth, Harrison. "Motif-Index and Analysis of the Early Irish Hero Tales." Ph.D. diss. Yale University, 1956. 829 pp. DAI 52:158A.

Butterworth's motif-index is devoted primarily to Ulster sagas, excluding "The Cattle Raid of Cooley," and is significant for its study of values that ultimately emerge in Arthurian romances and Icelandic sagas, values that reoccur in children's literature derived, directly and loosely, from early Irish literature.

Carson, Shirley Anne. "The Effect of Thematic Fantasy Play upon Development of the Concept of Beginning, Middle, and End as First-Graders Write in Response to Literature." Ed.D. diss. University of Oklahoma, 1991. 214 pp. DAI 52:1237A.

The purpose of this dissertation is "to examine the effects of thematic fantasy play upon understanding of story structure, specifically, beginning, middle, and end." Carson read picture books to first-graders and analyzed their written responses to them. She also had students dramatize the stories to determine whether acting out stories "warrant[s] the extra time needed" to produce better understanding. The intrinsic value of reading to children and their ability to make oral and dramatic responses is a secondary concern here, although Carson found that dramatization allowed students to reconstruct stories without leaving out the middle of them. She concludes that dramatization is beneficial and requires "little time as to its effect."

Chatton, Barbara Ann. "Pastoralism and Pastoral Romance in Twentieth Century Children's Literature." Ph.D. diss. Ohio State University, 1982. 206 pp. DAI 43:2665–66A.

Chatton evaluates four basic types of pastoral literature for children: literature set on the American frontier, which is essentially agrarian; wilderness literature; pastoral romances, replete in rural settings, farm life, and past times; and novels devoted to sheep and shepherds. She is particularly concerned with how an "author's attitudes about childhood may influence pastoral writings" and notes two distinct ways in which the pastoral is used in award-winning books for children. Many of the novels have an ironic tone that emphasizes the simplicity of the rustic life as it comes in contact with "civilization." "Others take the form of pastoral romances reflecting a nostalgia for simpler times . . . and for the wisdom and innocence of children, but unfettered by the ironic sense of loss."

Corcoran, Marcia Largent. "Seventh-Graders' Literary Preferences and Responses to Literature in and out of the English Classroom." Ph.D. diss. University of California—Berkeley, 1990. 420 pp. DAI 52:1237–38A.

In this year-long study Corcoran tries to develop "a global view of students' literary preferences" and to describe the students' attitudes toward themselves as both readers and writers. For the most part she found responses distinctly idiosyncratic, dependent on students' personal views of self, previous involvement with literature at home and in school, and preferences as to subject matter, theme, and setting. She concludes with a plea for educators "to better understand the role of literature in the daily lives of students."

Deschene, James Michael. "Joy in a Minor Key: The Mystery of Gender and Sex in the Thought of C. S. Lewis." Ph.D. diss. University of Rhode Island, 1991. 239 pp. DAI 52:545–46A.

Deschene is interested in the perception that Lewis contributed to "sexism and gender prejudice and oppos[ed] those values held by modern egalitarian and feminist thought," particularly in his adult fictional and nonfictional writing. But he concludes that Lewis is "solidly egalitarian and opposed to all brands of domination of any person or party over any other." This view of Lewis as a writer fully capable of differentiating between fantasy and myth on one hand and raw human nature and reality on another invites a new look at Lewis's work for children.

Duncan, Ralph Randolph, II. "Panel Analysis: A Critical Method for Analyzing the Rhetoric of Comic Book Form." Ph.D. diss. Louisiana State University, 1990. 237 pp. DAI 51:3942A.

Duncan develops a methodology for analyzing comic strips and comic books. His "panel analysis focuses on how the unique form of the comic book medium communicates content." The three components, "historical context, micro analysis, and macro analysis," deal, respectively, with the artist's personal history; psychological, psychoanalytical, and semiological approaches to individual panels; and the way "montage, the combination of comic book panels, creates meaning and manipulates time."

Folkes, Karl Constantine. "An Analysis of Wilhelm Grimm's 'Dear Mili' Employing von Franzian Methodological Processes." Ph.D. diss. New York University, 1991. 311 pp. DAI 52:931–32A.

Folkes analyzes Grimm's recently discovered religious-miraculous fairy tale "Dear Mili," first published worldwide in 1988, and concludes that it is a member of Grimm's *Kinderlegenden* genre. He shows that "the child-heroine experienced the highest possible level of individuation through self-reliance . . . and through an incomparable capacity for faith, hope, and abiding love," even though these traits ultimately lead her to a redemption possible only through death. He concludes that the "child-heroine, unnamed in the tale, was the Holy Virgin Mary, the Lady of Miracles."

Frost, Linda Anne. "Thinking Language to Be a Body of Thought: Reading Ralph Waldo Emerson, Henry David Thoreau, Louisa May Alcott and Margaret Fuller Ossoli." Ph.D. diss. State University of New York—Stony Brook, 1990. 322 pp. DAI 52:1328–29A.

Of particular interest here is Frost's study of Alcott's *Little Women, Little Men,* and *Jo's Boys* "guided by the feminist revisions of Lacanian psychoanalytic theory proposed by Julia Kristeva and Margaret Homans." She concludes that Alcott "demonstrates the way in which the instruction of language perpetuates polarized conceptions of femininity and masculinity, further ensuring women's exclusion from a public and expressive power." On the other hand, Frost concludes that Fuller, Emerson, and Thoreau "give us a better understanding of the way in which patriarchal structures occur in language as well as the way these structures have served to further the critical glorification of American Transcendentalism itself."

Granzow, Thomas William. "Children's Universal Requirement for Exact Repetition of Stories: A Unique Type of Memory?" Ph.D. diss. Catholic University of America, 1990. 99 pp. DAI 51:3590B.

While acknowledging children's marked desire to have a story read or repeated exactly the same way each time it is read or told, Granzow also recognizes that few data exist to demonstrate or analyze this phenomenon even though "theoretical interpretations have ranged from themes of powerful memorization, joy in mastery, a need for regularity, and the pursuit of object constancy, to Piaget's reproductive assimilation, Freud's repetition compulsion, or the manifestations of a belief that stories are historical." Working with groups of four- and six-year-olds who were read stories unfamiliar to them, both in original and variant versions, Granzow found that a significant number of the children noted a deviation, although many did not respond because they "did not see fit to interrupt." While trying to shed light on what has been considered "infantile dogmatism," it appears that Granzow ran into politeness of a particular classroom variety. Further studies that duplicate "the real-life social situation of reader listeners" might be profitable.

Gremore, Constance Fritz. "Characteristics of Stage Adaptations of Works of Children's Literature." Ph.D. diss. University of Minnesota, 1984. 343 pp. DAI 45:2696A.

Gremore analyzes plays adapted from works for children and produced between 1890 and 1980, particularly in terms of their treatment of character, plot, theme, style, and dialogue. "Selected for inclusion are five versions of *Cinderella*, five of *Treasure Island*, four of *The Adventures of Pinocchio*, and four of *The Pied Piper of Hamelin*" because they exemplify "traditional literature, realistic fiction, imaginative or fanciful fiction and poetry." Given the lack of faithfulness in the reworking of the stories and the general vacuity and insipidity of the adaptations, it is no wonder that Gremore concludes that adaptation of narration to the stage "should be seriously reassessed and generally discouraged."

Heard, Doreen B. "A Production History of the New York City Children's Theatre Unit of the Federal Theatre Project, 1935–1939." Ph.D. diss. Florida State University, 1986. 465 pp. DAI 47:4237–38A.

Heard's history of the Children's Theatre Unit of the Federal Theatre Project of New York City from its beginnings in 1935 through 1939 is essentially uncritical, although she draws conclusions about "the educational and social values of the work . . . and the legacy left by the Unit to future generations of workers in children's theatre." She discusses festivals that were presented for children, as well as plays, and the study is assisted by a large body of material, including scripts, programs, and photographs, as well as audience surveys from the period.

Heflin, David Duane. "The Contribution of Carlota Carvallo's Short Stories to Peruvian Children's Literature." (La contribucion de la cuentistica de Carlota Carvallo a la literatura infantil peruana. In Spanish.) Ph.D. diss. Texas Tech University, 1991. 229 pp. DAI 52:1758A.

Given the richness of Peruvian folklore, both that which survived the Spanish conquest and that enhanced by the comingling of cultures, we would expect its characters and themes to pervade the children's literature; but according to Heflin, the two traditions remain separate. A notable exception is in the work of the Peruvian painter Carlota Carvallo, who, concerned with the paucity of literature to read to her own children, began a writing career that has won her national and international repute; she was the single impetus for promoting indigenous folkloric literature for children in Peru. Heflin notes that Carvallo's short stories can be categorized into two main groups, "those based on Peruvian folklore and those from her own creative genius," both of which "contributed to the preservation of native folklore, and accomplished her goal of establishing a truly indigenous children's literature in Peru."

Hill, Elizabeth Frances. "A Comparative Study of the Cultural, Narrative, and Language Content of Selected Folk Tales Told in Burma, Canada, and Yorubaland." Ph.D. diss. University of Alberta, 1990. N.p. DAI 51:2482A.

Hill develops a method to help teachers of English as a Second Language to assess the potential of folktales to enhance "cross-cultural understanding." She analyzes characterization, setting, plot, narration, and language in Burmese, Euro-Canadian, and Yoruban folktales and concludes that "the tales must be supplemented with ethnographic resources" if they are to be useful. Even though many of the tales show strong similarities in values, "major differences in world view surface in the portrayals of gender, age, and nature."

Hood, Gwenyth Elise. "The Lidless Eye and the Long Burden: The Struggle Between Good and Evil in Tolkien's *The Lord of the Rings*." Ph.D. diss. University of Michigan, 1984. 232 pp. DAI 45:3645A.

Hood uses Tolkien's own critical ideas to analyze his trilogy and the struggle between good (a vision of harmony and earthly paradise) and evil (a vision of domination), exemplified by the ring and by the lidless eye through which Sauron makes "telepathic attacks on the imagination." She is concerned with Tolkien's depiction of the limits of free will and concludes that he believed in "a beneficent Providence at work which knows the difference between free choice and apparent choice and which brings good out of both good and evil actions."

Hurst, Mary Jane Gaines. "The Voice of the Child in American Literature: Linguistic Approaches to Fictional Child Language." Ph.D. diss. University of Maryland—College Park, 1986. 374 pp. DAI 47:2158A.

Hurst applies "linguistic information drawn from child language acquisition research" to the direct discourse of selected fictional juveniles," basing her study on works primarily intended for an adult audience (*The Scarlet Letter, The Turn of the Screw, Grapes of Wrath, Lolita, Call It Sleep*). Although her approach has not been informed by the study of children's literature, it might yield interesting results if applied, for instance, to the Alice books. Hurst concludes that an "author's gender seems to influence the portrayal of sexual differences in characters' language [and that] most American writers have depicted children and their speech in insightful life-like ways."

James, Michael E. "Teaching the American Myth: Children's Presidential Biography and the Development of the American Character." Ph.D. diss. Claremont Graduate School, 1987. 210 pp. DAI 49:1360A.

James believes that "children's biography is an oft-maligned genre. Criticism outdistances applause, and, if one believes the majority of reviewers and critics, for all the right reasons." Preeminent among its faults is the authors' willingness to distort facts and sublimate any weakness of character in an attempt to produce hero worship. Put in the kindest terms, James finds that American presidential biography for children is "mythology" and that the "folktales" created by the authors are best "interpreted through a unique model of human development that uses Carl Jung's theories of myth and psyche" to analyze both their "moral didacticism" and the unconscious "projections of our collective identity."

Kennedy, Anne Margaret. "Louisa May Alcott: Culture, Family, Fiction." Ph.D. diss. Bowling Green State University, 1990. 149 pp. DAI 52:972A.

Kennedy's purpose in this American Studies dissertation is "to explore the connections between 'how to' books and home/parenting manuals in the nineteenth century; the history and function of the Alcott family; and Louisa May Alcott's domestic fiction: The March Family Trilogy." Kennedy concludes that there are more similarities than differences between the Alcotts and the Marches; that the Alcotts are not especially strange in the light of nineteenth-century doctrine; and that the March family, like the Alcotts, "actually adhered to restrictive and claustrophobic ideas of the time."

Kerek, Yvonne. "Changing Family Structure and Teen Attitudes/Behaviors as Reflected in Selected Works of Adolescent Literature, 1950–1955 to 1980–1985." Ph.D. diss. Miami University, 1991. 170 pp. DAI 52:1239–40A.

Kerek studies twenty-four novels published between the early 1950s and the early 1980s to determine "changes in family structure and in social attitudes and behaviors related to sexuality, unwanted teen pregnancy, use of controlled substances, teen suicide, and use of strong and/or taboo language." Predictably she finds dramatic differences over time: the dissolution of the fictional portrayal of a nuclear family; a "shifting toward harsher, more severe, less socially constrained manifestations"; unconstrained language. She believes that literature in the 1980s gives "a realistic portrayal of the profound social changes in American society."

Klein, Jeanne Marie. "Fifth-Grade Children's Processing of Explicit and Implied Features of Live Theatre as a Function of Verbal and Visual Recall." Ph.D. diss. University of Kansas, 1987. 209 pp. DAI 49:1966B.

In her dissertation in developmental psychology Klein studies the differences between watching live theater and live television and their effects on perception and learning. She concludes that the majority of fifth-graders studied "preferred theatre over television primarily for its live values" and for their stronger sympathy or empathy with characters. But they also preferred the comfort of watching television at home and the ability to manipulate a television set over sitting in a theater.

Kuivasmaki, Riitta. "A Chaste Mind with a Noble Longing for Beauty: Finnish-Language Children's Literature, 1851–1899." (Siwollisuuden tuntoa ja ylewata kauneuden mielta: Suomenkielinen nuorisokirjallisuus, 1851–1899. In Finnish.) Dr.Phil. diss. University of Jyvaskyla, 1990. 259 pp. 52:307C. [Not available from University Microfilms.]

Kuivasmaki offers a literary and sociological analysis of Finnish children's literature written between 1851 and 1899, noting that prior to 1859 only 101 works for children had appeared in Finnish and Swedish and that the impetus for the development of a major children's literature is attributable to Finnomania, the work of J. V. Snellman, and the concept of "public enlightenment." The preeminent types of children's literature during this period are folk and fairy tales, poetry, songbooks and, in later years, the novel—all of which were intended "to adapt . . . youth to the Christian and patriotic cultural ideology of the time and at the same time to introduce Finland among the civilized nations."

Kuivila, Janet Leigh Hoebing. "Children of Schizophrenics—Using Bibliotherapy in Their Treatment." Ph.D. diss. Union Institute, 1990. 88 pp. DAI 51:3570B.

Kuivila's dissertation in clinical psychology focuses on children with a schizophrenic parent and the interventional benefits of books and bibliotherapy, with or without a trained therapist, to their ability to cope. She includes "a comprehensive annotated bibliography of books currently available to young children which deal with emotional issues" and, because no such literature exists for very young children, the text of her original work entitled "The Cat with the Crazy Mom."

Lake, Claudette. "Young Adult Literature and Kenneth Burke." Ph.D. diss. University of Oklahoma, 1991. 220 pp. DAI 52:2132A.

Lake applies Burke's rhetorical theory of motivation to young adult literature to elucidate coming-of-age situations and rites of passage from childhood to adulthood, and Twain's *Huckleberry Finn*. She sees literature as "an active participant in history, human development, [other] literature, and sociology" and "suggests that Young Adult Literature can function in a multiplicity of actions that range across disciplines and over cultural trends."

Lehman, Barbara A. "Children's Choice and Critical Acclaim in Literature for Children." Ed.D. diss. University of Virginia, 1986. 287 pp. DAI 48:1137A.

Lehman looks at books written between 1975 and 1985 that have either won or been runner-up for the Newbery Medal, the Horn Book Award, Children's Choice, and other literary awards to determine the differences and similarities between child and adult preferences. Differences "were more marked for characteristics of style and structure, while themes showed considerable similarity." Specifically, children preferred books that exemplify "an optimistic tone, a lively pace, and complete resolution."

Lindvag, Anita Lydia. "Elsa Olenius and Var Theatre." (Elsa Olenius och Var Teater. In Swedish.) Fil.Dr. diss. Lunds University (Sweden), 1988. 286 pp. DAI 49:525C.

Lindvag provides a history of the Var Theatre, established in the children's library of the Civic Hall in Stockholm in 1942, and characterizes Elsa Olenius as a forerunner in creative dramatics because she pioneered storytelling and dramatic reenactment of literature both in a library setting and during book reviews and discussions. "Points of contact are demonstrated between her views on the importance of children's self-activity and the progressive educational ideas of the 1930s and 40s."

Nelson, Craig Allen. "A Content Analysis of Female and Male Authors' Portrayals of Sex Roles in Science Fiction for Children from 1970 to 1990." Ph.D. diss. University of Minnesota, 1991. 236 pp. DAI 52:100A.

Nelson believes that "an underlying question" concerning sex roles in contemporary science fiction for children is "whether recent authors . . . have projected present societal structures into the future or if they have created new social and sex roles." He analyzes thirty-six books in terms of their depiction of age, sex, occupation, and social role and concludes that nothing has changed very much: female authors portray female protagonists more often than male authors do, although male characters prevail, as do male concepts of power and domination. "This implies the continuation of the stereotypical image of the power of the older, wiser man and the denial of the existence of the older, wiser woman," particularly because "female authors gave their female characters more masculine characteristics [but] were less willing than male authors to give feminine characteristics to their male characters."

Peddicord, Mary Hill. "Linguistic Stylistics and Children's Literature." Ph.D. diss. University of Southern Mississippi, 1980. 293 pp. DA 41:4700A.

Peddicord's goal is to determine "a visible and quantifiable means of assessing objectively what the sensitive reader intuitively recognizes as style." To do this she randomly selected sentences from fourteen Newbery Medal books and concludes that "the difference in complexity between literature for children and literature for adults lies not in the kinds but in the degree of complexity."

Rateliff, John D. " 'Beyond the Fields We Know': The Short Stories of Lord Dunsany." Ph.D. diss. Marquette University, 1990. 325 pp. DAI 52:2153A.

Rateliff's study, the first one based on the prolific work of Edward John

Moreton Drax Plunkett, Lord Dunsany (1878–1957), demonstrates that Dunsany was a pioneer of modern fantasy literature and an author who had considerable impact on Tolkien, among others.

Robinson, William Andrew. "The End of Happily Ever After: Variations on the Cinderella Theme in Musicals, 1960–1987." Ph.D. diss. Bowling Green State University, 1990. 318 pp. DAI 52:742A.

Robinson compares and contrasts the rags-to-riches Cinderella-like characters of musicals in the 1920s with the Cinderella heroines from 1960 through 1987 and concludes that "contemporary audiences reject traditional interpretations of the Cinderella myth. They are no longer satisfied with stereotypes and unrealistic plots." He does not address revivals.

Sarti, Ronald Christopher. "Man in a Mortal World: J. R. R. Tolkien and *The Lord of the Rings*." Ph.D. diss. Indiana University, 1984. 205 pp. DAI 45:1410A.

Sarti acknowledges Tolkien's aesthetic link to medieval literature and *Beowulf* through a theme of mortality—the concept that life is transitory. He shows how Tolkien works and reworks the theme through "change, choice, leave-taking and death," each of which deals with "the grim reality of a mortal world." But he further sees Tolkien's link with the past through two prevalent codes: Nordic and Christian. "The Nordic code is expressed in the values of despair, pride, vengeance and earthly fealty," which he contrasts with "the Christian values of hope, humility, mercy and fealty (or submission) to God and His Purpose." He believes that Tolkien resolves these warring concepts by vanquishing "the despair of death. Death itself is not to be despaired, for it is not a punishment, but a gift."

Smith, Karen Patricia. "The Keys to the Kingdom: From Didacticism to Dynamism in British Children's Fantasy, 1780–1979." Ed.D. diss. Columbia University Teachers College, 1982. 459 pp. DAI 43:3327–28A.

Smith identifies four major stages in the history of British fantasy literature: the Didactic (1780–1840), the Enlightenment (1841–99), the Diversionary (1900–1949), and the Dynamic (1950–79). Each stage is examined in terms of "character, plot, setting, mood, tone, point of view, language, and symbol." The primary authors are Dorothy Kilner, Sarah Trimmer, Lewis Carroll, Jean Ingelow, Mary Louisa Molesworth, Edith Nesbit, Enid Blyton, C. S. Lewis, Susan Cooper, and Alan Garner. "The literary elements analyzed against the backdrop of social and educational change in the four stages demonstrate the evolution of British fantasy from primarily an instructive form to one which embodied evidence of great imagination and creativity."

Stokes, Kathy Jo. "Children's Journey Stories as an Epic Subgenre." Ph.D. diss. University of Nebraska—Lincoln, 1988. 160 pp. DAI 50:131A.

Stokes compares six modern fantasies for children with *The Faerie Queene* and *The Pilgrim's Progress* in terms of plot, theme, characterization, language, general purpose, and underlying intent to teach. She concludes that "the epic tradition of didacticism in the works of centuries ago is brought gracefully into contemporary fiction."

Sullivan, Dale Lee. "A Rhetoric of Children's Literature as Epideictic Discourse." Ph.D. diss. Rensselaer Polytechnic Institute, 1988. 306 pp. DAI 49:3204A.

Sullivan believes that "children's literature can be seen as a modern genre that functions as epideictic rhetoric ('a form of rhetoric traditionally devoted to educating the young in orthodox values and reinforcing those values among adults'), and—as such—may be a powerful instrument for rebuilding our cultural life world." He applies his hypothesis specifically to C. S. Lewis's *Chronicles of Narnia*, a work intended "to combat A. J. Ayer's emotive theory of values [for] educating children in just sentiments and by introducing them to the Western literary heritage."

Vandell, Kathy Scales. "The Everlasting If: American National Identity in Children's Historical Fiction, 1865–1965." Ph.D. diss. University of Maryland—College Park, 1991. 584 pp. DAI 52:2186A.

In this American Studies dissertation Vandell examines historical fiction for children "as a mechanism of cultural transmission" of values associated with the national identity. She includes popular periodicals as well as books for children. The earliest works are characterized by "honesty, industry, loyalty, bravery, perseverance, sacrifice, duty, and obedience to (divinely appointed) leaders." Later definitions of national identity include "more political dissent, fairness, justice, responsibility, and negotiating solutions that accommodate all view-points." Two major changes are a shift from political to social history and "greater representational authenticity in children's books."

Weber, Carolyn Jefferson. "A Multidimensional Unfolding Model of Children's Preferences of Literary Style." Ed.D. Rutgers, the State University of New Jersey—New Brunswick, 1990. 259 pp. DAI 51:468A.

Weber believes that little research has been done on children's reading preferences, and she addresses the deficit by asking two questions: "What are the major literary dimensions affecting reading preferences? Are these dimensions gender-dependent?" She bases her study on Newbery Medal and Children's Choice books, notes some gender-based differences, and concludes that children like best what they understand, what they can feel comfortable about, and what is real.

Woods, Robert Michael. "Imagination, Religion, and Morality in the Shorter Imaginative Fiction of George MacDonald." Ph.D. diss. Florida State University, 1990. 166 pp. DAI 51:3070A.

Woods emphasizes the influence of MacDonald's moral and religious convictions on his more than fifty novels and works of shorter imaginative fiction with particular attention to "recurring images, ideas, archetypes, religious themes, moral issues, and symbols." He also traces MacDonald's influence on Lewis Carroll, C. S. Lewis, J. R. R. Tolkien, G. K. Chesterton, and T. S. Eliot.

Also of Note

The dissertations are not annotated if the title is sufficiently descriptive.

Anokye, Akua Duku. "Linguistic Form and Social Function: A Discourse Analysis of Rhetorical and Narrative Structure in Oral and Written African-American Folk Narrative Texts." Ph.D. diss. City University of New York, 1991. 238 pp. DAI 52:1729A.

Austern, Linda Phyllis. "Music in English Children's Drama, 1597–1613." Ph.D. diss. University of Chicago, 1984. N.p. DAI 45:2294A. [Not available from University Microfilms.]

Addresses Renaissance boys' companies and those players and dramatic poets who employed boy musicians in their plays.

Ayers, Margaret Rose. "An Exposition and Appraisal of C. S. Lewis and His Theology of Suffering: A Roman Catholic Perspective." Ph.D. diss. Duquesne University, 1991. 392 pp. DAI 52:1783A.

Backes, Nancy C. "An Adolescence of Their Own: Feminine Coming of Age in Contemporary American Literature." Ph.D. diss. University of Wisconsin—Milwaukee, 1990. 308 pp. DAI 52:536A.

Brady, Frank Robert. "Student Responses to Classic Novels and Their Television Adaptations." Ph.D. diss. New York University, 1991. 259 pp. DAI 52:1931A.

Challenger, Anna Terri. "An Introduction to Gurdjieff's *Beelzebub:* A Modern Sufi Teaching Tale." Ph.D. diss. Kent State University, 1990. 177 pp. DAI 51:3063A.

Elfant, Patricia Chiarelli. "The Cognitive and Metacognitive Strategies of First-Graders During a Shared Book Experience." Ph.D. diss. Fordham University, 1991. 246 pp. DAI 51:2328–29A.

Franko, Carol S. "The Productivity of Ambivalence: Dialogic Strategies in the Utopian Narratives of Wells, Huxley, Lessing, and Le Guin." Ph.D. diss. University of Wisconsin—Madison, 1990. 465 pp. DAI 51:3068A.

Gates, Spencer Charles Galpin. "Angry Young People: The Working-Class Adolescent in Contemporary English Drama as Portrayed in Selected Plays by Peter Terson, Barbie Keeffe, Nigel Williams, and Stephen Poliakoff." Ph.D. diss. New York University, 1990. 357 pp. DAI 51:2567–68A.

Granier, Douglas Mark. "The Effects of the Discussion of and the Drawing of Political Cartoons as Prewriting Activities to Increase Fifth- and Sixth-Graders' Ability to Write Persuasively." Ph.D. diss. Louisiana State University, 1990. 250 pp. DAI 51:4043–44A.

Halberstam, Judith Marion. "Parasites and Perverts: Anti-Semitism and Sexuality in Nineteenth Century Gothic Fiction." Ph.D. diss. University of Minnesota, 1991. 196 pp. DAI 52:2149A.

    Examines *Frankenstein, Dr. Jekyll and Mr. Hyde,* and *Dracula,* among other texts.

Harper, Marcia Mitchell. "The Literary Influence of Sir Edmund Gosse upon the Victorian Age." Ph.D. diss. Northern Illinois University, 1988. 347 pp. DAI 49:2229A.

    Significant for the discussion on the influence of Gosse on Robert Louis Stevenson.

Johnson, Gloria Carniece. "The Folk Tradition in the Fiction of Black Women Writers." Ph.D. diss. University of Tennessee, 1990. 190 pp. DAI 52:917A.

    Traces major influences of folklore, ritual, legend, and myth.

Keenan, Thomas Winslow. "Difficult Responsibilities: Rights of Fable." Ph.D. diss. Yale University, 1990. 243 pp. DAI 52:157A.

    Noteworthy for its analysis and comparison of Caxton and Nietzsche's Aesopic fables and Sade's *Philosophie.*

Kuhel, Patty Joan Farris. "Remembering the Goddess Within: The Functioning of Fairy Tale and Mythic Motifs in the Novels of Hurston, Walker, Morrison, and Shange." Ph.D. diss. University of Tulsa, 1991. 374 pp. DAI 52:539A.

Lia, Douglas Vincent. "A Study of Second-Grade Students' Inferences During and Following Participation in Three Types of Read Aloud Story Sessions." Ed.D. diss. Northern Illinois University, 1988. 200 pp. DAI 49:2166A.

McBratney, John Stuart. "East-West Meetings Under the Raj: Rudyard Kipling, E. M. Forster, and Paul Scott." Ph.D. diss. University of California—Berkeley, 1987. 378 pp. DAI 49:1464A.

McKinley, Virginia Susan Gallaher. "Rendering up 'The Tale of What We Are': Gothic Narrative Methods in Selected Novels of Godwin, Brown and Shelley." Ph.D. diss. Michigan State University, 1986. 246 pp. DAI 47:2597A.

    Horror fiction as exemplified in *Frankenstein.*

Mason, Pamela Ann. "Citizen of Geneva: Calvinist Themes in Rousseau's Political Thought." Ph.D. diss. University of North Carolina—Chapel Hill, 1990. 354 pp. DAI 51:2404A.

    Focuses on *Emile.*

Osborn, F. E. Ann. "A Computer-Aided Methodology for the Analysis and Classification of British-Canadian Children's Traditional Singing Games." Ph.D. diss. Ohio State University, 1986. 357 pp. DAI 47:1109A.

Parker, Gloria E. "Through the Eye of a Child: Their Societies Viewed by Five Black,

Francophone Authors: Zobel, Ega, Laye, Dadie, and Oyono." Ph.D. diss. Fordham University, 1991. 605 pp. DAI 52:1353–54A.

The influence of Richard Wright's *Black Boy* on five authors.

Retan, Katherine Allison. "Opening the Floodgates: The Construction and Transgression of Gender and Class Boundaries in the Novels of Charlotte Brontë, Charles Dickens and Elizabeth Gaskell." Ph.D. diss. University of Minnesota, 1991. 302 pp. DAI 52:1754A.

Robertson, Michael Lee. "*Frankenstein* and the *Odyssey:* Subverting the Gendered Structure of the Epic Tradition." Ph.D. diss. Florida State University, 1990. 203 pp. DAI 51:2373A.

Ross, Cheri Louise Graves. "Transforming Fictional Genres: Five Nineteenth-Century American Feminist Novelists." Ph.D. diss. Purdue University, 1991. 177 pp. DAI 52:2144–45A.

Significant for its treatment of Alcott with Catharine Maria Sedgwick, Anna Katharine Green, Fanny Fern, and Marietta Holley.

Rubio, Mary Henley. "F. P. Grove's Children's Novel: Its Text and Larger Context." Ph.D. diss. McMaster University (Canada), 1982. N.p. DAI 43:2996A. [Not available from University Microfilms.]

An analysis of Grove's semi-autobiographical novel for children entitled *The Adventure of Leonard Broadus,* first published in a serialized, truncated version in the *Canadian Boy,* 1941.

Ruff, Felicia J. "Suffering Angels: Images of Children in Nineteenth Century Drama." Ph.D. diss. City University of New York, 1991. 213 pp. DAI 52:1576–77A.

Ruppel, Richard Jeffrey. "Kipling, Conrad, and the Popular Exotic Short Fiction of the 1890's." Ph.D. diss. University of North Carolina—Chapel Hill, 1987. 215 pp. DAI 49:2234–35A.

Notes that Kipling may be criticizing imperialism in his jingoistic stories.

Sharps, Ronald LaMarr. "Happy Days and Sorrow Songs: Interpretations of Negro Folklore by Black Intellectuals, 1893–1928." Ph.D. diss. George Washington University, 1991. 455 pp. DAI 52:973A.

Skelton, Robert David. "The Narrative Discourse of Deaf Children: A Concept of Story." Ph.D. diss. University of Nottingham (U.K.), 1991. 320 pp. DAI 52:2796–97B.

Sukprapan, Kopkun. "The Literary Perception of India in *Kim, Gora,* and *A Passage to India.*" Ph.D. diss. State University of New York—Stony Brook, 1991. 228 pp. DAI 52:1345A.

Tobin, Lee Ann. "To Seek Another World: Arthurian Romance as Cultural Critique." Ph.D. diss. University of Colorado—Boulder, 1991. 223 pp. DAI 52:2155A.

Weiss, Robert Mark. "The Hidden World of Gogol: A Study of the Irrational in *Dead Souls.*" Ph.D. diss. University of California—Los Angeles, 1985. 187 pp. DAI 46:996A.

Includes a long comparison of Gogol and Lewis Carroll, with an emphasis on the Alice books.

Williams, Michael Eugene. "Coding Systems and the Question of Determinacy in Victorian Fiction." Ph.D. diss. University of Colorado—Boulder, 1982. 210 pp. DAI 43:1157A.

Interprets the Alice books via Barthes and Robbe-Grillet.

Wright, Aaron Eugene, Jr. "The 'Nuremberg' *Aesop* and Its Sources." Ph.D. diss. Princeton University, 1991. 347 pp. DAI 52:910A.

Wytenbroek, Jacqueline Robyn. "Structure, Imagery and Vision in the Romances of Ursula K. Le Guin." Ph.D. diss. University of Toronto, 1986. N.p. DAI 48:2871A.

Contributors and Editors

PHYLLIS BIXLER is a professor of English at Southwest Missouri State University and the author of *Frances Hodgson Burnett* (G. K. Hall, 1984). She recently published an essay entitled "Gardens, Houses, and Nurturant Power in *The Secret Garden*" in *Romanticism and Children's Literature in Nineteenth-Century England,* edited by James Holt McGavran, Jr.

FRANCELIA BUTLER, founding editor of *Children's Literature,* has published many books on children's literature, including *Skipping Around the World: The Ritual Nature of Folk Rhymes.*

JOHN CECH, book review editor of *Children's Literature,* teaches in the English Department at the University of Florida. He is the author of a book for children, *My Grandfather's Journey* (1991), and recently completed a book on the works of Maurice Sendak.

R. H. W. DILLARD, editor-in-chief of *Children's Literature* and professor of English at Hollins College, is the longtime chair of the Hollins Creative Writing Program and is adviser to the director of the Hollins Graduate Program in Children's Literature. A novelist and poet, he is also the author of two critical monographs, *Horror Films* and *Understanding George Garrett,* as well as articles on Ellen Glasgow, Vladimir Nabokov, Federico Fellini, Robert Coover, Fred Chappell, and others.

ANGELA M. ESTES is an associate professor of English at California Polytechnic State University, San Luis Obispo, where she teaches American literature and creative writing. She has published articles on Louisa May Alcott and is currently at work with Kathleen M. Lant on a book-length study, *Their Own Sweet Will: Resistance and Relationship in the Works of Louisa May Alcott,* for the University of Tennessee Press. She has also published her poems widely and is the author of a collection of poems, *Boarding Passes.*

RACHEL FORDYCE, former executive secretary of the Children's Literature Association, has written four books, most recently *Lewis Carroll: A Reference Guide.* She is dean of humanities and social sciences at Montclair State College.

BONNIE GAARDEN teaches in the English and Theatre Department at Edinboro University of Pennsylvania and is a doctoral student at the State University of New York at Buffalo, where she is writing a dissertation on the fantasies of George MacDonald. She also reviews books on children's literature for *American Literature.*

ELIZABETH GOODENOUGH, who teaches Victorian writers and children's literature at Claremont McKenna College, has written articles on Virginia Woolf and Carl Jung. She is coeditor of the forthcoming *Infant Tongues: The Voice of the Child in Literature.*

PETER HOLLINDALE teaches English at the University of York, England, specializing in children's literature and Renaissance drama. His essay "Ideology and the Children's Book" received the Children's Literature Association award for the best essay in the field in 1988.

MARY V. JACKSON is completing two volumes on early children's literature: *Aspects of the Hanoverian and Victorian Children's Book Trade* and *Pygmalion Print: Molding Class, Gender, and National Consciousness in British Children's Literature, 1740–1878.*

CHRISTA KAMENETSKY is a professor of English at Central Michigan University, where she teaches children's literature and comparative literature. She has published *The Brothers Grimm and Their Critics* (1992) and *Children's Literature in Hitler's*

Germany (1984), as well as articles in the *Journal of American Folklore, Children's Literature* (volume 6), *Journal of the College Language Association,* and other periodicals.

ELIZABETH LENNOX KEYSER, editor of volume 22, is an associate professor of English at Hollins College, where she teaches children's literature, American literature, and American studies. She is the author of *Whispers in the Dark: The Fiction of Louisa May Alcott* (University of Tennessee Press, 1993) and of numerous articles on American women writers, including Frances Hodgson Burnett.

KATHLEEN MARGARET LANT is a professor of English at California Polytechnic State University, where she teaches American literature and women writers. Her publications include work on Harriet Beecher Stowe, Kate Chopin, Tennessee Williams, Charlotte Perkins Gilman, and Louisa May Alcott, and with Angela M. Estes she is completing a book on Alcott. Her essays on Stephen King and Sylvia Plath are forthcoming.

CYNTHIA MARSHALL, associate professor of English at Rhodes College, is the author of *Last Things and Last Plays: Shakespearean Eschatology,* and of many articles on Shakespeare. She has also published essays on George MacDonald's fiction for children.

PERRY NODELMAN, professor of English at the University of Winnipeg, Canada, is author of *The Pleasures of Children's Literature* (Longman) and the children's novel *The Same Place but Different* (Groundwood).

LISSA PAUL is an associate professor at the University of New Brunswick, Canada. She teaches children's literature and literary theory and was a finalist for the 1990 Children's Literature Association Criticism Award for her article "Escape Claws: *Lolly Willowes* and *Crusoe's Daughter*," *Signal* 63 (September 1990).

ANNE K. PHILLIPS is an assistant professor of children's literature at Kansas State University. Coauthor of *Resources for Teaching "The Bedford Introduction to Literature"* and coeditor of *Children's Literature,* volume 21, she is studying the connection between canonical "adult" literature and popular children's literature in nineteenth-century America.

SUZANNE RAHN, associate professor of English at Pacific Lutheran University, is an associate editor of *The Lion and the Unicorn.* She is also the author of *Children's Literature: An Annotated Bibliography of the History and Criticism* (1981) and *Rediscoveries in Children's Literature* (forthcoming).

GLENN EDWARD SADLER teaches English and children's literature at Bloomsburg University of Pennsylvania and has recently edited *Teaching Children's Literature: Issues, Pedagogy, Resources* for the Modern Language Association. He has also edited an illustrated edition of George MacDonald's *Lost Princess: A Double Story* and MacDonald's *Selected Letters* (forthcoming).

CAROLE SCOTT is dean of undergraduate studies at San Diego State University and a member of the English and Comparative Literature Department. She has published in children's literature and pedagogy and is currently working on the function of parallel worlds in literature for children.

SANJAY SIRCAR wrote the first Australian higher degree in children's literature within the discipline of English and has published articles on various aspects of the area in England, the United States, Australia, and India. He is writing a book on the stylistics of nineteenth-century fantasy fiction. He has taught in Australia and China and is at present working in arts administration in the Australian Public Service.

ANNA SMOL teaches medieval literature and children's literature at Mount Saint Vincent University, Nova Scotia, Canada. She has recently published an article on the Old English poem *The Seafarer.*

SHARON SMULDERS is an assistant professor of English at the University of Lethbridge, Alberta, Canada. Her interest in nineteenth-century poetry has led to articles on Alice Meynell, Christina Rossetti, and Dante Gabriel Rossetti in a variety of journals.

J. D. STAHL is the author of *Mark Twain, Culture and Gender* (University of Georgia Press) and editor of a special issue of *The Lion and the Unicorn* on recent European children's literature theory. He teaches in the English department of Virginia Polytechnic and State University.

Award Applications

The article award committee of the Children's Literature Association publishes a bibliography of the year's work in children's literature in the *Children's Literature Association Quarterly* and selects the year's best critical articles. For pertinent articles that have appeared in a collection of essays or journal other than one devoted to children's literature, please send a photocopy or offprint with the correct citation and your address written on the first page to Gillian Adams, 5906 Fairlane Drive, Austin, Tex. 78731. Papers will be acknowledged and returned if return postage is enclosed. The annual deadline is May 1.

The Phoenix Award is given for a book first published twenty years earlier that did not win a major award but has passed the test of time and is deemed to be of high literary quality. Send nominations to Alethea Helbig, 3640 Eli Road, Ann Arbor, Mich. 48104.

The Children's Literature Association offers three annual research grants. The Margaret P. Esmonde Memorial Scholarship offers $500 for criticism and original works in the areas of fantasy or science fiction for children or adolescents by beginning scholars, including graduate students, instructors, and assistant professors. Research Fellowships are awards ranging from $250 to $1,000 (the number and amount of awards are based on the number and needs of winning applicants) for criticism or original scholarship leading to a significant publication. Recipients must have postdoctoral or equivalent professional standing. Awards may be used for transportation, living expenses, materials, and supplies but not for obtaining advanced degrees, for creative writing, textbook writing, or pedagogical purposes. The Weston Woods Media Scholarship awards $1,000 and free use of the Weston Woods studios to encourage investigation of the elements and techniques that contribute to successfully adapting children's literature to film or recording or to developing materials for television and video. For full application guidelines on all three grants, write The Children's Literature Association, c/o Marianne Gessner, 22 Harvest Lane, Battle Creek, Mich. 49015. The annual deadline for these awards is February 1.

Order Form Yale University Press, P.O. Box 209040, New Haven, CT 06520-9040

Customers in the United States and Canada may photocopy this form and use it for ordering all volumes of **Children's Literature** available from Yale University Press. Individuals are asked to pay in advance. We honor both MasterCard and VISA. Checks should be made payable to Yale University Press.

The prices given are 1994 list prices for the United States and are subject to change. A shipping charge of $2.75 is to be added to each order, and Connecticut residents must pay a sales tax of 6 percent.

Qty.	Volume	Price	Total amount	Qty.	Volume	Price	Total amount
____	8 (cloth)	$45.00	_____	____	15 (paper)	$16.00	_____
____	8 (paper)	$16.00	_____	____	16 (paper)	$16.00	_____
____	9 (cloth)	$45.00	_____	____	17 (cloth)	$45.00	_____
____	9 (paper)	$16.00	_____	____	17 (paper)	$16.00	_____
____	10 (cloth)	$45.00	_____	____	18 (cloth)	$45.00	_____
____	10 (paper)	$16.00	_____	____	18 (paper)	$16.00	_____
____	11 (cloth)	$45.00	_____	____	19 (cloth)	$45.00	_____
____	11 (paper)	$16.00	_____	____	19 (paper)	$16.00	_____
____	12 (cloth)	$45.00	_____	____	20 (cloth)	$45.00	_____
____	12 (paper)	$16.00	_____	____	20 (paper)	$16.00	_____
____	13 (cloth)	$45.00	_____	____	21 (cloth)	$45.00	_____
____	13 (paper)	$16.00	_____	____	21 (paper)	$16.00	_____
____	14 (cloth)	$45.00	_____	____	22 (cloth)	$45.00	_____
____	14 (paper)	$16.00	_____	____	22 (paper)	$16.00	_____
____	15 (cloth)	$45.00	_____				

Payment of $_____ is enclosed (including sales tax if applicable).

MasterCard no. _____

4-digit bank no. _____ Expiration date _____

VISA no. _____ Expiration date _____

Signature _____

SHIP TO: _____

_____

_____

See the next page for ordering issues from Yale University Press, London.

Volumes 1–7 of **Children's Literature** can be obtained directly from John C. Wandell, The Children's Literature Foundation, P. O. Box 370, Windham Center, Conn. 06280.

Order Form   Yale University Press, 23 Pond Street, Hampstead, London NW3 2PN, England

Customers in the United Kingdom, Europe, and the British Commonwealth may photocopy this form and use it for ordering all volumes of **Children's Literature** available from Yale University Press. Individuals are asked to pay in advance. We honour Access, VISA, and American Express accounts. Cheques should be made payable to Yale University Press.

The prices given are 1994 list prices for the United Kingdom and are subject to change. A post and packing charge of £1.75 is to be added to each order.

Qty.	Volume	Price	Total amount	Qty.	Volume	Price	Total amount
____	8 (cloth)	£40.00	_____	____	15 (paper)	£14.95	_____
____	8 (paper)	£14.95	_____	____	16 (paper)	£14.95	_____
____	9 (cloth)	£40.00	_____	____	17 (cloth)	£40.00	_____
____	9 (paper)	£14.95	_____	____	17 (paper)	£14.95	_____
____	10 (cloth)	£40.00	_____	____	18 (cloth)	£40.00	_____
____	10 (paper)	£14.95	_____	____	18 (paper)	£14.95	_____
____	11 (cloth)	£40.00	_____	____	19 (cloth)	£40.00	_____
____	11 (paper)	£14.95	_____	____	19 (paper)	£14.95	_____
____	12 (cloth)	£40.00	_____	____	20 (cloth)	£40.00	_____
____	12 (paper)	£14.95	_____	____	20 (paper)	£14.95	_____
____	13 (cloth)	£40.00	_____	____	21 (cloth)	£40.00	_____
____	13 (paper)	£14.95	_____	____	21 (paper)	£14.95	_____
____	14 (cloth)	£40.00	_____	____	22 (cloth)	£40.00	_____
____	14 (paper)	£14.95	_____	____	22 (paper)	£14.95	_____
____	15 (cloth)	£40.00	_____				

Payment of £_____ is enclosed.

Please debit my Access/VISA/American Express account no. _____

Expiry date _____

Signature _____ Name _____

Address _____

Volumes 1–7 of **Children's Literature** can be obtained directly from John C. Wandell, The Children's Literature Foundation, P. O. Box 370, Windham Center, Conn. 06280.